NARRATIVE

OF THE

TENTH INTERNATIONAL

CHRISTIAN ENDEAVOR CONVENTION

HELD AT

MINNEAPOLIS, MINN., U. S. A.,

JULY 9 TO 12, 1891.

First Fruits Press
Wilmore, Kentucky
c2015

First Fruits Press
The Academic Open Press of Asbury Theological Seminary
204 N. Lexington Ave., Wilmore, KY 40390
859-858-2236
first.fruits@asburyseminary.edu
asbury.to/firstfruits

1891.

NARRATIVE

OF THE

TENTH INTERNATIONAL

CHRISTIAN ENDEAVOR CONVENTION,

HELD AT

MINNEAPOLIS, MINN., U. S. A.,
JULY 9 TO 12, 1891.

COPYRIGHTED (1891)
BY THE UNITED SOCIETY ....
..... OF CHRISTIAN ENDEAVOR.

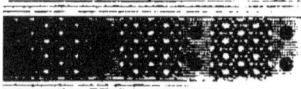

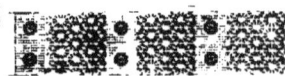

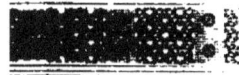

OFFICERS OF THE CONVENTION.

PRESIDENT.

Rev. FRANCIS E. CLARK, D.D., Boston, Mass.

HONORARY VICE-PRESIDENTS.

Rev. O. H. Tiffany, D.D., LL.D., Minneapolis, Minn.
Rev. H. T. McEwen, New York, N. Y.
Rev. Robert E. Caldwell, Louisville, Ky.
Rev. Elbert R. Dille, D.D., Oakland, Cal.
Rev. James A. Worden, D.D., Philadelphia, Penn.
Rev. William Patterson, Toronto, Ont.
Rev. R. M. Tinnon, D.D., Fort Worth, Texas.
Rev. Charles F. Deems, D.D., LL.D., New York, N. Y.
Rev. D. E. Bushnell, D.D., Chattanooga, Tenn.
Rev. J. F. Cowan, Pittsburg, Penn.
Rev. J. L. Parsons, St. Louis, Mo.
Rev. A. DeW. Mason, Brooklyn, N. Y.
Rev. Smith Baker, D.D., Minneapolis, Minn.
Rev. R. R. Meredith, D.D., Brooklyn, N. Y.
Rev. T. E. Vassar, D.D., Kansas City, Mo.
Rev. J. J. Hall, D.D., Raleigh, N. C.
Rev. J. A. Rondthaler, D.D., Indianapolis, Ind.
Rev. A. A. Fulton, Canton, China.
Rev. A. J. Turkle, Omaha, Neb.
Rev. J. B. Jordan, Pawtucket, R. I.
Rev. E. C. Ray, D.D., Topeka, Kan.
Rev. Alfred C. Hathaway, Richmond, Ind.
Rev. Frank R. Millspaugh, Minneapolis, Minn.
Rev. Hugh Walker, Birmingham, Ala.
Mr. Breedlove Smith, New Orleans, La.
Rev. A. B. Cristy, Albuquerque, N. M.
Rev. W. E. Judkins, D.D., Richmond, Va.

SCRIBE.

Rev. H. W. Gleason, Minneapolis, Minn.

COMMITTEE OF ARRANGEMENTS.

Franc B. Daniels, Chairman.
Grove A. Gruman, Recording Secretary.
Fred W. Dean, Treasurer.
Willis M. McDonald, General Secretary.

HOTEL. Edward M. Conant, Minneapolis, Willis M. McDonald, Minneapolis, Lawson Lindsley, St. Paul, Julian Millard, St. Paul.

FINANCE. Fred W. Dean, Minneapolis, Trafford N. Jayne, St. Paul.

EXCURSION. Trafford N. Jayne, St. Paul.

PRESS. J. J. Symes, St. Paul, F. G. Atkinson, Minneapolis.

PRINTING. Lew A. Huntoon, Minneapolis.

HALL. Grove A. Gruman, Minneapolis.

TRANSPORTATION. J. E. Thwing, Minneapolis.

RECEPTION. Harry A. Kinports, Minneapolis, W. G. Breg, St. Paul.

BULLETIN. Lew A. Huntoon, Minneapolis, Lawson Lindsley, St. Paul

MUSICAL DIRECTOR.

Mr. Lewis F. Lindsay, St. Louis, Mo.

SOLOIST.

Mr. Ira D. Sankey, the Evangelist.

CORNETIST.

Mr. Robert E. Burleigh, Rochester, N. Y.

PIANIST.

Miss Alma Norton Johnson, Minneapolis, Minn.

Francis E. Clark.

NARRATIVE

OF THE

TENTH ANNUAL CONFERENCE

OF THE

YOUNG PEOPLE'S SOCIETIES OF CHRISTIAN ENDEAVOR,

HELD IN

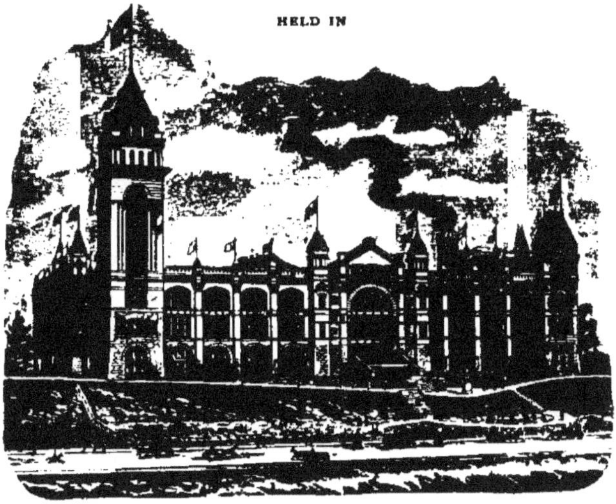

THE EXPOSITION BUILDING,

MINNEAPOLIS, MINNESOTA,

THURSDAY, FRIDAY, SATURDAY AND SUNDAY,

JULY 9, 10, 11 and 12, 1891.

WITH ALL ADDRESSES AND PAPERS READ AT THE CONFERENCE.

PUBLISHED BY
THE UNITED SOCIETY OF CHRISTIAN ENDEAVOR,
No. 50 BROMFIELD STREET, BOSTON, MASS.

PREFATORY NOTE.

THIS stenographic report of the Tenth Annual Convention of the Societies of Christian Endeavor is sent forth in the hope that all that was said and done during the four memorable days of the "Twin City" Convention may be still further blessed in spreading broadcast the spirit and practical suggestions for Christian work given by all who participated in the conference.

Hearty thanks are due Rev. H. W. Gleason, the convention scribe, for his complete and accurate report; to the authors of the papers herein printed, for their kindness in revising them, and to the Daily *Journal* and Daily *Tribune* of Minneapolis for the loan of the illustrations which are herewith reproduced from the columns of their excellent reports published during the sessions of the Convention.

THE TENTH INTERNATIONAL CONVENTION

OF THE

YOUNG PEOPLE'S SOCIETIES OF

CHRISTIAN ENDEAVOR.

MINNEAPOLIS, JULY 9-12, 1891

THE Tenth International Convention of Young People's Societies of Christian Endeavor was held at Minneapolis, Minnesota, July 9-12, 1891. The sessions of the Convention were held in the Exposition Building, the interior of which had been specially prepared for the occasion, providing an auditorium seating nearly 12,000 persons. Delegates began arriving as early as Wednesday afternoon, and when the Convention was over it was found that the actual registration amounted to 11,000. Besides this, it was estimated that at least 3,000 delegates and visitors were present who omitted to register their names. Delegates were present from nearly every State in the Union and the Provinces of Canada.

THURSDAY AFTERNOON.

At half past three o'clock the doors of the Convention hall were thrown open, and the vast throng of delegates entered and took their seats. They found an auditorium which, though crude in certain features, commended itself to all. The seats were arranged in the amphitheatre form, the speakers' platform being midway the longest distance of the hall and in height a little below the level of the gallery. Back of the platform rose the tiers of chorus seats, accommodating 800 persons. The hall was prettily decorated, especially about the platform, with bunting, foliage plants and evergreen. The only motto was a tastefully designed arch over the platform bearing the words, "For Christ and the Church."

Immediately upon the entrance of the delegates, the large chorus choir, under the direction of Mr. L. F. Lindsay of St. Louis, with accompaniment of piano, organ and cornet, rendered several of the new Christian Endeavor hymns, and at 4.15 o'clock the hymn, "All hail the power of Jesus' name," was given out and sung by the whole Convention. Pres. F. E. Clark called the assembly to order, and the organization of the Convention was completed by the appointment of Rev. H. W. Gleason, of Minneapolis, as scribe, and the authorizing of the president to appoint the usual committees on nominations, resolutions, greetings and business.

Rev. T. E. Vassar, D. D., pastor of the First Baptist Church of Kansas City, led in prayer, followed by the hymn, "Hear us, O Saviour."

The first addresses of the afternoon were words of welcome.

President Clark: From whom shall we be glad to hear the first word of welcome this afternoon? I think if I were to put this to vote, you would all say, "From the Committee of '91" — the committee that has done so much to make this meeting possible and to whom we shall owe so much before we leave Minneapolis. I have great pleasure in introducing to you the chairman of that committee, Mr. Frank B. Daniels. [*Loud Applause.*]

ADDRESS OF MR. F. B. DANIELS, CHAIRMAN OF THE COMMITTEE OF '91.

Mr. President, Ladies and Gentlemen—Fellow Endeavorers: It is with no ordinary joy and happiness that I, representing the committee of '91, step forward to bid you welcome in their name. At our bidding you have come from the East and from the West, from where the gulf stream washes our tropica shores to where the good queen's domains touch the eternal snows, and from our hearts we bid you welcome. Would it had been the task of one greater gifted of tongue and voice to extend our greeting. And it is also a happy hour for us, because for the preparation for this great gathering, which has given hard, ceaseless labor for weeks and months, is finished; and we see our work complete. If we have in any measure failed, forgive us. It has been no child's play. We have done the best we could to prepare for your coming; your approval is our reward. Have you ever heard that the denizens of the Twin Cities were proud and boastful? If not, I let you into the secret. We are proud of our weather, whether the mercury toys with 100 above or with 50 degrees below. But honestly, our ice palaces will not keep all summer, and speaking for the committee of '91 I give you visible proof of this today

We are proud of our cities, proud of their rush and bustle and enterprise and push, proud of our manufactories, proud of our mercantile interests, proud of

our newness and freshness, of our rapid growth and our future prospects, proud of our homes, of our laughing waters and our lake resorts, proud that we have chained the Father of Waters flowing at our very feet, and bidden him grind the flour for the nations, and we are proud of our hospitality, proud of the fact that year by year we welcome here mighty gatherings from all parts of the land, religious gatherings, medical gatherings, gatherings political, musical, educational and military. The railroad magnates, the secret orders, the editors and the travelling men have all been to see us and to each and all have our cities given a hearty welcome.

But to the chairman of the committee of '91 is given the greater and prouder privilege of welcoming to this building the greatest gathering of Christian workers which not only these goodly cities but our good land has ever seen. I look into the eager faces of Endeavorers, 15,000 strong, with the rear guard of a million, meeting for no personal gain, for no selfish purpose, but to raise aloft our banner with its single motto, "For Christ and the Church," and to reason together how we may best honor our Lord and Master. Our Endeavor movement has been called a crusade, and rightly is it so named. The name crusade warms the heart and stirs the blood. The poet and historian never tired of singing the glories of the old crusades and the heroic deeds of the crusaders. We love to read the brave deeds of Peter the Hermit, and St. Bernard, of Richard the Lion Hearted, and of Godfrey, how they raised great armies, led them across the continent and over seas, how they counted their lives not dear, but gave their all in the great struggle to regain Palestine and the holy sepulchre. But they fought in vain. The star and crescent still floats over the great dome in old Jerusalem and the moslem still rules the Holy Land. Shall we likewise fail? No. And why? They fought for a land, we fight for no earthly possessions, but for souls. They fought with swords and spears and left a bloody stain across the continents and through the seas. We, too, fight with a sword. It is not girded by our sides, the scabbard is thrown away and each Endeavorer bears it in his right hand; but no blood stains mark its brightness, no tears of sorrow fall upon it. It is the sword of the Spirit, the word of God. Dear it is to us; dearer than life itself, and we draw it in defense of our loved countries, our free institutions and our homes. They fought for an empty tomb. We fight for a Saviour's honor. Today it is for us with bowed heads and thoughtful hearts to consider the future of our crusade. Upon the little we do here much depends. The eyes of the land, yes, of the world, are upon us, and His all-searching eye is watching us. Shall the glories of the past ten years be repeated and magnified in the coming ten? With God's blessing I believe they shall, and to the consideration of such a glorious consummation, I again bid you welcome to this building, to our loved cities, to our homes and to our hearts. [*Applause.*]

President Clark: Christian Endeavor societies never forget their motto, "For Christ and the Church." Since this is so, our pastors are the most honored men among us, and we desire especially to have words of welcome from representatives of these many pastors who are here. We shall hear in the first place from Rev. H. H. French, pastor of the Centenary M. E. Church, Minneapolis. [*Applause.*]

ADDRESS OF REV. H. H. FRENCH.

Mr. President and Delegates to the Tenth International Convention of Christian Endeavor: I count it a high honor to stand before such a magnificent assembly as this and bid you welcome; and I especially appreciate the honor, since these words of welcome are to represent the pastors of Minneapolis—a body which I joined some eighteen months ago and which I have learned to believe is a body hard to be beaten in any city of this size on the continent. It is a body of men which includes such men as Dr. Smith Baker, who for a period of years moved the heart of New England with his common sense methods and his apostolic zeal, and who bids fair to repeat his earlier successes in this stirring Northwest; Dr. Otis H. Tiffany, who for a quarter of a century has enjoyed the reputation of standing in the front rank of the pulpit and platform orators of Methodism; Dr. Wayland Hoyt, of the Baptist church, genial and versatile and always popular with Christian Endeavorers; and while Dr. David James Burrell has recently removed from us, and the Presbyterian church has suffered a loss thereby, it is no less an honor to represent such men as Dr. J. S. Black, who will by and by conduct the pastor's hour, or the Rev. Mr. Wells, who for many years has made himself felt in every measure of municipal reform proposed in this city. Now this company of honored men and their colleagues all over the city are not mere figure heads, I assure you, in the conduct of the affairs of this city. They wield an immense influence for good. Their power was demonstrated very clearly only a few months ago when the friends of the liquor traffic announced that they were going to extend the patrol limits in the city. The ministers rose and said No, and the issue was fairly joined. The contending legions marched out in battle array. The enemy was proud, contemptuous, overbearing, threatening in their madness that if we did not keep still they would not only extend the limits but destroy them altogether. On went the battle, and when the smoke of the conflict had cleared away, it was found that the patrol limits were exactly where they were when the fight began.

Let me say a word as to the constituency of these men. Minneapolis is proud of the pre-eminence of being the city of churches. While Boston and Philadelphia have one church to 1600 inhabitants, Chicago one to 2100, New York one to 2400, St. Louis one to 2800, Minneapolis has one church to every 1052 of the population, [*applause*] with a church property aggregating in value nearly five million dollars, with church attendants averaging nearly 80,000, with a list of communicants numbering upwards of 30,000, and a great army of Sunday-school scholars. We believe that we can rightly rejoice in the fact that God has been among us and has worked through and by us.

I desire now, in the name of this body of men which I have indicated, backed by such a constituency, to offer you a hearty welcome to our hearts and homes. And I desire also to say that these ministers have a very warm place in their hearts for Christian Endeavorers. We believe that this Society is the child of providence, raised up specially for the purpose of helping Christ to win this world. We believe in it because it has the "go" in it. Ingersoll says the church must go. Certainly it must go — go into all the world, and preach the gospel to every creature, [*loud applause*] and Christian Endeavorers are to help the church take on new methods and stronger appliances for this magnificent conquest of the world. The world, "he do move" today. The calcium light, the telegraph and telephone, the electric car, the different agencies that we have today for crossing the ocean and the continent, these all indicate that the time is past when we can use the things that we have used in days gone by; and so, spiritually, the farthing candle and the stage coach and the messenger runner must be superseded by better appliances if we are to win the world for Christ. And because Christian Endeavor stands for all that is progressive and aggressive in Christian labor, we as pastors sustain it in our hearts and in our churches. We believe in it because it affords the best federation of Christian effort the world has ever seen. [*Applause.*] It arose not a moment too soon to point out the way by which we might change what had been in the past, by which the wasting of Christian resources might be stopped, and the bickerings and jealousies among denominations might come to an end, so that forevermore there might be one church, one vast brotherhood, cemented together by Christian love and moving out at the call of Christ for the conquest of the world. [*Applause.*]

One other thing. We love Christian Endeavor and give it our enthusiastic support because of its hopeful spirit. As Christian Endeavor has driven the long face and the weary groan out of the individual experiences of the people to a large extent, so it is exorcising that demon of all blasphemies, pessimism in the Christian church. [*Applause.*] We have a new philosophy today, and we believe that it is a sin for any man to believe that the mission of Jesus Christ to this world is a failure, or that He is not to see of the travail of His soul and be satisfied. Already signs of promise are looking us in the face, and we believe that the time is coming very speedily when nations shall be born in a day, and the great work of Christ shall be accomplished in the earth. Slumbering nations are awaking, strangely awaking, under the call of God. In the Flowery Kingdom there is beginning to blossom the Rose of Sharon and the Lily of the Valley. In India, that land of the nodding palm and the marigold, thrones and temples are tottering before the breath of God, and on their ruins are rising temples to our Lord Jehovah. On the dark bosom of Africa are blazing jewels even now that shall flash one day in Christ's crown. And so all over the world, the kingdoms of men are becoming kingdoms of our Lord and of His Christ. We take note of the disturbances everywhere, but we refuse to believe that these betoken the impending crash of all things good and great. No, no; they betoken only the breaking and the cracking of the glaciers and the ice banks under the heat of the awakening spring. We see the reddening glare deepening all around the horizon; but we believe that this is only the glow from Christ's face as He walks into the dawn of the millennial day. We listen, and we hear God's chariots rumbling, and we are able even now to believe that the kingdoms of this world are speedily to become Christ's kingdom. Hark!

> "He is sounding forth the trumpet that shall never call retreat,
> He is sifting out the hearts of men before His judgment seat:
> Be swift my soul to answer Him, be jubilant my feet,
> For God is marching on."

And in response, the moving legions are thickening the air all about us, and success is ahead of the Christian church if we do the will of God.

And so, because I believe this Convention is to help on the glorious consummation and bring in the day of the Lord, I bid you a hearty welcome once more to the churches of Minneapolis. We offer you the freedom of our hearts and our homes, and we offer it not in a casket of perishable gold, but in the tried metal of Christian brotherhood, impearled with the prayers and the best wishes of the pastors of Minneapolis. [*Loud applause.*]

President Clark: This Convention, you know, is a "Twin City" Convention in fact as well as in name, as many of you who are indebted to the hospitality of St. Paul can well testify. We shall now hear from Rev. Robert Christie, D.D., pastor of the House of Hope Presbyterian Church, St. Paul, one of the earliest and stanchest friends of the Christian Endeavor Society. [*Applause.*]

ADDRESS OF REV. ROBERT CHRISTIE, D.D.

Mr. President and Members of the International Convention: It has been made my pleasant duty to represent the other twin city in bidding you welcome to this portion of the great Northwest. Would that my soul had the power to feel, and my lips the eloquence to express the friendly interest that is felt by our citizens in this unique and magnificent assemblage. It has been the privilege of these cities to entertain many important conventions—political, educational, religious; but whether judged by its composition, its magnitude, its aims or its possibilities, this Convention overshadows them all. It is not made up of age, with its fixed habits and receding memories, but of youth, with its plastic power and forward look. It is not animated by sectional, sectarian, national, or race feeling, but has one grand motto: "For Christ and the Church." And when we think of the power that is represented by this Convention, the imagination declines to set limits to the influence that must flow out from this gathering, reaching all parts of Christ's visible kingdom. Permit me to say that you could not have selected another section in this great land where there would have been so many elements congenial to such a gathering as this. In this section you will not be expected to apologize either for your youth as members, or for your youth as a movement. Look around in this section and you will find that nearly all great enterprises are conducted by those who would be called young men. Neither will you meet that prejudice which in old communities always confronts novelty or new movements of any description. In this community we do not cling to tallow candles when electric lights flash on the darkness. We set aside the time-honored quill when type-writers make their appearance. And when Christian Endeavor came to our doors it had not to wait or knock for a welcome. It was taken at once as among the great agencies that were needful for carrying on the work of Christ's kingdom. [*Applause.*] Allow me to say also, that in a community that is familiar with printing presses that throw off 40,000 newspapers an hour, that is familiar with wheat fields 10,000 acres in extent, that has a milling system that produces 40,000 barrels of flour a day, we are not afraid of the power that dwells in an organization that grows at the rate of 150 societies every seven days. [*Applause.*] The throb of the life of this Convention will be congenial to the energies of this great Northwest.

And permit me to say, Mr. President, that it must be obvious to every candid mind that this movement was not begotten of the prevailing disposition of our time to organize something. It grew out of a felt need,—a need that had been felt by every living pastor and which he had tried to meet by organizing his young people into various forms. Run back over the history of any active congregation, and you will find it dotted here and there with the graves of defunct young people's societies. But when Christian Endeavor, with its manifest simplicity, its adaptability and its longevity, came along, every discriminating pastor said, "This is the way I long have sought, and mourned because I found it not." [*Applause.*] Hence I bid you welcome in the name of every pastor who believes that this Christian Endeavor movement was suggested to this brother (Dr. Clark) by the Lord Jesus Christ as an agency to carry forward as never before the enterprises of His visible kingdom. I imagine that nothing has been so injurious to the Christian name as denominational jealousies. Christians of different names have looked upon each other as belonging to hostile camps, and could see little good in that camp to which they did not belong, and they found it more difficult still to acknowledge the good that they did see. But such meetings as this clarify the vision and increase candor. Here you discover that the Christian life is just as beautiful in a Baptist as in a Congregationalist, in an Episcopalian as in a Presbyterian, and just as beautiful in a Methodist as in either. [*Applause.*] Hence I bid you welcome in the name of that better day when loyalty and brotherhood shall not be tested by a particular ensign, but by fealty to the one blood-stained banner which is over all and above all. Look into the Scriptures, and you will find that the idea of a Christian there differs very essentially from what you usually see embodied in the man of that name living in society. The Bible Christian is one who can pray, one who can say to his fellow-men, "Come thou with us and we will do thee good, for the Lord hath spoken good concerning Israel." The average Christian of today would almost as soon be led to the stake as to speak that into a living and listening ear. The time was, when, if a young man would speak to a comrade concerning religious matters, or lead in prayer, it was thought that it was by a gift, as directly from heaven as the gift of tongues on the day of Pentecost; but we have discovered that it is no such thing. It comes, like all our aptitudes, by training and by practice. The exercises of your Society all proceed on that single assumption. Therefore I bid you welcome in the name of all those who believe that this movement has been endowed by the Lord Jesus Christ with power to say to the church of the future, "Thou dumb and deaf spirit, I charge thee come out of her and enter no more into her." [*Laughter and applause.*] Look at that company of recruits that have just been brought to the parade-ground. What means that marching and counter-marching, that handling of muskets and those manœvres of body? Is it simply to give a measured step, to give an erect body, or a graceful carriage? These are important, but the object of all that drill and discipline is to give the habit of unquestioning obedience to the word of command from a superior, to give endurance for the march, and efficiency on the field of conflict. Your societies are drill grounds where you listen for the command of the great Captain of our salvation, and where you gain efficiency for the march and for the day of conflict.

Away down in Kentucky, during the war and before the emancipation, there was a slave named Sam. He was past middle life, considered somewhat lazy, always doctoring for fancied ailments, and not very well reported of for courage. One day Sam came into the house under great excitement and said to his mistress, "Miss Cornelia, Ise done gone and 'listed." "You 've done what, Sam?" "Ise 'listed." "Why, what do you mean, Sam? You know you are doctoring half the time, and you know, also, that you are an awful coward. How then do you expect to fight the rebels?" "Oh, Miss Cornelia, Ise 'listed in de invalid corps." [*Laughter.*] Nearly all the enlistments in the army of the Lord in the past have been in the invalid corps. Now, Mr. President, I welcome the members of Christian Endeavor because I believe they are animated by the one thought that no invalid corps ought to belong to the army of the Lord. [*Applause.*] There is a school of medicine that has for it motto, "*Similia similibus curantur*," that is, Like things are cured by like. I pass no judgment upon this principle as applicable to the science of healing, but I do know it is true in other and important directions. I know that youth has the power to influence youth for good when age will fail. "As in water face answereth to face, so the heart of man to man." Did you ever notice that, whilst Jesus never slights age, that He seems always to be looking out for the young? There was a profound reason in this choice. He had set in motion a movement that was to change the whole face of society. He was to lift society out of its old grooves and send it forward on new lines of advancement. It required men not of fixed habits and thought to conduct this great movement. It is said that when Harvey discovered the circulation of the blood, not a physician over forty years of age in Europe would accept his theory. Age is very suspicious of innovations that impinge upon fixed theories or fixed habits. Hence the Saviour called the youthful James and John, and left the aged Zebedee. He ordained the young and ardent Saul, and passed by the venerable Gamaliel. When He met that funeral cortege in the way, it was to say to that one on the bier, "Young man, I say unto thee, arise." And when His church had become corrupt, He called the youthful Luther, and passed by the aged Staupitz for the great work of reformation; and when that church had again become somnolent, and that precious command, "Go ye into all the world and preach the gospel to every creature," like Christian's roll in the vision, had fallen from her hand, whom did He awaken out of sleep in order to apprise the church of her neglected duty? Was it some great doctor of divinity? No. Was it some Archbishop of Canterbury with his gown and lawn sleeves? No; it was a young man named Carey who had just been making shoes for a living. Now all souls in themselves are equally valuable, but not so in their relation to other souls. A soul that has fifty years of consecrated endeavor before it in this life is much more valuable as an instrument to place in the hands of Jesus than a soul whose race is almost run. Let an old man be brought into the kingdom at 60 or 70 years of age, and he goes home without a single sheaf; but when a youthful Moody is brought into the kingdom it means multitudes of souls for God. Therefore I welcome you in the name of all who believe that in the consecrated youth of our generation is the hope of the church of God in this and future generations.

And now, finally, let me say that there may be citizens in either of these cities who have no sympathy with your Christianity, who have no sympathy with the form that it has taken in Christian Endeavor; but I do not believe that there is a lover of his kind, or a lover of his Lord, who does not look upon this magnificent gathering with a heart that is kindly,—yea, with a soul full of admiration, and silently say to you, Welcome. It will be a contradiction of my six years' experience, if this people do not treat you with such hospitality as will enable you at least to understand better than you ever did before the feelings of him who wrote the lines:—

"When death's dark stream I ferry o'er,
And that time surely will come,
In heaven itself I ask no more
Than just a Highland welcome."

I welcome you, then, in the name of the pastors of St. Paul and in the name of all Christian people of that city. [*Applause.*]

President Clark: The Society of Christian Endeavor loves not only the mother church, but also her other brothers and sisters. Mr. John H. Elliott, general secretary of the Minneapolis Young Men's Christian Association, will speak for one of the older brothers of Christian Endeavor. [*Applause.*]

ADDRESS OF MR. J. H. ELLIOTT.

Mr. President and Delegates to the Convention: I do not quite see why I should have been put at the tail end of so much eloquence, except by way of assent to the warm welcome already given. Or, to change the figure, it seems singular that you should have been treated to the cream first, and left to make the most of the skimmed milk at the last. There seems little else left to do than to offer a few simple words of welcome. I am somewhat in the predicament of the brother who was to speak in a colored church. Two others were to precede him, and so when the pastor of the church, in the opening prayer, prayed for the first that he might have liberty of speech, and for the second that he might have power, he added, "and God have mercy on the last man." [*Laughter.*] Perhaps the audience, however, will need the sympathy more than myself in this case, but it does seem fitting that you should receive at this time a special word of welcome on behalf of our Association which is so closely allied to your Society in its various lines of Christian work

Every true-hearted Association man the world around, as a loyal son of the church, rejoices in any organization, such as the one represented so grandly here at this time, that has for its aim the advancement of the work of our common mother, the church, or honor of our one Father in heaven, or the exultation of our great

Elder Brother, the Lord Jesus Christ. Therefore, I extend to you the greetings of the Young Men's Christian Associations of all lands, and especially of our own international, State and local organizations in North America. So far as our own organization is concerned, the relationship between these two children of the church in this city has been not only peaceful, but affectionate. In fact, I have known of instances where young men who were members of our Association have become so much interested in certain ladies — members of the Endeavor Society — that they were not contented to let them quietly remain as a sister you know, but insisted on forming a new Christian endeavor for life, for better or worse. [*Laughter*.]

But in the moments that remain I must not forget to welcome you, and this I do very heartily, because, *first*, we bear in common the one significant name, Christian, which is after all the best badge. I am sure that the true Christian bearing which we expect to be exhibited on the part of delegates to this Convention as they pass in and out of the homes in this city, will make a much deeper impression than all the ribbon and gold and silver badges in existence.

Then I welcome you because, *second*, we are interested in a kindred work, about which you are come together here to consult. Knowing something of the history of our own work, as I believe you do, you will understand that it is but natural that we should desire that the work be strongly aggressive. It is a significant fact that while the young people of the church are banded together to push forward Christian work as never before, at the same time all the influences of the evil one are being exerted to reach and destroy the youth of our land.

Third, you are welcome because we recognize the fact that you seek to exalt the same Lord, and so we are bound very closely together. In these days of blessing we believe that you will be careful to put Him first, that in the midst of so much that will entertain the ear, attract the eye and move the emotions, that you will not forget to crown Him Lord of all.

Last, we welcome you because we believe that your chief desire with us is to honor the word of God, and we believe that there will be no questions arising here about the new theories so prevalent in our day, but that there will be a sturdy clinging to the safe, old-fashioned Bible road. We gladly bow to the ability of some of the new teachers; the only trouble is that they teach too much, have too many ways, and they leave us more perplexed than we were at first. They remind me very much, in the multiplicity of views which they hold on given topics, of the old colored woman in Virginia, who, when asked by a gentleman if he could not make his way through her master's plantation and so take a short cut in reaching a certain road that he desired to follow, said to him:

"Why, certainly, master, you can go this way. All you have to do is simply to follow this path as far as the old black hen's nest."

"But," he said, "I don't know where the black hen's nest is."

"Why," she said, "every child on the plantation knows that, but if you don't know where it is, you follow this path until you come to a crooked fence and on the other side of the fence you will see three roads. If you take the wrong one you will wish you hadn't." [*Laughter*.]

So we believe that the safest thing for us to do is to cling closely to the old-fashioned, plain way laid down in the word of God, and not get lost in the endeavor to find new ways which are vague at best.

We are glad to have come; we expect a blessing from your presence, and hope you will stay as long as you can. [*Applause*.]

President Clark: You will hear the word "inter" used many times during this Convention,— interdenominational, interurban, international. I am glad to say that Rev. Geo. H. Wells, D. D., of Montreal, one of the trustees of the United Society and one who is a representative of this international feature of our work, will respond to these addresses of welcome. [*Applause*.]

ADDRESS OF REV. GEO. H. WELLS, D.D.

Mr. President and friends,— one and all, ladies and gentlemen, residents and visitors, hosts and guests together in this great gathering of Christian purpose and endeavor, mine is a heavy, though a pleasant task.

It is not easy to respond in fitting terms to the welcomes that have been so cordially and generously pronounced. We have received right royal greeting. The various interests and institutions of this community have risen up together, and vied with one another in speaking glowing words of salutation and in giving gracious assurance of their gladness for our coming to their cities and their homes. The committee of arrangements, upon whom have rested so great burdens of anxiety and responsibility, have not only performed cheerfully their duties, but they have had the further and surprising grace, to rejoice in tribulation, and to thank us for the toil and the trouble we have caused them. The churches through their honored pastors have expressed their hearty sympathy and voiced their warm approval of our work. The Young Men's Christian Association has met us with a warm, fraternal grasp. It is but meet and right that it should do so, for that organization is the elder brother and fore-runner of our own,—the solitary and severe Elijah that has led the way for a gentler and more socially inclined Elisha. [*Applause.*] What it has accomplished in bringing together young men of different churches and conditions, and binding them into one brotherhood of Christian life and work, has well prepared and prophesied the coming of our wider effort, the Christian Endeavor movement. Its high aim is to gather and unite in a single society of Christian fellowship and labor all young people of both sexes and of every class. [*Applause*]; its ardent hope is to be itself herald and helper of that broader and better union which shall include all Christians, in which there shall be "neither Jew nor Greek, neither bond nor free, neither male nor female," neither old nor young, for all shall be one in Christ Jesus. [*Applause.*] Most wonderful and beautiful of all — a thing so sweet and strange that it seems miraculous and millennial,— is the fact that St. Paul and Minneapolis, these twin, keen rivals of the North, for once forgot their strife and forbear to provoke one another any more, except to love for us and to good works in our behalf. [*Laughter and applause.*] The representatives of both these cities have spoken us so fair, and each has painted in so glowing colors the charms of his own place, that we have been in a strait betwixt two, not knowing which one to prefer, and have felt like exclaiming "How blest could we be with either, were t'other fair charmer away." [*Laughter.*] Fortunately we are not compelled to choose between them. They have both received us to their homes, and we will respond by taking them both to our hearts and holding them in equal honor and esteem.

Gentlemen who have spoken: we thank you all for your good words of hail and cheer, and we pray that while we meet in these great assemblies, the one Lord and Master may be so visibly among us, that we shall all be conscious of His presence and shall see no man but Jesus only.

We are glad to come hither to this favored and attractive region. If environment be so potential, as the scientists now say, we surely ought to catch encouragement and inspiration from these scenes. We stand here upon lofty and central ground. At this point we are about midway between the eastern and the western, and not far, also, from equidistant between the northern and southern seas. Over these wide prairies the pure winds of heaven breathe with free and open force. From these high plains start streams to flow across the continent and to fall into distant and diverse seas. The mighty Mississippi springs from one of the seven thousand silver lakes that Minnesota bears upon her ample breast and speeds away to the great southern gulf.

The Red River of the North leaps from another of these lakes close by and runs in the opposite direction to empty into the Bay of Hudson in the far North. If I am rightly informed, these two streams approach each other so nearly, that at one point the portage of a single mile will carry a canoe from the current of the one and launch it upon the other, thus crossing the one brief break in the great waterway that stretches from tropical to arctic climes. The magnificent St. Lawrence, that monarch of the rivers, — well, no, it doesn't rise in Minnesota; [*Laughter.*] we cannot grant you that honor; the St. Lawrence is Canadian at its source as at its mouth; but it flows from the Lake of the Woods, a sheet of water, that sits astride the boundary fence between this State and Canada, — this king of rivers, which by its reservoirs forms the chain of the great lakes, which marches seaward to the music of Niagara's thunder, which widens towards its end to a majestic gulf and grasps the great Newfoundland in its teeth, this truly regal stream draws many of its headwaters from this region, and is ready to bear your vessels from Minnesota's harbors half way upon their voyage to Europe. [*Applause.*] Is not this a fitting and inspiring place for our Convention? While we are met in these exalted scenes, may we not hope to be raised up and made to sit together in heavenly places in Christ Jesus? May we not believe that the breath of the Holy Spirit will blow powerfully upon us? May we not think that from our assembly shall burst streams of sacred influence to reach and to refresh the farthest corners of the land?

We have come up hither from every part of this vast continent. The United Society of Christian Endeavor has said to the North, "Give up," and to the South, "Keep not back; bring my sons from afar and my daughters from the ends of the earth," and they have listened and obeyed. From the rocky portals of the East and from the golden gateways of the West our hosts have come, in ever gathering and growing force, until prophetic vision is fulfilled and the beholders cry, "Who are these that fly as a cloud and as doves to their windows?" I believe that every State and Territory in the Union, and every Province and portion of the Dominion has sent its representatives to this, the greatest Christian convocation that has ever met on this round world of ours. [*Applause.*] We have come, too, from every section of the Christian church. We have not yet attained that perfect union in which all differences disappear, and we wear no name but that belonging to our common head. We still retain our separate camps and titles, and each one bears aloft that banner which he believes most truly represents our common faith. Here are sober Congregationalists, boasting their descent from the Puritans and bent on proving themselves the worthy sons of noble sires Here are sturdy Presbyterians, talking much of John Calvin and John Knox and bound to prove their orthodoxy by practising as well as by preaching the perseverance of the saints. Here are stately Episcopalians, who claim the grace of apostolical succession and are ready to make it good by showing apostolical faith and works. Here are beloved friends who bear the name of that grand Christian hero, Martin Luther, who come to us a splendid contribution from the German and the Scandinavian fatherlands. Here are fervent Methodists, fresh from keeping the centennial of John Wesley's death and resolved to make their second century of history yet grander than the first. Here are sturdy Baptists, sometimes thought a little narrow, but who will yield to none in this Convention for Christian charity and breadth. I have heard it said that Methodists are fiery and Baptists watery, and that it is not safe to put them together lest they should quench each other. Well, that depends upon the mode in which they are applied. Rightly mingled, fire and water make steam, [*Loud applause.*] and steam is the great motor that drives the world's machinery and turns the wheels of travel and of trade. We are going to put them skilfully together here and we expect that they will produce tremendous power, and, under the guidance of our wise and practised engineer we look to see our gospel train show great speed and staying power. [*Applause.*] But what can I more say of all our Christian tribes and sects, for the time would fail me to tell of the Gideons and the Baraks, the Jepthahs and the Samsons, the Samuels and the Davids, the prophets and the worthies who make up our mighty host. Suffice it to confess with sorrow that our divisions are too many, and to breathe

the earnest prayer that the spirit of this Convention and the influence of our Society may always be strong toward the making of more Christians and fewer sects. [*Applause.*] Meanwhile, let us rejoice most heartily in this. We can come together, no one abating a jot of his own denominational loyalty or preference, neither denying nor forgetting one of the many points in which we differ and yet grasp one another by the hand, call one another brother, and thank God for real and blessed unity. We have "all obtained like precious faith through the righteousness of God and our Saviour, Jesus Christ." "We have one Lord, one faith and one baptism of the Holy Spirit." This Convention is neither denominational nor undenominational, but interdenominational, crossing without obliterating all lines between the churches, and stimulating all to work more earnestly for the coming of God's kingdom and the doing of His will on earth as it is done in heaven.

We leave behind us here the jars and wrangles of the sects and schools. Questions of the new theology and the higher criticism and the advanced ritual come not to offend or vex us here. Rather will we confer together upon the great practical and pressing themes of Christian life. Especially upon this problem will we seek for light and help: — How may we discover and develop the talent and unknown power of the Christian church? How shall we train most surely and wisely our young Christians, so that "our sons may be as plants grown up in their youth; that our daughters as corner stones, polished after the similitude of a palace"? How shall we roll away the reproach of slothfulness and silence from our membership, and bring in that happier day when amid all Christ's followers there shall not be left one idle hand or one dumb tongue? These are the matters that we meet to consider and discuss; and while we talk of them, may He, whose we all are and whom we seek to serve, draw nigh and join Himself to us, so teaching us from His word, so filling us with His Spirit, that we shall go down better instructed and prepared in mind and heart to do His will and to accomplish greater things than we have ever done before.

This Convention is international as well as interdenominational. In behalf of the Canadians here present, I owe an especially warm and grateful acknowledgement for the welcome you have given. We come from homes in the far North. We trust that our hearts are not cold; but if they were as frigid as the Canadian climate is sometimes supposed to be, they must quickly soften in the sunshine of your presence. [*Applause.*] It is good for citizens of different countries, as well as for members of different churches, sometimes to meet together. Such intercourse broadens views, dispels prejudice and promotes respect for one another. It teaches us that all the virtues and advantages do not belong to any single clime or country. It shows us that beneath our seeming differences there lies our common manhood, having the same great hopes and needs. Especially is such fellowship helpful and pleasant when the nations represented are near neighbors and closely connected with one another, as in the present case. We have, indeed, our separate forms and names. You call your highest legislature Congress; we call ours Parliament. You celebrate your national birthday on the fourth of July; we are a little more alert and keep ours on the first. Your chief magistrate is the President; ours is the Queen. God bless and keep them both! Your flag is the beauteous banner of the Stars and Stripes; [*Loud applause.*] ours is the time-honored standard of the Union Jack. [*Applause.*] Here they hang twined lovingly together on this wall. We are glad that almost a century has passed since they last met in battle shock. We pray that they may never be opposed again. [*Loud applause.*] May all their future meetings be as peaceful as is this. May all their rivalries henceforth be those of generous friends and not of bitter foes. Meeting here beneath their ample and encircling folds today, we may well thank God for the rich past to which we both lay equal claim, and may both look forward to the future that is big with promise and radiant with hope.

Mr. President, it seems to me that we may draw a noble and inspiring lesson from these very flags. Look at them for a moment. At first they seem quite different, and one might say they had no common term nor ground. But gaze a little longer, and you shall see that after all they are very much alike. They are composed of like material. Why, sir, the bunting from which these flags are made might have grown on the same sheep, been dyed in the same vat, woven in the same loom and cut from the same piece. The very same colors, the red, the white and the blue, are blended in them both. [*Loud applause.*] They both stand for the same great principles of freedom, justice and progress in the earth. [*Renewed applause.*] The difference betwen them is not one of matter, only one of order and arrangement. Both nationalities have used the same materials, but each has cut and shaped them to its own character and needs. Each banner tells the story of its people in characters so plain that he who will may read. I look upon your banner, and I count 13 stripes, representing the original colonies which won their liberty and their self-government a hundred years ago. I count also 44 stars which typify the States that glitter in the goodly constellation of today. I look upon our flag and I see there three crosses, placed one upon another. They are the standards of St. Patrick, St. Andrew and St. George, the patron saints of Ireland, Scotland and England. Together they represent the union of those countries, and so they fitly form the flag of the united realm. My friends, no other standards upon earth so closely resemble one another as do these. No other nations are so closely kindred and connected as those they represent. [*Applause.*] Let us never forget our common heritage of blood and creed. Let us "look diligently lest any root of bitterness springing up" should trouble and estrange our hearts. As Abraham said to Lot: "Let there be no strife, I pray thee, between me and thee, and between my herdmen and thy herdmen, for we are brethren;" so let us say here today, Americans and Canadians, to each other, "Let there be no strife between you and us, nor between your fishermen and our fishermen, [*Cheers and prolonged applause.*] whether in the East or West, whether they catch cod or seal." [*Renewed applause.*]

But there are French Canadians as well as British. A large portion of our countrymen speak a language that is not English, and hold a faith that is not Protestant. It might be thought at first that these could furnish no link of union to our countries and bring no theme of interest to our Convention. The very opposite is true. Why, do you know that it was French Canadians, or Frenchmen who came through Canada, who discovered and explored this region where we stand today? Spreading from the valley of the St. Lawrence westward and southward, those brave men rested not until they reached the Gulf of Mexico and the Pacific Coast. You call this region new, and Dr. Christie has been telling us of its superlative youth. It is new in settlement and development, but those brave priests and pioneers of France were here two centuries ago. They pierced the virgin forests; they skirted the great streams and inland seas; they crossed the pathless prairies, and everywhere they went, they planted the pennant of the lily and the cross in sign that they claimed this continent for King and Pope. They have left lasting memorials in the names which commemorate themselves and which bear witness to their Christian faith and their Gallic speech. This continent is strewn all over with these names. Champlain, La Salle, Joliet, Marquette, Detroit, St. Ignace or Ignatius, founder of the Jesuits, Duluth, St. Anthony, St. Paul, St. Louis, La Crosse, Prairie du Chien, Dubuque, New Orleans, and westward Les Mauvaises Terres (Bad Lands), La Roche Jaune (Yellowstone), Lac Pend D'Oreille,—these and many others are instances of what I mean. Two of the chief streets in Minneapolis are Nicollet and Hennepin,—named for two of those old French discoverers. Why, think of it, dear friends; if it hadn't been for French Canadians, this country might never have been discovered, [*Laughter*] and St. Paul and Minneapolis might not have been at all. [*Renewed laughter.*] My tongue falters and my mind shrinks in terror at the thought. Surely, we Canadians, who are the successors, though not the sons of those hardy explorers, cannot be foreigners or strangers on this soil. If we were not so modest, we might lay claim to this whole region, [*Laughter*] and at one fell swoop annex the homes and persons of this whole Convention. Be not alarmed. We are not so ambitious. Canada has land enough already; she only lacks somewhat for people.

Now, Christian Endeavorers are the very kind of settlers we desire. You have sent us some emigrants that we have prized but very little. Your boodling aldermen, your absconding bank officials and your defaulting county treasurers have been more fond of us than we have been of them. [*Laughter and applause.*] But if such men and women as I see before me now will come to Canada, we promise to receive them all with open hearts and arms. Indeed, so anxious for your coming are we, that we will woo you with our sweetest and most persuasive strains. I give you this early and timely warning that the Canadian delegates to this Convention have come hither on purpose to capture and annex the grand International Christian Endeavor Convention for 1892. [*Loud applause and cheers from Canada delegates.*] And we propose to do it. We should have done it this afternoon, but the New York delegation is belated, and has not arrived. We understand that they have put in a rival claim; and with that magnanimity and generosity which always characterize the subjects of our beloved Queen, we give them a chance; I hope they will get here; but understand, the next Convention is to meet in Montreal. [*Applause.*] You are to come to us and see the broad fair land in which we dwell and make acquaintance with our goodly city of the Royal Mount. We confidently expect that many of you will be so pleased that you will stay with us, and we are sure that those of you who must go back will carry with you a kind remembrance and regard for us and for our northern land.

But I trespass too far upon your patience. I have not time to marshal all the good and cogent reasons that should bring you to Montreal next year, but there is one that I cannot omit. Many of you have supposed that our portion of Canada is wholly Roman Catholic and French. Persons who knew that I lived in Montreal have been surprised to hear me speak English and have asked if I did not always preach in French at home. [*Laughter.*] You have thought that the Province of Quebec was a poor, priest-ridden, benighted country, a very Nazareth out of which no good thing could ever come. Now, what will you say when I tell you that the Christian Endeavor movement comes from the Province of Quebec? Whom do you most love and praise as the leader and founder of this work? Who is the man whom Christian Endeavorers most delight to honor, talking of him with filial affection, and calling him "Father Endeavor" Clark? [*Applause.*] Who do you think he is? Whence do you suppose he comes? I will tell you, for I am sure a great many of you do not know. He is a native Canadian; he was born in the Province of Quebec, not far from the city of Montreal. [*Applause.*]

Now, last winter many of us went on a loving pilgrimage to Portland, that we might keep the decennial of our Society beside the cradle where it had its birth. Next year had you not better go a little farther back, and pay a visit to the country from which the discoverer and promoter of Christian Endeavor comes? I have heard of a tourist who visited an Irish Cathedral and was shown a human skull and was told that it was the skull of St. Patrick. He looked at it somewhat doubtfully and said, "Oh, but I saw a much larger skull of St. Patrick in Dublin the other day. How do you explain this?" Well, the Irish beadle's wit was equal to the demand, and he replied at once: "Ah, sir, this is the skull of St. Patrick when he was a boy." [*Laughter.*] Now, Portland and Boston may plume themselves upon the residence and ministry of Dr. Clark in later years, but we shall always boast that he first belonged to us. He was ours when he was a boy. Now, all Canadians are not like Dr. Clark, not even those that are born in Quebec and live near Montreal. I wish they were. Would that our people were all prophets, and that the Lord would put His Spirit upon them all! But come and see for yourselves, and you may make some great discoveries upon your own account.

In closing I wish to say, in behalf of this vast throng — and I wish I could say it with the power of ten thousand lungs and tongues — a deep and hearty "Thank you" and "God bless you" to these our friends and generous hosts. My last word is this; Come all of you to Montreal next year, for we are filled with thankfulness for this reception and welcome, and we are burning to display our gratitude by deeds as well as words. [*Prolonged applause.*]

The hymn, "Blest be the tie that binds," was then sung, after which the benediction was pronounced by Bishop Samuel Fallows, D. D., of Chicago.

THURSDAY EVENING.

During the half hour preceding the exercises of the evening session, the delegates as they assembled in the great convention hall joined in singing a number of the new Christian Endeavor songs from "Gospel Hymns, No. 6," prepared by Mr. Sankey and others with this Convention in view. The singing was deeply impressive and the new tunes won instant approval.

The auditorium was almost completely filled at eight o'clock, when Rev. O. H. Tiffany, D. D., LL. D., who presided, announced the hymn, "Stand up for Jesus." Following this, Dr. Tiffany requested the audience to join in repeating the 23d Psalm, which was done heartily — the vast volume of sound, in this declaration of faith, producing a profound impression. Prayer was offered by Rev. S. L. B. Speare, of Minneapolis. "Nearer my God, to Thee" was then sung as perhaps it was never sung before, after which Dr. Tiffany announced, as the first item on the programme, the annual report of General Secretary J. W. Baer. Mr. Baer was received with much enthusiasm, and many of the statements given in the report awoke emphatic applause.

REPORT OF GENERAL SECRETARY BAER.

Another year has gone and we meet again. Divinely blest be the tie that binds our hearts in Christian Endeavor, and I am to tell you of the breadth of the Christian Endeavor movement. Its wide outreach has been unexpected from the first by its human leaders. God has caused its swift, continuous, and successful progress. He has directed its irresistible momentum.

After ten years, and in the morning light of its second decade, we pause to consider what God hath wrought. Last year, at the St. Louis Convention, we rejoiced in the great extension of our fellowship which had been made in the twelve months previous to that time, and with thankful hearts attempted to overcome our astonishment when we were informed that there were 11,013 societies in the world, an increase over the previous year of 3,341 societies.

Another year, what would it bring forth? It has been said, "He enjoys much who is thankful for a little." Then who can measure our enjoyment and thankfulness when we know that the growth of that year has been outstripped, and now we must add one thousand, yes, two, and a third, and still another, and yet another thousand to the St. Louis figures? And more, for now we have regularly reported societies to the number of 16,274. Verily, "A grateful mind is a great mind"; and what minds then are ours tonight!

AN INTERNATIONAL MOVEMENT.

The Christian Endeavor movement has become world-wide. Three hundred and seven societies have reported from across the waters; there are others from whom we have not heard. Travel where you will, land where you will in journeying around the world, and you are likely to find Christian Endeavor societies. You will be interested to know of the five foreign countries that have reported the greatest number of societies, as shown by my records: England, the old mother country, leads, and has 120 societies; Australia has 82, and more forming each week; India, 30; Turkey, 12; and China, 7; By another year we hope through our superintendents to gather more complete statistics from the foreign fields.

And now as to our friends, brethren and sisters across the imaginary line, who have adopted the Christian Endeavor principles so enthusiastically. Canada has reported societies in every single Province throughout the Dominion. The five Provinces having the greatest number of societies are as follows: Ontario. having 458; Nova Scotia, 156; Quebec, 63; New Brunswick, 36; and British Columbia, 25. In all Canada there are 829 societies. Loyal as they are, every one of them, to the Union Jack, with its cross of St. Andrew and St. George, and with hands clasped in ours in Christian Endeavor, while over us wave the Stars and Stripes, we both take step, and shoulder to shoulder, with a united front, place in the van and above all other emblems the blood-stained banner of the cross, believing it to be a portent of disaster to the hosts of sin and a pledge and prophecy of victory for the army of the living God. Surely, surely, ours is an international movement.

But what of the United States, the land of its nativity? Briefly, let me name the five States which have the largest number of societies within their borders. New York, long the "banner" State, still leads the list with 2,354 societies; then Pennsylvania comes along with 1,464; Ohio, with 1,061: Illinois has 1,043; and Massachusetts 918; and a number of other States are not far behind, crowding one upon another, for every single State and Territory is represented.

The annual conventions, held in the various States, Territories, and Provinces, have been wonderful gatherings. They grow materially and are becoming great springs of spiritual refreshment. Their helpfulness in the past suggests even greater fields of usefulness for the future. Shall we not, more than ever we have, aid the officers of these various unions in their services, which are always freely and gratuitously given, busy pastors and busy men and women as many of them are? Follow the histories of the State, Territorial, and Provincial unions, from the first one, organized in Connecticut in 1885, up to the one formed last month in North Carolina, the youngest, and you will find sufficient warrant for their existence. May God continue to bless them abundantly.

WINNERS OF THE BANNERS.

At St. Louis, last year, a badge banner, made up, as it was, of badges from hundreds of societies, was displayed amidst much enthusiasm. Acting upon the suggestion made by a delegate, it was decided to place that banner for one year in the custody of the State, Territory, or Province that should show the greatest proportionate increase in its number of local societies during the year just closing. Therefore with pleasure I desire to inform you of the five States, Territories, or Provinces that have made the largest percentages of gain since the St. Louis Convention. The Territory of Oklahoma stands first and gains the banner. British Columbia is second, Nova Scotia comes third, Virginia a very close fourth, and Alabama, Arkansas, and Mississippi each have the same ratio of gain and take fifth place. The work in Oklahoma speaks for itself and has been a faithful one. With one society last year, that figure has increased thirteen times. The work in Canada I have already spoken of, and now with pleasure I desire you to note the excellent record made by our sister States from the South, who have been aggressively marshalling their forces under the Christian Endeavor banner. We who live in the States that have been longest blessed with this movement shall have to look out for our laurels.

It was also decided at St. Louis that another badge banner should be made this year and given here to the State, Territory, or Province that should show the greatest *aggregate* gain in the past twelve months. Pennsylvania, having gained in the last year 645 local societies, is therefore entitled to hold that banner for one year. New York is second, with 559; Iowa has increased her list 382; Ohio, 380; and Kansas, 278. Think of it! Even the fifth State in this list, Kansas, has gained more societies in the past year, within her own borders, than the whole number of societies reported to the United Society during the first five years of its history.

LOCAL UNIONS.

One of the later developments and one of the most helpful in the practical emphasis of our fellowship is the formation of town, city, and district unions throughout the world. Many of these unions are doing aggressive missionary work in the cities, and in passing I desire to mention the five largest city unions of Christian Endeavor societies. Philadelphia is the largest, and has 182 societies; Chicago, 160; New York City, 80; St. Louis, 67, and Brooklyn, 65. Greatly tempted am I to stop and tell you of the evangelistic and missionary work done through the various unions, but lack of time will prevent. Mention must be made, however, of the twenty-five societies which have been organized in public institutions, among which are the societies in reform schools and prisons. There are also four Floating Societies of Christian Endeavor to be found on men-of-war, and it is hoped ere long we may have made some advance in the army as we have in the navy.

JUNIOR SOCIETIES.

But I must hasten on and turn our attention to a branch of our movement that bids fair to rival any of its many streams that are making glad the city of our God,—the Junior Societies of Christian Endeavor. It has been a short time, comparatively, since the first Junior society was organized in Iowa, and now hundreds are springing up all over the land. Already local unions of Junior Christian Endeavor societies have been formed. The first meetings of that character reported to us convened in Winona and Minneapolis, in this good State of Minnesota. Literature has been provided, and in every way are the Juniors and their work recognized as one of the greatest of the many possibilities of the Christian Endeavor movement. No convention programme, be it local, State, or international, is complete without generous provisions being made for the Junior work. Their distinctive badge is rapidly becoming as familiar as the Christian Endeavor pin of the seniors, so well known now to all Christendom. It has been especially difficult to gather accurate statistics in regard to these societies, but 855 societies have already reported and many more are known to us. Illinois is the banner Junior Endeavor State, having 122 societies; Massachusetts next, with 75; Iowa, 61; Minnesota, 45; and New Jersey fifth, with 42, these five States leading the others in this branch of our work.

INTERDENOMINATIONALISM.

During the past year more than any other, the Society of Christian Endeavor has stood firmly and loyally under God's guidance as an increasing force to broad, genial self-respecting inter-, *inter-*, INTER-denominationalism. The spirit of federation and Christian fellowship increases. It is a legacy too precious to be held lightly, a possession too valuable to lose. Some who have heretofore called the Society *undenominational* and have consequently held aloof from it have become its ardent advocates and promoters as they have become familiar with the principles and aims of our Society. The Christian Endeavor Society has promoted Christian federation, and does not seek to establish any formal organic church union. "Christ," "Co-operation," "Conquest," it has been well said, are our watchwords. The first society was a Congregational society, and for several years that denomination led all others in point of numbers. As the movement spread, it was found that the Christian Endeavor principles could be applied to any church and every evangelical denomination. Then denominations one after another became represented until now societies are reported in thirty evangelical denominations. The five denominations having the greatest number of societies reported to me are: first the Presbyterian, with 4,019; the Congregationalist second, with 3,545; the Baptist third, with 2,381; the Methodist fourth, with 2,068, including thirty-five or more Epworth Leagues of Christian Endeavor, and the Christian (Disciples) fifth, with 801 societies. Believe me, each society is loyal to its own church and its own denomination, yet one with us in presenting a united front to the forces of sin. But let me express myself on this subject with the utmost economy of words and sum it all up by saying, "All hail to the growing power of interdenominationalism."

INDIVIDUAL SERVICE.

I have been speaking a good deal about the growth of local societies, local, State, Territorial, and Provincial unions, the forward movement denominationally, etc., and have not referred to our individual members. The importance of individualism is made manifest more and more in our work and in many ways. We do not forget our part and our work in this warfare. We believe in co-operation and all that, and we also believe in individualism, and emphasize it prominently by accepting for ourselves individually definite pledged service. You will agree with me, of course, that the growth of the local societies "is marvellous in our eyes," but what can we say when we number the recruits in this rapidly increasing international and interdenominational host? Listen. At Chicago in 1888, 310,000 members reported; at Philadelphia in 1889, 485,000; this number increased at St. Louis last year to 660,000, and then we began to look forward to the time when seven figures would be required in naming our grand legions. That time is here. It has come, and we individually have a certain place in this grand army. We march with our local societies, in our local union, with our State union, and at the same time loyally swing our denominational colors to the breeze, and yet we are individuals, each one, one of a million. O how like a sweet morsel under our tongue we have turned that word "million" when we have said "nearly a million," and now to be able to say a million and even more! Here in the tenth year of Christian Endeavor, with 16,274 local societies in the wide, wide world, we are delighted to announce a total membership of 1,008,980 soldiers of the Lord Jesus Christ.

SOME PRACTICAL RESULTS.

But the material and numerical growth is not all we would return thanks for at this time. Had I the time, and were the design of this report other than statistical, I would ask you to think of the earnest efforts which have been put forth for Christ's sake and consequently blessed. You can think of them as they are passing rapidly before your mind's eye. A determination to get good and do good; a desire for a modest and teachable spirit; hearts aflame with the love of Christ; a greater and increasing spirit of love for our own church; a closer bond of union between the society and the Sunday school; an increased attendance on the part of the young people upon all regular church services and the mid-week prayer meeting; the definite and practical work of the various committees; the acceptance of the new revised pledge by hundreds of societies previously organized with the first pledge; the systematic study of the Bible and an ever-increasing knowledge of its use in hand-to-hand work for the saving of souls; the cordial, heart-felt words of praise and commendation from pastors who with thankful hearts praise God for the movement which has been one of the instruments in His hands for making their young people effective; a vigorous attack upon all forms of doubtful amusements; open hostility to every plan for destroying in any way the sanctity of the Sabbath Day, illustrated by the united desire to exert an influence upon the directors of the Columbian Exposition that will prompt them to keep their doors closed on Sunday; aggressively waged war against the cause of intemperance and the sale and manufacture of intoxicating beverages of all kinds; the interest in missions which is sweeping through our societies, evidenced not only by their pledged contributions to our regular denominational missionary boards, home and foreign, but by the fact that many of our members have given themselves to Christ's work in bringing all to know His name; the excellent education our young people are deriving from the plans for proportionate and systematic giving which have been carried on in many societies; a clearer understanding that the Society is only a means to an end; a more thorough knowledge on the part of all that the relationship of each local society to the United Society is only the bond of a common name, common methods of work, and a common warfare against a common enemy, and that the United Society exerts no authority over any local society, levies no taxes, and asks for no contributions, and that every society can be affiliated with its own denominational union and conference, and can at the same time have the delightful fellowship that is to be found in interdenominational conventions such as this.

THE WORK OF THE PRESS.

But I must stop, for I might go on for some time to come, reporting the results of the past year. I can only take time to tell you that the printing department of the United Society has prospered, largely through the good business management of our agent, Mr. Wm. Shaw. Mention is made of this, as it is often asked how so large a work as that accomplished by the United Society of Christian Endeavor can be carried on without asking the societies for a penny to pay expenses from one year's end to the other, while at the same time the only source of income is from the sale of the badges and literature, and the printing done for local societies. The answer is that everything is conducted in the most economical way, and that very much service is rendered to the societies "free gratis for nothing." We do not know of any organization to which so much time and labor is gratuitously and gladly given.

One of the most important factors in the promotion of Christian Endeavor during the last few years, particularly the year just ending, is the work of the press, particularly the denominational religious press. There is scarcely a leading religious journal in the country that does not have its regular column devoted to news from the societies and to the exposition of the uniform prayer-meeting topic. This work has been invaluable, and, in turn, by an offer of generous prizes, the United Society has called forth many valuable essays instructing Endeavorers as to the introduction of denominational papers into all the homes of our church, and I take further occasion, at this time, to urge the claims of the whole denominational press upon our young people.

And what shall I say of *The Golden Rule?* Occupying a field of its own, it is supplementary to all other papers. Standing, as I do, in no way connected officially or financially with *The Golden Rule* or its publishers, the Golden Rule Company, I can say with all the personality I can put behind my words, that *The Golden Rule* has been always, and is today, a great blessing to the cause of Christian Endeavor. It has modestly made its own way, seeking to give the best methods of work to young people who are striving to work "for Christ and the Church." Its editor and the officers of the United Society have constantly said by voice and pen that it believed that it had its own field, and in no way made itself a substitute for any denominational paper. "If you can take but one paper, let it be your regular denominational paper, rather than *The Golden Rule*," has always been insisted upon.

THE GAIN TO THE CHURCHES.

Believing that there are many important matters I have not even touched upon, let me, last and above all, for your prayerful consideration, give you the best of the statistics I have collected for your interest. If I have tired you up to this time, take encouragement, for you will be refreshed now. God only knows all the results of our labors, but we do know of 82,500 members of our societies who have become church members since last we met in St. Louis. Eighty-two thousand five hundred in one year! "Praise God, from whom all blessings flow." The past year's history has been the most notable and prosperous in all the history of the Society, its growth unprecedented and astonishing; and to all that add the fact that 82,500 have joined churches and can say, "We are laborers together with God." Eighty-two thousand five hundred who are, under God's guidance, fast transfiguring the word "duty" to the word "privilege." How much or how little the societies have influenced this grand result we know not; sufficiently thankful are we to know that these young people became church members from the ranks of our societies. How much more expressive are those figures in proclaiming our motto to the world, "For Christ and the Church," than the most eloquent appeal one could make. Eighty-two thousand five hundred! Yes, it seems a great many, and we thank God for them, every one; but let us not forget, in this hour of glad hallelujahs, the possibilities and the future before us. One hundred and sixty-eight thousand one hundred and sixty-two of our members today are in the associate lists. How many can we win for Christ the coming year? How many? Eighty-two thousand five hundred? More! Shall it not be more? God grant it.

PAST AND FUTURE.

This Convention marks the close of the tenth year of Christian Endeavor. A marvellous decade! Little did Dr. Clark, or any one else, think, on Feb. 2. 1881, in Portland, Me., that he was sowing the seed which in God's hands contained the germs of this world-wide movement. Ten years! And what a written history and what a history unwritten! Young people attached to their church as they never were before, given work to do at home and abroad for Christ's sake; youthful enthusiasm; youthful sacrifice; youthful consecration, — all this revealed during this first decade of Christian Endeavor. Let us sum it up in one sentence, with simplicity, plainly, all in all. *A strong grasp upon evangelical, evangelistic gospel truth, and a common longing for the power of the Holy Spirit to make effectual all forms of organized effort in the Christian endeavor to win the whole world for Christ.*

Now turn, turn, dear friends, from this backward look, pleasing, cheering, comforting, and encouraging as it may have been, and with the spirit for the exaltation of Christ in our hearts and very lives, let us think, plan, and act for the future.

Being better than any words of mine, and particularly appropriate at this time, let me quote to you these verses, written by a pastor well known to us all, the Rev. David J. Burrell, D. D., of New York City, a sentiment which I hope will stir your heart as it has mine, after ten years of Christian Endeavor: —

An angel came from heaven down
 To speak one word, and speak it ever,
To quicken hearts and kindle eyes,
And move dull souls from sloth to rise
And win a glorious renown,
 With one brave word, "Endeavor!"

Ten years in service thus he wrought,
And then at heaven's gate besought,
 "My Lord, what wilt thou now?"
"Return," said He, "and ten years more
Proclaim thy message o'er and o'er;
 Be faithful thou."

"And then?" "And then serve ten years more,
And ten years more, and so forever.
For angel ne'er had nobler task,
Nor of his Lord could nobler ask,
Than to proclaim forevermore,
That potent word, 'Endeavor!'"

Another hymn was then sung by the united choir and congregation, after which Dr. Tiffany introduced Mr. Ira D. Sankey, the well-known evangelist, as "the leader of Christian song and the inspirer of many souls." Mr. Sankey sang, "Throw out the life-line," the audience listening in perfect stillness.

The following cablegram was then read by Secretary Baer and received with great enthusiasm:

"Melbourne Australia, July 8. Australia rejoices with you."

Dr. Tiffany then announced the annual address by President F. E. Clark. Dr. Clark was greeted with a genuine ovation, the whole audience rising and joining in the "Chautauqua salute."

THE PRESIDENT'S ANNUAL ADDRESS.

We have come together tonight for the tenth international and interdenominational gathering of a great and spontaneous movement among the young Christians of America. It is fitting that we should consider for what, in God's providence, this movement stands. Can we decipher the handwriting upon the wall? Not the handwriting, please God, that tells of unfaithfulness and speedy destruction, but that which reveals His divine purpose in calling the Society into being.

As such a movement develops, we can see many reasons for its existence, all, doubtless, embraced in the divine plan, such as the promotion of outspoken discipleship, the increase of faith in youthful piety, the development of well-trained workmen for the church, and the increased respect paid to covenant vows; but above and beyond even these priceless blessings, I think we may mention two elements that pre-eminently mark the history of the Christian Endeavor Society. These two features are FIDELITY and FELLOWSHIP; FIDELITY to the local church to which each society and each member of each society belongs, a fidelity without which a true Christian Endeavor Society cannot exist; FELLOWSHIP, a fellowship cemented by a common name, and common vows, and common methods of service,—a fellowship that is exemplified by this magnificent assembly.

Are these two features antagonistic? Nay; I contend that they are necessary one to the other; they supplement and complement one another. Our fidelity will become narrow and bigoted without our fellowship, our fellowship flabby and sentimental without fidelity; but *fidelity* AND *fellowship* may win the world for Christ.

FIDELITY.

Unhesitatingly I say, challenging the most searching criticism, that from the second day of February, 1881, to this ninth day of July, 1891, the Society of Christian Endeavor has stood for *fidelity*, unswerving and unswervable, to the church of God; and not to the abstract church universal, which embraces all good men and all creeds, but to the local, individual, particular church to which each society belongs. Examine the history of the Society with a magnifying lens, read its Constitution with a microscope, weigh its trend and tendency with balances that turn with a hair's weight; and see whether you can find anything that does not speak to the young Christian of allegiance to his own church.

The society related to the church! The word "relation" is too tame and cold a word, unless you say that the daughter is related to the family. So the Society of Christian Endeavor is not a relative of the church; she is, wherever admitted, one of the church family. If there are any words that can make this plainer, if there are any acts that can demonstrate this truth more fully, let us speak these words and perform these acts in this great representative gathering.

I dwell on this point a moment because there are some who, by direct statement and by insinuation, by covert newspaper paragraphs and occasionally by open attack, strive to create the impression that the Christian Endeavor societies are not loyal to their own churches and denominations, and who thus seek to stab our interdenominational fellowship to the heart.

It has been said before, but I say it again, that the words may be emphasized by your indorsement: The Society of Christian Endeavor, by its very principles, when they are understood and adopted, *necessarily* increases church loyalty and denominational fidelity. It makes the young Methodist a better Methodist, the young Presbyterian a better Presbyterian, the young Baptist a better Baptist, the young Congregationalist a better Congregationalist, the young Lutheran a better Lutheran, the young Disciple of Christ a better Disciple of Christ.

FELLOWSHIP.

But since this principle of fidelity is established as securely as words and deeds and history and tendencies can establish anything, why, let me ask, should we not take for our other watchword *Fellowship?* Fidelity and Fellowship, the two wings which will bear upward and onward the Christian Endeavor cause to final victory. "*I believe in the communion of saints.*" This sentence of the Apostles' Creed has awakened an echoing sentiment in every church and in every Christian heart. We have an opportunity of showing, not only of saying, but of demonstrating, in a way never before possible for young Christians in the history of the world, that *we believe* in the communion of saints. The church has waited long for the glad day when, without yielding conscientious scruples, or sacrificing the principles that her different branches held dear, she might unite not only in singing, but in living, the hymn: —

"Blest be the tie that binds
Our hearts in Christian love;
The fellowship of kindred minds
Is like to that above."

Now, for a million young hearts in thirty evangelical denominations, in every realm on the globe, the day has come when Christian fellowship is an inspiring reality. Thank God that the prayer of the ages has been answered, in some little degree at least, in this great Convention of youthful Christians.

Thank God that without endangering a doctrine for which the fathers fought, without imperilling a rite or custom that any sensitive heart holds dear, without weakening a tie that binds any soul to his ancestral church home, we can come together in this fellowship that is as broad and deep and lasting as the love of Christ.

A DUTY.

Moreover, I think the time has come for us not simply to accept in an easy-going way this inheritance, but to stand for it; yes, to glory in it, as we glory in the cross of Christ around which this fellowship gathers. I maintain that this is our duty: —

First, because every church will be stronger because of this fellowship. If I belonged to the most obscure church in the most obscure sect in all Christendom, I would pray and strive for this fellowship, had I only the interests of my own little church in mind. Every regiment, every company, every soldier in every company, is stronger when the great army to which he belongs is united and victorious. Guerilla warfare never wins any great triumphs. To do our work well within the most narrow horizon, we need to look onward and upward to the stars. To fight with bravest heart any little picket-guard skirmish with the enemy, we need to be inspired by the bugle call of victory from other divisions of the army.

I have said that Christian Endeavor stands for fidelity. *Because* it stands for fidelity it must also stand for fellowship, for we cannot be in the largest sense faithful to our own church without the spirit of fraternity with others. We cannot be fully faithful to the city mission, or to the little hillside church, or to our fellow-disciples in the frame schoolhouse where we worship, without the inspiration that we may draw from keeping time with the innumerable hosts that are marching on to victory.

AN IMMEASURABLE BLESSING.

I have heard such a splendid convention as this criticised because it cost money and time and many months of effort, and I must say that such criticism always seems to me to savor of the Judas spirit. This "might have been sold for more than three hundred pence and have been given to the poor." Weigh the fellowship of such a meeting in the balances,—impossible! Reckon its influences in dollars and cents! Measure it with your foot rule! You might as well try to compute the value of the sunlight, or the worth of the dew that distils from heaven, or the commercial value of the rain after a long drought. The good fellowship, the Christian fraternity, the blessed friendships of such a meeting as this cannot be set over against a Minneapolis flour-mill, or a Chicago stockyard, or a New England cotton-factory. And this fellowship, this sense of comradeship among the youthful hosts of God, you need, O brother or sister mine, to take back with you to the little church from which you have come, to enable you to do courageously the work of these coming days.

Does such fellowship make any of you less loyal to your own church? Will you go home from here dissatisfied, listless, and unwilling to do "ye nexte thing"? I leave the answer with you, and I know what it will be. This Convention will never adjourn. This fellowship, which these days of holy communion will cement, shall flow back in refreshing rills of spiritual power to churches in every State and Territory and Province between the two oceans; and even to the churches across the sea the electric thrill of this fellowship will go, and wherever it goes it will carry strength and cheer. Who will voluntarily cut himself off from such a reservoir of power? For the local church, for the individual Christian soul, I plead when I pray that our fellowship may remain unbroken.

Again, the united strength of the common enemy demands that we oppose to him the united strength of our common fellowship.

There are no divisions among the hosts of darkness. "No Sects in Heaven," is the title of a familiar poem; it is quite as true that there are no sects in hell. The evil one marshals all his forces in his assaults against Mansoul. He attacks eye-gate and ear-gate, the citadel and the outworks, simultaneously and hotly. His forces are not weakened by factious disputes. Let not the children of the pit be wiser than the children of the light. Never before did the clans of evil seem so persistently to marshal their united forces for a desperate assault. The watchword of the day is combination. Rumseller is combining with rumseller, distiller with vender, speculator with speculator, libertine with gambler, to resist good laws, to obstruct righteous legislation, to bring about a reign of terror and confusion among the hosts of God. Shall we who represent the coming generation of Christ's warriors play into the enemies' hands by weakening our ranks and dividing our hosts? I cannot believe that we shall.

Mark me, I am not reflecting on denominations, any more than I would reflect upon the regiments, corps, and divisions of an army, but I do depreciate, and so I am sure do you, the spirit that is unwilling to allow any common bond between young disciples, the spirit that would shun a common name and similar methods of work, and that would perpetuate differences and promote rivalries. Here, we believe, in this name, "Christian Endeavor," which recognizes the supremacy of Christ and the supremacy of effort for Him, a common bond of union is found, while at the same time unswerving, steadfast loyalty to the particular division in which we have enlisted is secured. Shall we, I say, make light of such a bond of strength against the united foe? Oh, I believe the fiends in the pit would laugh to see our bonds of union disintegrate and disappear; but I also believe that, God helping us, no such sight will provoke their fiendish glee.

CHRIST'S PRAYER.

Once more, I plead for this interdenominational and international fellowship of the societies because Christ commands it and prayed for it. Listen to this prayer, O young disciple. For you it was offered, and for those whom you represent. It was near the very end; Gethsemane and Calvary, the betrayal, the denial, the scourging and the crucifixion are yet to come; but they are very near, and at this supreme moment our Lord's prayer is for the unity of believers. With the agony of the coming cross before Him, with the blood drops of Gethsemane about to bead His brow, in the longest recorded prayer that He ever uttered, and with reiterated emphasis, He prays: "Neither pray I for these alone, but for them also which shall believe on me through their word [that includes each one of us]; that they all may be one; as thou, Father, art in me, and I in thee, that they also may be one in us: that the world may believe that thou hast sent me. And the glory which thou gavest me I have given them; that they may be one, even as we are one: I in them, and thou in me, that they may be made perfect in one; and that the world may know that thou hast sent me, and hast loved them as thou hast loved me." Brethren and sisters, we have the opportunity in our Christian Endeavor fellowship to answer Christ's prayer, in some worthy way to usher in the glad day to which his petition points forward.

Even now I see that day dawning in the east. It is coming, brothers; it is surely coming. Its early light already gilds the mountain-tops. Of this good time coming one of the leaders* in this Christian Endeavor movement sings in exultant verse: —

* Rev. C. A. Dickinson.

O golden day so long desired,
  Born of a darksome night,
The swinging globe at last is fired
  By thy resplendent light.
And hark! like Memnon's morning chord,
  Is heard from sea to sea
This song: One Master, Christ, the Lord;
  And brethren all are we.

The noises of the night shall cease,
  The storms no longer roar;
The factious foes of God's own peace
  Shall vex His church no more.
A thousand, thousand voices sing
  The surging harmony;
One Master, Christ; one Saviour, King;
  And brethren all are we.

Sing on, ye chorus of the morn,
  Your grand Endeavor strain,
Till Christian hearts, estranged and torn,
  Blend in the glad refrain;
And all the church, with all its powers,
  In loving loyalty,
Shall sing: One Master, Christ, is ours;
  And brethren all are we.

O golden day, the age's crown,
  Alight with heavenly love,
Rare day in prophecy renown,
  On to thy zenith move.
When all the world with one accord,
  In full-voiced unity,
Shall sing: One Master, Christ, our Lord;
  And brethren all are we.

You have been accustomed to give a most kindly greeting at these Conventions to a suggested motto for the coming year. Let this beautiful hymn suggest our motto for 1891. Our great motto, *Pro Christo et Ecclesia*,—"For Christ and the Church," will never be superseded; it embraces all our creed. Our loyalty and our fellowship are expressed by it. But as our yearly watchword, we have said to each other, We are, "not to be ministered unto, but to minister," and again, "We are laborers together with God," while last year we took for our motto, "One is your Master, even Christ; and all ye are brethren." Can we do better, my friends, than again to make this our watchword for the twelve months to come? "One is your Master;" in that sentence is embodied our fidelity. We cannot be faithful to Him without being faithful to His church, our church. "And all ye are brethren;" there is our fellowship.

Let us say it once more, ALL YE, ALL WE, Baptists and Methodists, Presbyterians and Congregationalists, Lutherans and Disciples, Moravians and Memnonites; from East and West and North and South, from either side of that imaginary line called the forty-ninth parallel comes the glad refrain, "One is our Master, even Christ; and we are brethren."

Dr. Clark's address was followed by the singing of the hymn, "Victory through Grace." Secretary Baer then made several announcements and read a telegram of greeting from the New York City Union. Mr. Baer also announced that Bishop Vincent, who was on the programme for the annual sermon, was unable to be present. He had come as far as Chicago, hoping to be able to preach, but the state of his health had compelled him to cancel all his engagements. Mr. Baer stated that Dr. Vincent had said to him and to Mr. Sankey at Chicago, "Had I been a Presbyterian or Congregationalist, I should not have come thus far; but being a Methodist I thought I would try and come so that I might show my sympathy with the Christian Endeavor movement." The audience greeted this statement with prolonged applause.

Dr. O. H. Tiffany, pastor of the Hennepin Avenue Methodist Episcopal Church, of Minneapolis, at the urgent request of the trustees, had kindly consented to address the audience briefly at this point, taking the place of the sermon by Bishop Vincent. He spoke as follows:—

SERMON BY REV. O. H. TIFFANY, D.D. LL.D.

NOTHING but the most uncompromising loyalty to the idea of Christian Endeavor could induce me to attempt to fill a vacancy in a meeting over which I was called to preside, especially a vacancy created by the absence of such a man as Bishop Vincent — a man selected for this position because, by common consent, he is the best qualified of men to speak of Christian educational movements among young in this country. [*Applause.*] A man who, moreover, has had opportunity of prolonged and careful preparation, so that he had thought out all that was to be said and thus he would not need to think while he was speaking; and a man who had the opportunity to pray over every word that he intended to utter, that each expression might receive the baptism of the Holy Spirit. I have not had the opportunity for this preparation; and while I have been earnestly engaged in prayer, it has been for the revival of God's work in our hearts rather than for the success of any individual address or sermon. But the brethren of the trustees have said that some Methodist must take the place of the Methodist bishop and must announce a text and indicate a regular order of procedure. I do not know what text Bishop Vincent would have taken had he been here, but I should not have been at all surprised if he had selected that passage of Scripture to which Dr. Clark called our attention at the close of his most admirable paper, — words that may be found in the seventeenth chapter of the Gospel by St. John, the twenty-first and twenty-second verses. "That they all may be one; as thou, Father, art in me, and I in thee, that they also may be one in us: that the world may believe that thou hast sent me."

We all know that this is Christ's prayer for the *unity* and the *usefulness* of His disciples. It lay so heavily upon His heart, that it was crushed out of His lips; and the thoughts that lay back of His utterance were that this unity and usefulness once achieved would be for the glory of God, for He says, "I pray for them, for I am glorified in them." He also knew and felt that it was desirable for the growth of the disciples themselves to be all one in Him, "that they may be *made perfect* in one." And then he felt that when the time should come, in the diffusion of His gospel, that men could see eye to eye and all be one in the true unity of the Christian faith, then men "may know that thou hast sent me." These were the thoughts in His mind, pressing to His lips this most wonderful petition. I think we are nearer to its realization tonight than the world has ever been before. I doubt if so many earnest and consecrated Christian souls were ever gathered under one roof before, in the oneness of the faith, in loyalty to Christ. [*Applause.*] The world has complained of our segmentary arrangements, of our segregations and our separations. It has made much of our denominationalism and our sectarianism, and it has claimed to be unable to see the oneness of the Christianity which we all profess. There is to be seen here tonight, and there is to be heard in the air of this building and to be felt in the hearts that have been beating here this afternoon and evening, a realization of oneness in Christ which makes us gladsome and fills us with rejoicing. The world forgets that we are brethren, brethren jealous for the Father's honor, brethren contending for the mastery and supremacy in the way of serving Christ which seems best to our individual judgments. And we are here as brethren, with different interpretations of passages of Scripture, with different forms of worship, with somewhat of difference in our creeds; but every man and woman of us loyal above all things else to Jesus as Christ, the Head of the living church. [*Applause.*] The world is unable to see it, for the world looks at those distinctions which separate us and does not perceive the unity which joins us. The world, as one has beautifully expressed it, sees no difference between the eternal ever-living church and the temporary denomination or sect; or as David Thomas still more beautifully puts it, the world has not had its vision clear to see the enormous difference between the eternal Rock of Ages and the temporary tabernacles that we build against its giant breast. But we are building for Christ and the church. The unities which bind us together are becoming stronger than the differences which separate us. We are learning; we rejoice to know that the days of controversialists are past, that the time when a man was mighty according to the size of the trees against which he lifted up his axe has gone, and that now we may all of us, everywhere, in loyalty to that blessed Lord and in the realization of the fidelity and the fellowship of Christian Endeavor, strike hands this side of the river as we expect to join hands when we meet upon the other side. [*Applause.*[

I am glad that I live in a day when there are so many indications of the coming of millennial glories. I am glad to live in a day when the Young Men's Christian Association has shown that it is possible for Christians of every belief and of every denomination to work side by side, none to hinder, all to help. I am glad to live in a day when the Evangelical Alliance has made it possible in all things essential to agree and in all things unessential to differ, and I am glad that we have brought the thought and feeling of the Christian church into that ripening organization. But I am gladder still — though a year or two ago I would not have dared to say that I expected to live to see it — that we have the Christian Endeavor, on top of the Y. M. C. A., in advance of the Evangelical Alliance. What is it brethren, but a great band that is to unite together all the dynamos that are producing Christian forces separately and swing the whole power of the Christian church against the enemies of the Lord Jesus? [*Applause.*]

I have faith in it because it is the *Young People's* Society of Christian Endeavor. [*Applause.*] St. John knew the sources of power. Wisely discriminating in the efficient energies for Christian work, he wrote unto young men because they were strong. The strength of young manhood is back of the Christian Endeavor movement. He wrote to them because they were strong and because the word of God abode in them — the loving, living principle of Christlikeness, growing and developing on the basis of the abiding word. And he also wrote to the young men because they had overcome the wicked one. And so today, with the young people back of the Christian Endeavor movement, I look at it as an expression of loyalty to Christ which makes me think that the time draws near when the Messianic prophecies are to be completely realized, and all the differences that have separated men are to be hushed and stilled before the fidelity and the fellowship in which we live and labor and pray. I should not wonder if I lived to see the lion and the lamb lie down together. Nor should I be surprised to see a great churchly procession, headed by an Arminian and a Calvinist, arm in arm. [*Applause.*] I should not be amazed to see a presbyter and a bishop — whether of the first, second or third order would be immaterial — walking along the streets thanking God for His love; and it would only make my heart rejoice if the members of conferences and the members of councils and the members of synods and the members of assemblies should all forget the names of their organizations and every one feel his heart going out to his brother as he pronounced the shibboleth, "Love to God and love to the brethren." [*Applause.*]

So let our churches and our nationalities be united together, welded by the heat of the Divine love into an inseparable unity. As the twelve tribes made the one nation of Israel and when their priests took up the ark of the covenant all the people rose and shouted together, so from the various nations of the world, in all the babbling tongues of modern speech, with the one great love for Jesus in our hearts, let us all rise and pray to God that He may come with the ark of His strength, that He may cause us to shout together for joy, as in fraternal recognition we realize our oneness in Christ Jesus in answer to the closing prayer of His life. May God's abundant blessing rest upon us all. [*Applause.*]

Mr. Sankey then sang the well-known hymn, "The Ninety and Nine," prefacing his singing with an account of the way in which he first came to sing the hymn in Edinburgh, in 1874.

The session closed with the benediction pronounced by Rev. J. T. Beckley, D.D., of Philadelphia.

FRIDAY MORNING.

Delightful weather again favored the delegates. At 6:30 o'clock the early morning prayer meeting was held at the exposition building, Mr. William Shaw, treasurer of the United Society, conducting. In spite of the distance of the building from most of the places of entertainment of the delegates, there were upwards of 2,000 present, and the meeting was an inspiring one.

At 9·20 the regular exercises of the morning began with the singing of the favorite hymn, "Blessed Assurance," followed by Scripture reading by Rev. S. M. Ware, of Omaha, and prayer by Rev. W. H. McMillan, D. D., of Allegheny City. Another hymn, "At the Cross," was sung, and President Clark appointed the following committees:—

Resolutions—Rev. J. H. Barrows, D. D., Chicago; Rev. H. B. Grose, Dakota; Mr. Geo. R. Lighthall, Canada; Mrs. R. P. Lee, Alaska, Mrs. V. S. Barber, Florida.

Nominations for Honorary Vice-Presidents—Rev. B. F. Boller, Missouri; Rev. S. M. Ware, Nebraska; Mrs. A. C. Hathaway, Indiana; Mrs. E. N. Hardy, Massachusetts; Rev H. P. Welton, D.D., Michigan.

Greetings—Prof. W. W. Andrews, Nova Scotia; Rev. E. M. Poteat, Connecticut; Miss Clara Kellam, Georgia: Mr. E. B. Clark, Colorado.

Business—Secretary Baer; Miss Annie Baker, Utah; Rev. G. R. F. Hallock, New York; Dr. Francis Carothers, Iowa; Mr. Thomas Morris, Ontario.

President Clark: Next we come to a most delightful part of our programme, as we believe, called the Free Parliament. I congratulate myself on being here this first hour of the morning and all of you who have come to this opening hour of our Convention. I predict that it will be one of the most delightful and memorable hours of all our sessions. It will be entirely in the charge of Rev. J. A. Rondthaler, D.D., of Indianapolis. [*Applause.*]

ADDRESS OF REV. J. A. RONDTHALER, D.D.

THE FREE PARLIAMENT.

Let us get the plan of these sixty minutes well in hand before we start off. We desire to carry up into this great assembly the best features of our State and district conventions. In those gatherings it often happens that some of the finest thoughts and best suggestions come from the floor,—they are not always brought down from the platform by the sky-scrapers and spell-binders who talk from thence. When one gets to talking in a set speech, he is apt to get beyond the practical into the midst of theory. Therefore I want to say that the success of these sixty minutes depends upon the floor and the galleries. First of all, you must speak loud; secondly, speak briefly; thirdly, speak sharp and to the point, so that these sixty minutes shall raise the roof and shake the floor and quiver the pillars. [*Laughter and applause.*]

I wish I could read you the letter Secretary Baer wrote me asking me to lead this conference. At the opening he was full of taffy; at the close he was awfully afraid that he had made a mistake and he wanted to take back what he had written at the beginning, and get somebody else to lead it. When he wrote the second letter he was still more in doubt, and I found I had to cut off all further correspondence if I wanted to show myself before this Convention —and that I was determined to do. [*Laughter.*]

The parliament will consist of one minute speeches — sixty seconds each. The best will not be any longer, and the worst need not be any shorter. So, if any of you have prepared any thoughts upon the subjects given on the programme, by all means cut off the introduction of your speech, chop off the end, pull out the middle, disintegrate what is left, and give us the remainder. [*Great laughter.*] Thus we will get at the golden thought that you have found in this great, magnificent Christian Endeavor movement. [*Applause.*]

Now, a look at your programme. "What the Society has done." This is Decennial Day;—ten years of life, ten years of labor, ten years of prayer, ten years of consecration meetings, ten years of faithfulness to the pledge. We will make a quick, comprehensive review of our first decade, not in minutiae, but in the general influence the Christian Endeavor movement has had upon the Christianity of the United States and of Canada and of the world at our doors. How those figures last evening thrilled us when we heard of 82,500 gathered into the churches through the effort and earnest work of Christian Endeavorers in this last year. Ten years, and 1,008,890 members! Ten years, and 16,000 societies! Is there anything in the history of Christianity or of New Jersey that can equal that? [*Laughter.*] What are the reasons of this success? We can number them off on the fingers of one hand, with perhaps a little finger on the other hand.

First of all, this Endeavor movement has been true to Christ, and He is beginning to see of the travail of His soul through the earnestness of the young people's work for Him, in Him, under Him, through Him. Secondly, loyalty to the Church, the representative of Jesus Christ. The Society has been consecrated to those things the church in its individuality believes in, lives by, and teaches. Thirdly, the pledge — so sensible, so biblical, so true to the idea that we get from God's Word and from the Holy Spirit, the pattern of what a church member should be in his devotions, in his life and in his work. I believe in the pledge. I know it has power, for I have seen it up and down through my own State and I have read of it in the results of the work in other States. I hope that some one on this platform will give special thought and time to earnest words, eloquent words, golden words — anything but flowery words, about this pledge of the Christian Endeavor movement. [*Applause.*] Fourthly, the prayer meeting. The church was born in a prayer meeting, and the church lives by the prayer meeting, and the Christian Endeavor movement founded in a prayer meeting holds its own, sustains its spirituality, is so effective in the church because of its prayer meeting. Whenever you think of the Christian Endeavor work, the prayer meeting stands forth first of all and is the index to the spirit and success of the Society. Fifthly, the consecration meeting, which brings up every individual to time, which makes every individual responsible and leads him to examine himself and to see whether he is true to himself, true to his pledge and true to his Christ. Sixthly, the faithful work of the lookout committee is one of the reasons of the success of this movement, because the lookout committee is neither ashamed to open the arms of the Lord Jesus Christ in welcome nor is it afraid to use the knife with indifferent and lukewarm Christians,—those who have grown away from their interest in the Lord Jesus Christ. I believe in the knife when it is not a butcher's knife that murders, but a surgeon's knife that simply cuts off for the health of the body. [*Applause.*]

And so I might go on to fourteenthly, but it would not be a good example to those who are going to speak only a minute each.

Now we come to the syllabus. Remember that during these sixty minutes we are not going to talk about the "Relation of the Society to the Church." There are several subjects on this programme which squint at the relation a little bit, but I am glad that the word "relation" has not come into this programme. For what is the use of establishing the relation of my brain to me or of my heart to me. *They are me.* Why should I be always looking at this hand and asking, What relation does this hand bear to this arm? What I want to do with this hand is to put it to work, use it as a part of me, no matter what somebody else says. This hand knows that it belongs to this body. So, by virtue of our constitution, by which every active member is a member of the church of Jesus Christ, the Christian Endeavor Society *is* the church of Jesus Christ [*Applause*], — not the whole of it and a part that is very sturdy and sometimes noisy, like that New York delegation that came in early this morning. [*Laughter.*] But it can always be called to order [*Applause*] and responds quickly to any suggestion from pastor, church officers or president of the Convention. And that is the beauty of it. Ministers and others sometimes used to say, "The Christian Endeavor Society is getting away with the young people." I am glad that no one is saying that any more; I have n't heard it for the last two years, and I am sure we are finding that nothing is so easily moulded into the ways of the individual church as the pliable Christian Endeavor movement. This society of young people is like a certain kind of stone. Fresh from the quarry it is easily cut and shaped, but when it is put into the building and exposed to wind and weather it becomes hard as adamant. So the young people, under the Christian Endeavor inspiration, can be shaped according to any church lines, but when once they are cordially recognized, they stand steadfast, true and immovable on the Rock of Ages. They strengthen the walls of Zion and are "a thing of beauty" in the eyes of the church and "a joy forever" to thousands of pastors.

I am going to make one little flowery remark — merely a reference to flowers. I, as a pastor, want to say that to me the Christian Endeavor Society is my "Heart's-ease." [*Loud applause.*] God bless it forever and ever. Oh, how I wear it on my bosom in pride and in joy! How in the evening of the Sabbath days, when discouragements have been many, the Christian Endeavor Society is my "Heart's-ease," and I fall to sleep with the remembrance of what my young people have said and prayed as a sweet fragrance. I am sure God's cause will go on. I can trust much of it to the young people. So I sleep sound and wake with encouragement and hope. A pastor can meet anything that is discouraging so long as he knows that his young people remain loyal, true and enthusiastic for Christ and His church.

Now we come to this syllabus. I will say nothing with regard to the subjects themselves save to announce them. Here we have the Society in the Sunday services, — at the church door, with the right hand extended in fellowship and welcome; at the church door also at the close of the services, with the same right hand extended in invitation to "come again." In the pew, the young head bowed in reverence, the ready ear to hear and the willing heart to do. By the way, there has happened in these last ten years something that pastors of twenty-five or thirty years standing only dreamed of. You have seen a fern bed in the early spring, have n't you? — those little brown fellows that come up and cover the rocks? Well, in former times we ministers used to look out over our congregations and we saw beautiful flower gardens, — the ribbons and the bonnets and the hats of our lady friends and members. But now the brown heads are coming up, the pompadours are beginning to show in our congregations. [*Laughter.*] The Christian Endeavor movement is bringing out the young men to our services, and we know not whereunto this will grow. And so also we have members of the Society in the mid-week meeting, where they have increased the attendance, where they have taught Presbyterians that all grace does not lie in long prayers, and Methodists that all glory does not lie in loud prayers, and Congregationalists that all beauty does not lie in exact prayers, and all the others that the blessing of the prayer meeting lies largely in *brief* prayers—sentence prayers. [*Applause.*] The sentence prayers of our church meetings today have been born of the Christian Endeavor movement, for nobody else knows how to be short but a young person, because he is so short in thought and shorter in experience. [*Laughter.*] Now, who will be the first one in this audience to make the first minute speech on the Society in the Sunday services.

Delegate from Hamilton, Ont.: The Sunday services afford golden opportunities for a live Christian Endeavor society. Let the president see to it that sentinels are stationed in different parts of the church, with note books in their hands, and that they take the names of strangers, welcoming them, and endeavoring to interest the young people in the work of the society.

Delegate from Madison, Wis.: Those members of our society who are best acquainted with the congregation take the back seats in the church services, and every new face in the congregation is spoken to, or recognized in some way.

Delegate from Michigan.: The Christian Endeavor Society has rescued the prayer meeting from a state of innocuous desuetude to a live, real thing. It has been the right arm of service to the pastor.

Delegate from Rochester, N. Y.: The Christian Endeavor Society stands for sociability in the church. I know a church in Rochester where it is said that a man cannot get out of the church without some one shaking his hand. The Christian Endeavor Society stands for young men who will waylay the outgoers and bring them into the after-meeting, bring them under the power of prayer. The Christian Endeavor Society stands for those who will sing for Christ.

Delegate from Western Springs, Ill.: I want to suggest to some of your societies of 150 members that you send them in squads of from 25 to 75 to these missions surrounding you in the cities.

Delegate from Newark, N. J.: We are about to organize in our societies at home an inner circle, composed of the members of the Christian Endeavor Society who will pledge themselves to take part once a month in the regular mid-week prayer meeting of the church, arranging them so that three will take part every week.

Delegate from Rochester, N. Y.: We have our society meeting at 6.30 P.M., with from 150 to 200 present. We form the backbone of the evening congregation and carry on an after-meeting every Sunday night the year round.

Delegate from Baltimore, Md.: We have a vestibule committee, with sentinels posted from the church door to beyond the street corner, so that all strangers passing by are welcomed to the services.

Delegate from Minnesota: Our Christian Endeavor society has held together a pastorless church for nine months.

Dr. Rondthaler: Oh, let us applaud that! [*Loud applause.*] I hear such testimony over and over again throughout this country, that the Christian Endeavor society is holding together a pastorless church. It is being done again and again; and when the new pastor comes he does n't find ruins, but he finds a beautiful palace.

Delegate from Minnesota City, Minn.: The Christian Endeavor society of our church has maintained the services of the church, although without a pastor, for one year. [*Applause.*]

Delegate from Pennsylvania: The Christian Endeavor Society in our State has greatly promoted the study of the Bible and drawn our churches closer together.

Delegate from Indiana: The Christian Endeavor society in Shelbyville will conduct the services next Lord's Day, while I, their pastor, am here enjoying these services.

Delegate from Boston, Mass.. The Christian Endeavor society of the People's Church, Boston, has found new work. We have gone among the Chinamen and brought them to our church. We have a grand Sabbath school carried on among them by members of our society. [*Applause.*]

Delegate from Chicago, Ill.: After the people have filled the pews of the church, the Christian Endeavor society fill the choir seats back of the pulpit and hold up the singing.

Delegate from Connecticut: We cannot exist in our State without the Y. P. S. C. E.

Dr. Rondthaler: Who can? [*Laughter.*]

Delegate from Syracuse, N. Y.: The union of Syracuse has closed Sunday saloons. [*Applause.*]

Delegate from Iowa: There is a church in our State which called a new pastor last year. He was taken sick after he had been on the field a week. The Christian Endeavor society of 20 members took hold of the church services and carried them all on. They had a revival; and on the first Sabbath that the pastor was able to be at church he received into membership 105 young people. [*Loud applause.*]

Delegate from Missouri: With a society less than a year old we have started three mission schools. In each of these we have organized a Y. P. S. C. E. and by this means have kept the Sunday schools alive.

Delegate from Long Branch, N. J.: We have had no pastor for three years and we are going yet. We have young men stationed in every hotel all summer to invite every guest to the church services. [*Applause.*]

FROM SOUTH CAROLINA, [a colored delegate, received with great cheering]: I stand here as the only delegate from South Carolina. We caught the inspiration three years ago, and I am glad to say that last year 100 were converted and baptized through the instrumentality of the Y. P. S. C. E. [*Loud applause.*]

DELEGATE FROM LITTLE ROCK, ARK.: The Y. P. S. C. E. is doing more in Arkansas than any other organization, through all denominations.

DELEGATE FROM NEBRASKA: We have a State union that has a representative from every town and village in the State. [*Loud applause.*] One church in Lincoln has three mission schools conducted exclusively by members of the Y. P. S. C. E.

DELEGATE FROM WEST DULUTH, MINN.: Our Society has built a prayer-meeting room, furnished it and presented it to the church. We propose to take part in every prayer meeting held in it.

DELEGATE FROM PHILADELPHIA, PENN.: Our society has brought 50 souls to Christ. Our special work is to save the boys and girls.

DELEGATE FROM BLOOMINGTON, ILL.: Our societies supply the repair shops and engine houses with good literature.

DELEGATE FROM MANITOBA: Christian Endeavor is spreading broadcast over our wheat fields and nearly every town now has a Christian Endeavor society in one church or another. Our motto is, "Manitoba for Christ." [*Applause.*]

DELEGATE FROM WINONA, MINN.: Our society has been of great help to Sunday-school teachers, inspiring them to work more earnestly for their pupils.

DELEGATE FROM CALIFORNIA: There are eleven delegates here from California. [*Loud applause.*] In our town, last year, we organized a Christian Endeavor society with 22 members, 12 active. Today we have 145 members, 60 active. Our last State union meeting was considered one of the best and most enthusiastic gatherings in the State.

DELEGATE FROM PAINESVILLE, O.: Our Christian Endeavor societies have succeeded in closing every saloon in the City. [*Enthusiastic applause.*]

DELEGATE FROM ST. LOUIS, MO.: Our Christian Endeavor societies are doing so much for mission work that one society supports a Sunday school of over 1000 children with money and teachers. [*Loud applause.*]

DELEGATE FROM MASSACHUSETTS: We have held gospel meetings for nine months with great success in a non-evangelical church.

DELEGATE FROM INDIANA: Our society of 40 active members has raised from $125 to $150 a year for missions aside from their own work. They do it by the help of the Sunday school, also by consecration, by self-denial, by system. We do not seek to convert people from Christianity by making them dyspeptics, feeding them with strawberries and cake. We give the money out of love to God. [*Applause.*]

DELEGATE (A BOY) FROM GALESBURG, ILL: Our Junior society formed a year ago has brought ten of its members into the church. [*Applause.*]

REV. JAMES E. ROGERS, D.D., OF CHATTANOOGA, TENN.: Our Young People's Society in the South has learned that there is a difference between systematic benevolence, which means well-wishing, and systematic beneficence, which is well-doing. We believe that there is no other way of giving to the Lord Jesus Christ acceptably except in that way which gives a certain definite and non-take-backable percentage of our income to the cause of the Lord Jesus Christ. If the 1,000,000 Christian Endeavorers should give on that basis, even if they received but $10 a month, they would gather into our churches $12,000,-000 a year, and this in the Presbyterian proportion, would amount to more for foreign missions and for home missions and for every other benevolent object of the Presbyterian church than they are receiving now. Let the watchword of the Y. P. S. C. E. be: A percentage of our income for the cause of Christ, according to the language of inspiration which says, "Let every one of you lay by him in store, as God hath prospered him, on the first day of the week," that there may be no collections when the cause of Christ is presented to you.

DELEGATE FROM MARSHALL, TEX.: The work in Texas is yet in its infancy, but it will very soon assume proportions, we trust, equal to the vast territory of the Lone Star State. In our church the Christian Endeavor movement has revolutionized the spiritual life of the church. We have in the last six weeks sent two young men into the ministry. We have sent one young lady into the foreign field, and the same Young People's Society has sent a representative of China to this Convention. [*Great applause and the Chautauqua salute to the young man from China.*]

DELEGATE FROM CHINA: The Chinese come very slowly but they come solidly and sure. I have been here nearly four years, and I am glad that I came to this country and found my dear Saviour. I trust in Him; He is my Friend. I am going home to take this wonderful story back with me. I am going to tell my parents and my friends about Jesus. [*Renewed enthusiasm and applause.*]

DELEGATE FROM CLEVELAND OHIO: In Cleveland we have a thousand in attendance at our quarterly young people's meeting. We have succeeded in closing up the Sunday theatres. The young people of our churches are doing the great bulk of the missionary work in the city, and what we want is that you will all come there two years from now and see how well they are doing it. [*Applause.*]

DELEGATE FROM KANSAS CITY: The Walnut Street Methodist Church of Kansas City, recently imported from the far South, a moss-back minister, (the speaker) and the first thing the Christian Endeavor Society did with him was to take him in hand and send him to this Convention in order to teach him how to be a pastor, and he is learning at the rate of a mile a minute from this lively corpse who is attending his funeral. [*Laughter.*] I want to say further, that the Methodist Episcopal church isn't anything without a collection, and in my church we have a dozen collections through the year, for church extension, home missions, foreign missions, colored education and so on. Every Methodist Episcopal church South has a collection for the education of the colored people. [*Applause.*] I put the whole matter into the hands of the Christian Endeavor society, and the money is collected and disbursed by them. [*Applause.*]

DR. RONDTHALER: And nobody from the Christian Endeavor society ever goes to Canada and carries the money with him. [*Laughter.*]

Dr. Rondthaler here called on Rev. C. F. Deems, D.D., of New York, who was received with cheers and the Chautauqua salute.

DR. DEEMS: Dr. Rondthaler says to me, "See what the young people think of you." Well, they ought to think a great deal or there would be much love lost. [*Laughter.*] If Dr. Clark had kept back three weeks longer, the first Y. P. S. C. E. would have been formed in the Church of the Strangers in the city of New York. [*Applause.*] But God gave him the right of way, and from that hour on we have been cheering him. Our New York delegation has come up through much tribulation, but we have come up. [*Applause.*] We determined that if we could only be in at the Doxology and the benediction, even if Montreal had captured the Convention for '92, we would be here and shout the glory at the end. [*Applause.*] We have had seventy-two hours of continuous camp-meeting, from Forty-second Street, New York, into this union depot. [*Applause.*] I thank God for this, one of the most extraordinary experiences of my life, in the course of over seventy years, over fifty years in the ministry and on four continents. I have never had seventy-two such hours. Hundreds of people were packed together in those cars. We have crossed and recrossed the Straits of Mackinaw, joined, been stopped, smashed up the "Soo" Railroad and laid part of it down again. We have had meetings with the Salvation Army in the cities along the way.

A DELEGATE: Tell us about it, Doctor.

DR. DEEMS: No; I never tell all I know the first time. [*Laughter.*] I will tell you what I am going to record, and that is this: I am firmer in the faith of Christianity as a doctrine, as a life, and as a passion than I ever was before. [*Applause.*] I want to tell you why. I am an optimist, with a touch of poetry in me. I have had my dreams and my visions; but I never before believed that that many Christian people, men, women, and children, old and young, not able to find a place to sleep sometimes, so cut off from food that we had to raid a town and then shout the inhabitants into good humor when we had taken what they had to eat,— I declare here in this presence, before the august God and my adorable Redeemer, I never believed before, that that many people could live together in that style, with not a word said in my hearing, not a deed performed, not a look given, which I believe the Lord Jesus would not approve. [*Loud applause.*] Glory to God! I know I have religion now. I have stood the "Soo" Railroad and still have hope of everlasting glory. [*Laughter and applause.*] And I know that the rest of those people have religion. I know that Dr. Farrar has religion now; I know that Dr. Tyler has religion now, though I suspected it before. [*Laughter.*] Blessed be the men and women that came with me; and if I have to return by the very next train, I thank God I came. Those seventy-two hours were wonderful; and if you don't give us the Convention next year, nevertheless we have had those seventy-two hours. [*Laughter.*] Blessed be the Young People's Society of Christian Endeavor, and blessed be all the obstructions which we met on the "Soo" Railroad! [*Laughter and applause.*]

Dr. Rondthaler: Sixty-three minutes and sixty-seven speeches. [Several spoke in so low a voice that it was impossible to record their remarks.— Sten.] Three cheers for the Young People's Society of Christian Endeavor that stands for brevity, sharpness, striking the nail on the head, spirituality and Christ! [*Loud applause.*]

This closed the "free parliament." Secretary Baer read a cablegram from Durban, Natal, South Africa, quoting Isaiah 54: 2, as follows: "Enlarge the place of thy tent, and let them stretch forth the curtains of thy habitations; spare not; lengthen thy cords and strengthen thy stakes." It was received enthusiastically. Several announcements were then given and Dr. Hoyt proposed the following:

Dr. Hoyt: We all know that the Rev. Mr. Spurgeon, whom we all love, is lying very sick at his home in London. It has seemed to me as though it were a fitting thing for us to send him our love and greeting by cablegram. I therefore move that the Secretary be instructed to send him a telegram, perhaps like this: "Love and prayers from the Young People's Society of Christian Endeavor, in Convention, more than 12,000 strong."

President Clark: Let me say that three years ago, when in England, Mr. Spurgeon gave me a very hearty and cordial welcome as I talked to his students in his college. I am sure that he is interested in this Society and that he will gratefully appreciate any such remembrance from us.

The vote upon the motion was taken by raising the right hand, and apparently every hand in the audience was raised.

A brief prayer service followed, conducted by Mr. J. A. Chase, president of the Minneapolis Union, after which the whole congregation united in singing "Blest be the tie that binds."

PRESIDENT CLARK: I think you will all agree with me that this meeting so far this morning has been perhaps the most interesting that was ever held in connection with one of these Conventions, and that is saying a good deal. We have heard about what the Society has done from sixty-seven people in the audience. Now let us hear what the Society may do; and first we will listen to Rev. F. O. Holman, D.D., of St. Paul. [*Applause.*]

ADDRESS OF REV. F. O. HOLMAN, D.D.

Mr. President: After the tremendous enthusiasm which has already been excited by this meeting, I feel as though for me to speak were very much like attempting to help on a cyclone with a hand bellows. I am to speak about "The Society and the Pastor." I want to call your attention to two or three fundamental propositions about this Christian Endeavor Society, and I think before I get through that I will bring it around to the pastor.

In the first place, I want to say that the Society is organized solely to increase the efficiency of the church of God. It is not a debating society; it is not a literary society; it is not a social club; it is not a fraternity for mutual advantage; but its sole business is to increase the efficiency of the church of God. And I want to say that the influence of the Society and its success is to be measured, not by the reports of your numerical increase, but by statistics which you cannot gather—statistics which lie in increased prayer meetings, in numberless conversions and in the entire advance in efficiencyalong the whole front of the church of God. That is our work.

Secondly, next to Jesus Christ, the local society owes sole allegiance to the local church. That is the only line along which it can possibly be interdenominational; and it is a sign of the divine wisdom that superintended its organization, that these brethren were saved from instituting a great connectional society, and understood from the start that the only allegiance of the individual society was to its local church. [*Applause.*] That makes it possible for the Society to be intensely Presbyterian in a Presbyterian church, intensely Methodist in a Methodist church, intensely Congregational in a Congregational church.

Thirdly, every local society ought to be organized constitutionally subordinate to the governing body of the local church. That is to say, if you are a Methodist society, you will be organized in constitutional subordination to the official board of the quarterly conference of the church. [*Applause.*] If you happen to be a Congregational society, you will be responsible to and subordinate to the church meeting or the committee, as it may be. If you are a Presbyterian society, you will be organized in subordination, constitutionally to the session. And so on through all the societies.

Fourthly, the official relation which the pastor should sustain to the society is the same which he sustains under the law and order of the local church and demonination to the other departments of the church work. That is to say, if you were to organize a Methodist Y. P. S. C. E.—and as I happen to be a Methodist I know more about that than anything else—you would make the pastor chairman ex-officio of all the important committees, because under the law and order of the Methodist church he is chairman ex-officio of all the important church committees. If you were organizing in a Presbyterian church, you would let the pastor sustain the same relation to your society which, under the Presbyterian form and order, he sustains to all the other organizations of the church work. Hence the pastor's official relation will be exactly the same—or ought to be—when you organize, as that which he sustains under the law of the church to every department of church activity.

Once more. I almost hesitate to make this statement because it is adducing such an extremely improbable condition of affairs; yet it is practical because I heard the question raised in a pastors' meeting not long ago. In case of irreconcilable difference of opinion between the pastor and the society, the ultimate and final appeal is to be, not to the United Society of Christian Endeavor, not to Secretary Baer, not to Dr. Clark, though these would all give you wise advice; it is to be made to the governing board of the local church, [*Applause*] because that is the only way this Society can be strictly interdenominational. I once heard a pastor ask this question, "What are you going to do when the Y. P. S. C. E. will not do the sort of work the pastor wants them to do?" I have to say that while that is a very unfortunate condition of affairs, and I should hope a very rare one, the answer is inevitable: The appeal is to the governing body of the local church and nothing else, [*Applause*] because the Y. P. S. C. E. is first, last and all the time loyal to the local church. [*Applause.*]

Once more. The practical relation which should exist between the Y. P. S. C. E. and the pastor may be expressed in the one word—Loyalty. It is a magnificent word. The pastor ought to be loyal to the society. He ought to see to it in his pastoral calling that there is no young person within the reach of his pastoral influence who does not receive an earnest, cordial and repeated invitation to become a member of the society. He ought to see to it that the society is all the time brought into cordial and constant relationship with the governing authorities of the church. He ought to work for the society all the time and everywhere. On the other hand, the young people ought to be loyal to the pastor. Thank God, they are loyal to the pastor in all our Young People's Societies! [*Applause.*] They ought to be loyal to his services. Once in a while, when the Rev. Dr. Quicktongue is giving a series of sermons across the way on "How I Courted and When I Married," the young people will be rather anxious to go over there and hear him, because they are all interested in the subject; but that is the time when you ought to be loyal to your own pastor, [*Applause*] and to your own church. Stand by your pastor every time. You are to be loyal in the prayer meeting. If your pastor don't know how to run a prayer meeting in real good shape—most pastors do—then you ought to go to the prayer meeting and make it such a meeting that it won't need any running, and in that case you will find all the difficulties will vanish. [*Applause.*] You ought to be loyal to him in what you say about him. Speak for him; brag about him on every possible occasion. [*Applause.*] "Well," you say, "I have a pastor that I cannot brag about much." That is not so. There is not a pastor in the country whom you cannot brag about concerning something. Away back East there was a man from New England who came to our little town once to lecture. He was a man with a prodigious voice and an immense lot of black hair. The lecture didn't amount to much as a lecture; but there was an old man, the postmaster, who always had something good to say about everybody, and my brother went to him the next morning and said, "What did you think of the lecture last night?" The old man scratched his head as if to think of something nice to say, and finally he said, "Well, he had a good stout voice and an amazin' head o' hair, now, didn't he?" Well, if you can't say anything more for your pastor than that, say it, and brag of him morning, noon and night. [*Loud applause.*]

I want to close with this one statement: the Y. P. S. C. E. is doing more to lift a load of anxiety from the hearts of anxious pastors than any organization in the church. [*Applause.*] The pastor who is earnest looks out on the tremendous activities of these modern days, with all the pitfalls and snares for the feet of the young, and the one cry of his heart is, "Oh, God, save my young people!" He has not known how this might be done until very recently. But now the pastor realizes that he has in his church an instrumentality that is teaching young men in his community that the kingliest manhood is the young manhood that consecrates itself to the Carpenter of Nazareth, and the queenliest womanhood is the womanhood that lies on the bosom of Jesus. [*Applause.*] That is being taught to the young people by the Y. P. S. C. E. It is raising up a sort of Christian character and Christian experience that has hitherto been comparatively rare in the church of Jesus Christ. Last week, on the Fourth of July, I stood in front of one of the engine houses in St. Paul. Now St. Paul has the finest fire department of any city in the United States—except Minneapolis. [*Laughter.*] I saw a lot of young men, strong, sturdy looking fellows, standing out there around the door. They were laughing, chaffing, telling stories, cracking jokes on one another, playing ball, and having a grand good time in every way. There were all sorts of fun and frolic going on. I said, "That does not look much like business," and I looked behind them into the engine house, and I saw everything in perfect readiness—the harnesses hanging over the places where the horses were to stand, the machines polished until they shone like mirrors; everything was ready, nothing was out of place in that room. Just as I stood there looking into that room and at the men outside who were having such a good time, clang! clang! went the gong inside, and it seemed as if a magician had instantly wrought a change upon everything. The story was stopped in the middle; the joke was quitted before the teller got to the point of it; the ball was tossed away, and in one instant there was a rushing of feet, there were the sharp metallic clicks as the harnesses were brought down into place, and the next moment the man at the alarm said "Go." Immediately there was a vision that went dashing down the street of plunging horses and flashing engines and rumbling wheels; and on those swaying, rocking machines were those same jolly boys, every man of them with a set face, every one of them ready to do and dare and die for life and for property; and I cried, "Hurrah for the fire department!" [*Applause.*] As I stood there I said to myself, that is the sort of Christian experience that we want in these days. We want young men and young women who can play and frolic with all the enthusiasm and gladness of youth, young men who are not unfamiliar with the base-ball bat and who are not entirely unfamiliar with the oar and the football; we want young women who know how to handle tennis rackets and who can be queens in society; but we want them so consecrated to God, so trained to service, so ready for usefulness, that when duty sounds its alarm, every one of them will leap to his place, trained, alert, eager, ready to do and dare and die "for Christ and the church." [*Loud applause.*]

Dr. Wayland Hoyt: Mr. President, this matter of the loyalty of the local society to the local church has been put straight. The loyalty of the members of the local society to the local pastor has been put straight. It has been suggested to me, and I warmly second the suggestion, that we have a vote of the pastors in this great assembly on this matter. All those pastors in this assembly who have found that Christian Endeavor does increase loyalty to the local church and to the local pastor, let them rise and by their rising set forth the fact of their own experience.

A large number rose all over the house, and the vote was received with applause. The hymn, "Faith is the victory," was then sung, after which President Clark introduced Rev. Elbert R. Dille, D.D., of Oakland, Cal., who was announced to speak on the topic, "The Society and the Church Officers."

ADDRESS OF REV. E. R. DILLE, D.D.

THE theme assigned me is "The Society and the Church Officers," and coming as it does on the programme between the discussion of "The Society and the Pastor," and "The Society and the Sunday-School Superintendent," I understand it to contemplate the relation of the local Christian Endeavor society to the temporal and spiritual interests of the church with which it is connected, and by the same token the mutual relation between the society and the godly and picked men who are office bearers in the church.

Until a few years ago, the burning question in all the official meetings of our church was, "How shall we reach and enlist and train and hold the young people for Christ and His church?" for the wisest minds in the pastorate and in the laity saw, in the solution of that question, the solution of that other crucial one, "How shall we reach the masses?" for if we can save our young people and train them for efficient Christian service, through them the masses will be reached and won.

It is to answer that question that God raised up the Christian Endeavor Society. It is the child of providence. God always supplies at the right time that which is needed for the unfoldment of individuals, of nations, of the church and the race. It is wonderful how, as we look back over the past, we can see that God has met — nay anticipated — the needs of mankind, material and spiritual by a timely provision for those deeds. God hid America away until the race needed it, and then He prepared two peoples — the Puritans of Holland and England, and the Hugenots of France to take possession of it for God and Protestantism and liberty.

The old appliances will no more meet the spiritual needs of today than will the stage coach as a means of transportation, the penny post as a means of communication, or the old flint-lock musket as an arm of precision, or naked muscular force in the industrial world. Is the spiritual realm the only one in which there is to be stagnation, while in the intellectual and material realm man is making such strides? I tell you He has mighty spiritual forces and resources that He is bringing to the front as fast as they are needed. The coming generation, potential now in childhood, has no evil habits, no prejudices, no superstitions. There are no enemies of the cross among the children. You will not find a child in any home in this land, whether that home be Christian or not, who will not say "Yes" to the question, "Ought you not to love Jesus?"

Yes, this movement means that the time has come in the history of the church, as never before, when this grand army of 1,000,000 Christian youth should be enlisted under the banner of Immanuel, so that He shall be speedily crowned King over this world, which He has bought with His blood.

Some have said that this is the woman's century. Nay, it is rather the young people's century.

Then here is the Young People's Society of Christian Endeavor. When we ask about its origin we are told that a young pastor, who is still young — though we affectionately call him "Father Endeavor" Clark — having had a revival in his church and feeling the need of getting his converts to work, called a few of them together for consultation at his parsonage and organized the grandest movement of this century — the Young People's Society of Christian Endeavor, now numbering more than a million members. This is the grandest movement of this age—the grandest Christian movement since the Reformation, except the second reformation under Wesley and Whitefield and Jonathan Edwards, and will be as much at home in the twenty-fifth as in the nineteenth century. But do you think that chance meeting explains the Young People's Society of Christian Endeavor? Chance indeed! "Eternal God that chance did guide." [*Applause.*]

I remark that our church officers should hail with gratitude and heartily co-operate with the Christian Endeavor movement, because it solves the great question, How shall the mighty lay element in the church be reached and utilized for God? There is a power latent here sufficient to evangelize the world, if it were fully aroused, consecrated, organized, trained and led to victory. It takes discipline to make an army. It was discipline, drill, training, that fashioned that rude mass, our volunteer army, into that all-crushing hammer of Thor that beat the Rebellion to pieces — that beat out on the hard anvil of war and finished a blade of more than Damascus edge and temper, that, in the hands of Grant, was never beaten down till it was sheathed in victory at Appomattox. Now every Christian is an enlisted soldier of the cross. He is enlisted to be duly instructed, drilled, and assigned to his proper place in the marching column and in the line of battle. He is under the most sacred obligations to go where duty calls and to do and dare, and die, if need be, for Him who has called him to be a soldier. Think of it! There are over 12,000,000 names on the muster roll of the American Protestant church today, with 92,000 commissioned officers, — ministers — and half a million non-commissioned officers — official members of our churches — and 114,000 recruiting stations — churches. Filled with the spirit of Christ, thoroughly organized and drilled; with such discipline as Loyola imposed upon his Society of Jesus — that force is sufficient to bring the whole world to Christ before the dawn of the twentieth century. Brethren, there was a time, but not now, when a passive, pietistic, contemplative, retrospective type of piety was in harmony with the spirit of the age.

The problem of the hour is the problem of our great cities. But the church of Christ in the great cities of New York, Boston, Chicago, San Francisco, and your Twin Cities here, is strong enough in numbers and wealth and influence, — if it were a disciplined, a concentrated, a united, moral and spiritual force, wisely generalled, and loyal to Christ and duty — to shut up every one of the liquor saloons that rule our politics, drive from power the bosses and corrupt politicians, and make these cities the distributing centres of moral power instead of the storm centres of our civilization. How is this state of affairs to be remedied? Why, in the youth of today we have the church of the twentieth century. It is in our hands to mould as we please. The church looks to the youth of today to carry forward her great Christian enterprises, to replenish her treasuries, to man her pulpits, to fill her offices, to snatch her missionary banners as they fall from the hands of a Scudder, a Turnbull, a Pierson, and a Taylor, and plant them on the last citadel of heathenism. She looks to you, O young people, to make this a land of churches and of schools; a land of happy homes and peaceful industries; to cast out of it that sum of all villanies, the liquor traffic; to make room for the kingdom of Christ, the New Jerusalem which is to come down from God out of heaven. And shall she look in vain?

Now, how admirably adapted is the Christian Endeavor as a school of Christian training. In the first place, it calls every soul to a sense of responsibility, influence and opportunity; it shows a boy that he need not wait until he is of age before he becomes a spiritual power. It cries in his ears, "Neglect not the gift that is in thee." It finds out for the youth what that gift is by placing before him certain lines of work. It shows a young man that if God has given him a tongue with which he may do business, and fill his place in society, and make love with persuasiveness, he can also use it for God. It develops executive ability by placing young people on committees, where they may have opportunity to develop their natural capabilities and where they can find where their strength lies.

Our young people must be enlisted in Christian service if we would attach them to Christ and His church. A young man, if he is of any account, has a horror of being a mere hanger-on, even to the best of things. He wants to feel that he is giving an equivalent for what he receives, even from the church, to preserve his self-respect; and when you have him at work in a responsible place, you have him sure. Then, how admirably adapted is this Society to solve another weighty problem which so often confronts the pastor and his official staff, namely, how to call out the laity of the church as witnesses for Jesus. The ability and willingness to declare his convictions is as vital to the Christian as to have those convictions. And this witnessing for Christ, which is the glory and the strength of this Society, is brought about by the simple expedient of the pledge — some call it the cast iron pledge — if it were wrought iron I should like it still better. [*Applause.*]

Now the Christian Endeavor movement — and somebody derives the name Christian Endeavor from the French *en* and *devoir*, "on duty" — has sounded to 1,000,000 young Christians the bugle note of duty. Go to meeting, confess Christ, work for Him, give for His cause whether you feel like it or not — nay all the more because you don't feel like it. History tells of the sacred legion who were always victorious because they were banded together under a vow of eternal loyalty. Upon their shields was inscribed "I will come back from battle with it or upon it," and upon their banners "Over us or around us." Has not our King Jesus equal claims upon this sworn band for fidelity to death?

Another problem that Christian Endeavor solves for the office bearers of Christ's church is indicated by the name, Society, for that means fellowship. The Christian Endeavor Society is an institution which deals with the whole being of man, and seeks to touch the youth on every side of his many-sided life. There is a gospel of the tongue; the truth must be preached. Of the life; it must be lived. Then, too, there is a gospel of the hand. There must be the warm, cordial handgrasp of Christian love. The hand is the biggest human power. Without thumbs, our race would live in caves, like bears; or in trees, like monkeys. The thumb, a small part, the humblest part of the hand, has created civilization.

And speaking of this Society's promotion of fellowship, I remark that one element of its permanence and power is its interdenominational character, the very feature that makes sectarians and bigots sometimes look askance at it. Some people can't enjoy anything, not even religion, without a denominational flavor to it. Like an old Missouri farmer, who, cashing a draft at the bank, was asked by the cashier what denomination he would have his bills in. "Wall,' said he, "you might give me $100 in Old School Presbyterian, my wife belongs to that, but gimme the heft of them in Hardshell Baptist." [*Laughter.*]

In matters of life we are one; in matters of theology not, not likely to be until thought runs, I had almost said stagnates, into one mould. That organic unity which some denominations propose is the unity the whale offered to Jonah. This society is undenominational; it does not say I am of Paul, and I am of Apollos, and I of Calvin, and I of Wesley, but it takes for its motto, one Lord, one faith, one baptism. The flag under which we march was not cut out of Methodist homespun, or Presbyterian blue, or Episcopalian lawn, but it is the old banner of the cross, equally dear to Christians of every name. It stands with all who stand with Christ and works with all who seek the upbuilding of His kingdom. Its energies, confined to no one channel, are diffused through the whole evangelical brotherhood, while at the same time each local society is steadfastly loyal to the local church and to the denomination with which it is connected, and so to the general church of Christ. I have nothing to say against denominational societies, I bid them Godspeed. But as a Methodist minister, I say here today, that we need this interdenominational society to keep our youth in touch and sympathy with the young Christian life around them, to broaden their outlook, to cultivate in them a spirit of fraternal catholicity, and to unite them as a solid phalanx that together they may meet and master the problems of the twentieth century, and together they may crown Christ, King. [*Applause.*]

The Christian Endeavor Society, then, commends itself to the sympathy and co-operation of the wise and godly men who have charge of the temporal and spiritual concerns of the church, because it is no independent institution moving on parallel lines with the church as its ambitious competitor, but a constituent part of the church, engaged in the church's legitimate work of bringing souls to Christ and building them up in Him, by methods adapted to young people, but not therefore unadapted to those who are older. The Christian Endeavor Society is as much a part of the church as the branch is part of the tree, or as my hand is a part of my body. All its active officers and members either are, or are eligible to be, members in good standing of some evangelical church.

This Society has long since ceased to be an experiment, and has won its way to the front by its downright merit. It is the church's own child, nursed on her bosom, grown to its present stature and fair proportions under her fostering care. It is the best child she ever had—the fairest and faithfulest of her numerous family. It is neither headstrong nor idle; neither a sponge nor a spendthrift, neither a drone nor a dead beat, but diligent, dutiful, devoted, it can be trusted to guard the ark of the covenant surrounded as it is by foes, and to capture this world for Christ, and to hang this old globe up in the temple of God as a trophy of His cross. [*Loud applause.*]

After singing the hymn "Throw out the Life-line," President Clark introduced the next speaker, Rev. James A. Worden, D. D., of Philadelphia,—his topic, "The Society and the Sunday School."

ADDRESS OF REV. J. A. WORDEN, D.D.

Mr. President: What should the Sunday school do for Christian Endeavor? Once upon a time there was a female elephant so built that she was a mate for Jumbo. It came to pass all on a summer's day that Mrs. Jumbo took a walk in a field of barley; and as she switched around with her trunk, gathering in her food, she unwittingly uncovered a nestful of young larks. The nestlings being suddenly disturbed, began to pipe and cry. Mrs. Jumbo stopped, looked down, took in the situation, and with the greatest sympathy said, "Ah, I too have the heart of a mother," and so she sat down on the nest. [*Laughter*] Well, it does not need any application, I see. That is one trouble with these Christian Endeavor Conventions: the audience always gets to the end before the speaker does.

Now, in opposition to this idea of repressing our young people, I say this: all in the Sabbath school, pastor, superintendent, officers, teachers, scholars—all above the primary class—ought to be heart and soul members of the Christian Endeavor Society. [*Applause*] I am not a radical, either; I am a conservative of the conservatives. I have given the thing a great deal of thought, and no man that is set in any department of Christian work in this, the latter part of the nineteenth century, can ignore the Christian Endeavor movement. Yet I think that there is such a thing as overdoing the matter of conservatism, and there are thousands of Sunday schools in these United States and Canada that are disgracing common-sense conservatism by what I might term anti-diluvian moss-backedness. [*Laughter.*] Why do I say that every Sabbath-school worker ought to be in the Christian Endeavor Society? If for no higher motive than just to keep up with the procession. Old Father Time has dropped his scythe. You don't have to picture him as an old man, with flowing hair and scanty raiment, prepared to mow us down and gather us in. He is a railway official, standing at the station gates, examining the tickets; and when the bell strikes for the train to start, he closes the gates, and in the very classic language of the Tennessee Jubilee Singers, I would like to say to every moss-backed Sunday-school worker, "The old ark's movin', chillun', get on board!" The Greatest and Wisest of all has said, "How is it that ye cannot discern the signs of the times?" This great uprising of Christian young people, inspired, as I firmly believe, by the Spirit of Almighty God, is a message from heaven, and is written in letters of living light, as across yonder sky, and the lesson which it brings, is not only more light breaking forth from the word of God, but new and better methods springing up in the church of God. Now, shall we join the onward march, or shall we sit down on the nest? [*Laughter.*] I think it is a sin against high heaven to have no heart that throbs to the time and the tune of the music of the footsteps of the coming Christ.

And for another reason we ought to be Christian Endeavorers, to maintain our youthfulness. My brother, my sister, did you ever think it was your duty to grow young again? What has a Christian to do with growing old, who has all eternity before him? How old he would get by the end of eternity [*Laughter.*] The Saviour had on His brow the dew of youth, and we are to be like Christ. I will give you a recipe for growing old, and if it does not perform all that I say, return it and I will pay you back your money. Stand aloof from the young people; criticise the young people; get out of sympathy with the young people; do not ever forget to call them bumpkins and self-conceited and callow; ridicule their awkwardness and mistakes, and then, in order to show your consistency, sit and sing, "I would I were a boy again," and just hear yourself grow older as you sing. [*Laughter.*] I will guarantee that it will make any man or woman ancient at thirty-five. But there are five thousand people at this moment within sound of my voice, who have learned the secret of youth. It is here; keep near young people; feel the fulness of the beating life of the young people; sympathize with them; work with them; keep the new baptism of the dew of fresh and tender love, and you will grow younger every week,—or in one word, meaning all this, be a Christian Endeavorer. [*Loud applause.*] The youngest man I know of is "Father" Clark. [*Applause.*] My friend out there, who is a little indifferent yet toward this great movement, you need not think that the young people are beyond you, and that you are regarded simply as an enemy of their enjoyment and a censor of their pleasures. Come into our charmed circle and you will be one of us, and you will fulfill that ancient prophet's word, "A child shall die a hundred years old."

Now I will tell you from the bottom of my heart why I like this movement. I believe with my brother who has taken his seat, that God is drilling this army of covenanters, pledged Christian workers, for the battle of Armageddon, for the battle with anarchism, atheism, materialism and Romanism. [*Applause.*] Another thing I like it for is because it includes the women. [*Applause.*] I never did like a stag prayer meeting. [*Laughter.*] I do not believe that any man — I will speak for myself and all the men I know — will attain the purity and nobility of Christian character without the constant help and purifying influence of Christian women. [*Applause.*] "Neither is the man without the woman, neither the woman without the man in the Lord." I believe in working, not along the line of pessimism or despair, or "awful responsibility," but of courage and joy, —

"Strong in the strength of youth,
Strong in the strength of truth,
Armed as with Moses' rod,
Armed with the word of God."

Now, as a profounder reason, what is the Sunday school for? Is it simply to run an institution, keep up a school and grind out fifty-two lessons a year? Why, you would think so. You may go to ten thousand Sunday schools that I know, and you would think that the whole end-all and be-all was the man down

WILLISTON CHURCH AND PARSONAGE, PORTLAND, MAINE. BIRTHPLACE OF THE CHRISTIAN ENDEAVOR MOVEMENT.

there turning a crank, and grinding out fifty-two opening exercises and fifty-two closing exercises, and fifty-two lessons a year. Is that all? The object of the Sunday school, as my brother has said, is to bring souls to Jesus, to train those converted souls in Jesus, to drill them for Christ and the church. Now, where do you find a drill ground or a training class equal to Christian Endeavor? Pastors, superintendents, teachers, where else will you put your young people to train them for just the membership in the church that you want? Where, in the whole one hundred and sixty-eight hours of the week, can you crowd so much of Christ, of Christian counsel and culture, as in that short, precious Christian Endeavor hour? There is the time; there is the place. One blow struck there for Christ is worth ten blows struck elsewhere. One word spoken there for Christ, outweighs five words spoken elsewhere. Why? I will tell you. Because those whom you address there are in the most critical period of their Christian life; because they love Christian Endeavor; because they will meet you more than half way; because they are just waiting for the tongue and the hand which will point them to Jesus Christ; because you are bringing them help and stimulus and courage, in their own chosen work.

In the fifth chapter of first Timothy, the first and second verses, we read: "Entreat the younger men as brethren, the younger women as sisters, in all purity." A great deal has been said lately about philosophy and science, and higher criticism. I am somewhat like the old lady who heard her minister preach a learned sermon on the evidences for the existence of a personal God. She came up to him at the close and said, "Pastor, that was a splendid sermon, but I do believe, nevertheless, that there *be* a God." [*Laughter.*] After all that has been said, I do believe that that Bible is the word of God as it stands: [*Loud applause.*] Just look at that one word to prove its inspiration: "Entreat"—not command, not order, not "boss" your young people. If Paul had had young Americans in view when he wrote that, he could not have hit the nail on the head any better. Young Americans can not well submit to being driven, and they do not overlike the idea of being bossed; but you can entreat the young men and the young women as brothers and sisters. Here is this one advantage about Christian Endeavor, too. In the church and Sunday school there is more or less of superiority and inferiority, and that has been nicely explained here this morning; but in Christian Endeavor we all meet on the same platform. "One is your Master, even Christ, and all ye are brethren." [*Applause.*] We all meet in one society; we are all equal, and the minister can entreat the young people as brothers and sisters in Christ.

Secondly, let the Sunday school not only send one million new members into the Christian Endeavor Society, but let them send them surcharged with the word of God. Give them the sincere milk of the word, and do not put in it any of the acid of German or higher criticism, either. [*Applause.*]

Thirdly, let the Sunday school teach the duties of Christian Endeavor, and the wisest methods of performing them.

Fourthly, let the Sunday school give a more hearty and more universal celebration of Christian Endeavor Day. Let the whole church devote that day to Bible reading and exercises in behalf of young people's work. For my part, I should like to make a contribution on that day for the United Society of Christian Endeavor. [*Applause.*]

One thing more. I plead now, as a humble Sunday-school worker; you Christian Endeavor young people, come and re-enforce us. Not only give us that Sunday-school committee, but send us word that you are ready to help us,—

First, in making a thorough visitation of our scholars;

Second, in training our teachers and,

Third, in the canvass for new scholars. We are going to begin the first of next October a special effort for six months with a three-fold purpose: first, to gather all the membership of the church into the Sunday school; second, to bring back all the young people, who for various reasons have lapsed; and third, to gather into it all the children and youth now outside. Christian Endeavorers, come to our help. [*Loud applause.*]

After a long list of announcements from Secretary Baer, Mr. Sankey sang a solo, "Fading away like the stars of the morning," asking meanwhile that the audience unite in silent prayer in behalf of Mr. Spurgeon. The benediction was pronounced by Rev. W. K. Marshall, D. D., of Minneapolis.

FRIDAY AFTERNOON.

The central thought of the afternoon's exercises was: "The Society as a Soul Winner." There was an immense audience present at two o'clock, when the opening exercises began with the hymn, "Showers of Blessing." The Scriptures were read by Rev. Geo. B. Stewart, of Harrisburg, Penn., and prayer was offered by Rev. J. K. Fowler, D. D., of Cedar Rapids, Iowa. The hymns, "Jesus of Nazareth" and "Army of Endeavor" followed, after which President Clark called attention to the programme for the afternoon and introduced as the first speaker, Mr. F. J. Harwood, of Appleton, Wis., who would lead a conference upon the subject, "Souls won through the work of Committees."

OPEN CONFERENCE:

SOULS WON THROUGH THE WORK OF COMMITTEES.

LED BY MR. F. J. HARWOOD.

The subject that we have before us is the most important one of the whole Convention. The work of our orgaization is to win souls; and I realize, as I stand before you this afternoon, that there are thousands in this audience that have come up here to know how better to win souls through the work of the committees. I realize also that there is no necessity for a speech from me, for no speech can carry the force that your statements of experience will have. We want, then, brief, pithy statements of experience from the floor concerning the work that you have done, or have seen done, through these various committees.

We have been likened in our organization, by one of our writers, to a perfect man. Our spirit is the Spirit of God, and our different committees have been likened to the different faculties that we have. For instance, our lookout committee is the eye of our association; the prayer-meeting committee is our heart; the social committee is our handgrasp; the missionary committee is our pocket, and so I might go on through the list. You will see what I mean. We want to know how to win souls through the eye of our society, through the heart and the hand of our society. Can we win souls systematically? Think of the systematic work that goes on in this Convention, for instance, in the railroads that brought us here; in these magnificent flouring mills; in all the business of the commercial world. Should we not have equally as good system in the Lord's work? Let us hear from you now.

In response to this invitation, delegates rose in all parts of the hall and spoke briefly. Their statements are here summarized.

"Our lookout committee secures a list of those eligible for membership and divides the list up among the different members of the committee for special work."

"The social committee has organized a hospitality circle among the ladies of the church, each promising to entertain at her home at least one evening every month some homeless young man or woman."

"Our society at Orlando, Fla., has found cottage hospital work very useful."

"As a pastor, I find it much easier to bring young people into the church after they have been induced by the lookout committee to join the Christian Endeavor society as associate members. Seventy-five per cent. of those uniting with our church during the past seven years have been associate members of the Christian Endeavor society."

"In welcoming strangers to the Christian fellowship of the prayer meetings, the lookout committee does a very valuable work."

"The prayer-meeting committee of the Congregational Society of Jericho, Vt. has secured pledges from 24 out of 47 members to hold district prayer meetings in outlying neighborhoods."

"Our young people have done an excellent work in bringing their young friends to the inquiry meetings during the revival services and standing by them."

"We find our lookout committee does the best work when each member fully realizes that every name on the associate membership list represents an immortal soul."

"Let the lookout committee take the warm heart of the society in its right hand and extend it to every stranger that comes within its gates."

"The Tulare, Cal., society has an organization committee which goes from place to place organizing societies."

"A Massachusetts society organized a Sunday school in a district school house, resulting in ten or twelve conversions during the summer."

"Our lookout and prayer-meeting committees feel that they are doing some of their best work in urging upon the members of the society their regular attendance upon the weekly church prayer meeting and the Sunday services." [*Applause.*]

"Our lookout committee divides up the entire active membership and urges every division to make special efforts to reach the associate members."

"The Allegheny County Union (Penn.) has a lookout committee of fifteen which goes through the county organizing new societies."

"The smallest Christian Endeavor society in Chicago constitutes all its members a lookout committee."

"Let all the committees meet together and agree upon a campaign for saving souls. Set apart a week of solid work in that line. If we have the spirit of winning souls, that sort of thing will be contagious, and the whole society will be one mass of workers in that line." [*Applause.*]

"The Fort Street Methodist Episcopal Society of Rockford, Ill., is educating one person in the foreign field, a native, for missionary work. Our prayer-meeting committee meets with the pastor every evening before the meeting for consecration. At the close of the meeting we have a social gathering for religious conversation."

At the conclusion of this conference, President Clark resigned the chair to Rev. J. H. Barrows, D. D., of Chicago, who announced the next conference to be on "Souls won through the Prayer and Consecration Meetings," led by Rev. J. Z. Tyler, of the Central Christian Church, Cincinnati, O.

OPEN CONFERENCE:

SOULS WON THROUGH THE PRAYER AND CONSECRATION MEETINGS.

LED BY J. Z. TYLER.

IF I read the signs of the times aright, we have reached that point in the Christian Endeavor movement when there needs to be placed greater emphasis upon the thought that we are enlisted to win souls for Christ. The Christian army is of necessity an army of conquest, and every active member of the Christian Endeavor Society ought, in virtue of his pledge, in virtue of his personal consecration to Christ, in virtue of his promised fidelity to his church, to be an active worker in winning souls to Christ. Moreover, no class of persons has the opportunity that the young people in our churches have for this glorious work. More than ninety per cent. of all those who are brought into our churches by conversion are brought in before they reach the age of twenty years; and these young persons are, by their social intercourse, by their daily associations, brought into contact with these who are to be won for Christ. If the ranks in Christ's army are not only to be kept full but to be increased according to the needs of the cause, every Christian must become a recruiting officer. We are now to consider the prayer and consecration meetings as opportunities and aids to this work. Let us speak out of personal experience and from personal observation. Let us speak earnestly, let us speak with deep solicitude. Let us speak this afternoon with the view of making this Convention memorable as the inauguration of a new endeavor to make the Christian Endeavor a great and widespread evangelistic movement. One million of young persons actively engaged in this work means more than one million of souls won for Christ before our next Convention. Now let us hear your experience along this line, and remember to speak briefly and to the point.

"Our prayer and consecration meetings have been the means of leading a number of young people to be active and earnest members of the church during the last six months."

"First, the prayers must be from the heart and the consecration must be real. Second, we must always have a distinct purpose to save souls. Third, let us take care that our conduct after the meeting is Christian conduct, that we do not dissipate the good impressions which may have been made during the meeting." [*Applause.*]

"Does the prayer-meeting committee meet with the leader and study each topic together? If not, why not?"

"We have fifteen minutes prayer service previous to our prayer meeting, covering prayer for special objects, including those concerning whom we are solicitous. We deprecate the mechanical reading of Bible verses in our prayer meeting. We have ceased to call the roll, expecting our members to testify without the roll call."

"Two things are necessary: one is to know the sinner and have a hearty sympathy with him, making a personal friend of him; the other is to know the way of salvation to present to him."

"Our prayer-meeting committee meets with the leader before the meeting and prays with him for the success of that meeting."

"Encourage the associate members to take part in the meeting."

"The First Congregational Society of Dedham, Mass., has its associate members pledged to regular attendance and participation in the consecration meeting."

"We have found the Bible to be the most potent factor in the hands of the members of the Christian Endeavor Society. The pastor sees to it that a few of the most earnest members are conversant with the most pointed Scripture passages and bring the awakened members face to face with God's word."

"Never close a Christian Endeavor prayer meeting without extending the invitation to accept Christ, and never let a man or woman who signifies a desire to accept Christ go away from that room without being personally spoken to and prayed with until he or she is converted, if it takes all night."

"Our prayer meeting is held on Sunday afternoon at four o'clock, and thereby—and by all other means—we try to discourage the desecration of the Sabbath by walking, driving, etc., in the afternoon."

"We find one of the very best things in our work is to look after the bashful and awkward boys and try to bring them to Christ. We have found that there is no heart so sensitive and tender and impressionable as a boy's heart."

"Our young people have used the prayer list, writing down the names of those asking for prayers and praying for them and working with them until they are brought to the Saviour."

"The prayer and consecration meetings have developed the conscience of our young people and have greatly assisted the pastor in leading some into the church who had refused to come."

"At our consecration meetings we make our associate members an object of especial thought and attention. They take part in the meetings more and more, and are rapidly becoming active members."

"Read the pledge at every consecration meeting after silent prayer."

"The lookout and prayer-meeting committees ought to confer together and take advantage of every opportunity to win souls. After a meeting of this kind the two committees ought to plan for definite work for the conversion of souls and begin early in the year, before the Week of Prayer, that they may be ready for God's blessing."

"In the consecration meeting let the active members take part so promptly and cheerfully that the associate members may be led to regard it not as a task but as a great and pleasant privilege."

Our prayer and consecration meetings have been the best meetings in our church life, productive of a great amount of good, resulting in the conversion and gathering into the church of many souls. I can speak as State evangelist for South Dakota that in the Congregational denomination the Christian Endeavor Society is doing more to win souls to Christ than all the older organizations that I know anything about. Among our earnest purposes is to enforce the prohibition law and save souls from temptation and to bring them fully into the fold of Christ." [*Applause.*]

"Our young people believe in prayer. They take each meeting to God in prayer before they come to it, praying for that meeting, for those members who are lacking in interest and for the unconverted."

"We call upon all the associate members at the consecration meetings just as regularly as we do the active members; and when we find them showing some interest we get them to join the church."

"One great means of winning souls is through song. Use frequently such songs as 'Just as I am,' 'I am coming to the cross,' etc."

"About a year ago a third of our society were associate members and we divided them among the members of the active list. About four of us would take one associate member and we had a special time each day that we would pray for them. Then, during the meetings we remembered them all the time. At the end of two months we had one associate member left." [*Applause.*]

"Let the active members be thoroughly consecrated to the work, and God will show them how to lead the associate members to Christ."

"The earnestness and consecration of our young people have so permeated the church that during the last six months we have received 56 new members into the church, 45 per cent. of the previous membership."

"At the Christian Endeavor meetings of the society of the girls' school of Hawaii, Sandwich Islands, each one of the girls takes part and there have been many conversions." [*Applause.*]

Mr. Tyler: The time for closing this conference has come. Let us try to make the Christian Endeavor movement a grand evangelistic movement during the coming year.

After the singing of the hymn, "Work for the night is coming," and the reading of several announcements, Dr. Barrows introduced Mr. W. H. H. Smith, of Washington, D. C., as the leader of the next conference on "Souls won through the influence of local, district, Provincial and State unions."

OPEN CONFERENCE:

SOULS WON THROUGH THE INFLUENCE OF LOCAL, DISTRICT, PROVINCIAL AND STATE UNIONS.

LED BY MR. W. H. H. SMITH.

CHRISTIAN workers, I shall take but a brief part of the time allotted to this conference; and in order that our thought may be centralized, I will state four points about which I think it would be well to cluster our words. They embrace, to my mind, what should be the chief features of our union work in these larger bodies. First, co-operation, a wide and deep front against a common and merciless foe; next, fellowship, a heart that beats glad and loyal for the success at either end of the line and all through the ranks; next, inspiration, the cumulative thought that we are identified with so great an host working together on these grand lines; and lastly, aspiration, that we shall go out in our thought and determination for a big victory for our Lord and Master, Jesus Christ. All who are or have been officers in local, district, Provincial or State unions, are requested to speak to this topic.

LUVERNE DISTRICT UNION, MINN.: It promotes Christian fellowship and shows to the world that Christians of different denominations dwell together in love.

LOCAL UNION IN NEW HAMPSHIRE: At the close of a day of Bible study in our local union an evangelistic meeting was held and quite a number rose for prayers.

LOCAL UNION, BETHLEHEM, PENN.: We have a committee appointed whose duty it is to go around to all the churches who have no Christian Endeavor societies and inspire and instigate them to form such societies. We have another committee whose duty it is to look after such societies as have grown cold and warm them up again.

A DELEGATE: In our local union we have a committee appointed to arrange for the interchange of visiting between societies.

FRANKLIN COUNTY UNION, VT.: At our last union meeting a number present were not members of the Christian Endeavor Society, and they expressed their desire to go home and form societies in the churches where they belonged.

BROOKLYN CITY UNION: The city is divided into five districts and each district has three committees: a reaching out, a visiting, and a social committee.

ROCHESTER LOCAL UNION, MINN.: We have special subjects for our union meetings, such as union work, missionary work, Bible study, etc. They have been very successful.

A DISTRICT SECRETARY, NEW YORK: The work is kept up by the district Secretary holding meetings throughout the county. He gets acquainted with the societies and keeps up a general interest. This is sustained by a few active members who assist the district secretary in his work. We also have another system. If I hear of a society that is weak, I call upon some lady friend to address a communication to that society,—a Christian word which cheers them in their work and draws them nearer to the heart of the Master.

STAMFORD LOCAL UNION, CONN.: During the past six months a committee has held a conference with every society in the union, talking over the work, the successes achieved and the plans for the future, closing with a union prayer meeting.

NEW YORK CITY UNION: Every church where we have held our quarterly meetings has been taxed to accommodate the large audiences. We have at these meetings addresses by the leading city pastors. The city is divided into districts and each district is attended to by a committee. Every church in the city is reached by these committees. It is needless to say that we have the hardest city in this union to work for Christian Endeavor, among a conservative business class of people; but we have a local union that in a few years has increased more rapidly in proportion than any other local union in the United States.

ESSEX COUNTY UNION, N. J.: We have two purposes before us continually: first, to bring all the societies regularly organized into the county union, also to communicate with other churches that have not societies to induce them to become members of the county union; second, we have organized a system of visitations whereby every society makes and receives three annual visits to and from all the societies in the union, the object being to convey Christian congratulations and to get into the fulness of the blessing of the gospel of Christ and to illustrate that we are all brethren. [*Applause.*]

LOCAL UNION, ONTARIO, CAN.: Our Christian Endeavor societies meet on Monday night and that night we call "Christian Endeavor night." We hold our union meetings on Monday night, and by setting aside this "Christian Endeavor night" we find it has a good effect in the city, the same as mid-week prayer-meeting night.

MONTREAL UNION, CAN.: Our union has a committee which visits every pastor in the city and brings before him the work of the Christian Endeavor Society. This has resulted in the formation of several new societies. We also have a committee which visits the societies every quarter.

ONTARIO PROVINCIAL UNION: The work of the union this year has been taken up with dividing the Province up into districts, holding district conventions and appointing district secretaries to work up an interest in the Society and above all to lift up the standard of Jesus Christ.

GEORGIA STATE UNION: Our State union was organized in 1889 and we have held two meetings. We have two local unions, one at Savannah and the other at Atlanta. We believe in capturing and making a Christian Endeavorer wherever we find him. We made two on the way up here from Atlanta. One was 6 years old, the other was 69. [*Applause.*] I want the privilege of introducing our youngest Endeavorer, Dr. Abraham P. Love, of Atlanta. [*Applause.*]

DR. LOVE: I did not expect to be called upon here, but I desire simply to state that my heart is altogether wilh the principles of this Society and in the work that it has undertaken and so successfully carried on. [*Applause.*]

KANSAS STATE UNION: We are making a special effort in Bible study. Also seeking to reach the unsaved young men and women in the country districts.

NORTH DAKOTA STATE UNION: Organized last November by Secretary Baer. We desire to do better work.

OKLAHOMA TERRITORIAL UNION: First Territorial Convention held last spring. Increase of societies, 200 per cent.

NEBRASKA STATE UNION: At our last meeting it was reported that we had gained 75 per cent. over the year before. This coming fall we shall report 150 per cent. gain. One of the results of our State union meeting has been to place increased value upon Bible study. We have an Indian Christian Endeavor society at Santee Agency with 35 members.

REV. J. Z. TYLER: I have been requested to state a method pursued by the Cincinnati Local Union because it is thought that it may prove helpful to some others. The executive committee of our local union has a regular meeting once a month. Our union has 35 societies. The plan adopted is this: at the meeting of the executive committee we have a normal corps; that is, at one meeting we call in all the lookout committees from the 35 societies and drill them in their work; at the next meeting we call in all the prayer-meeting committees and drill them in their work. We think that by thus doing we shall make the committees more efficient, it will keep the interest awake, and these committees will make every society in our union more successful in winning souls for Christ and doing every part of the work. [*Applause.*]

At the close of this conference the audience sang, under the direction of Mr. Sankey, the hymn, "Bringing in the sheaves." Mr. Sankey first divided the congregation into several sections, assigning to each section one line of the chorus. He then sang each verse as a solo, the audience joining in the chorus as divided. The effect was very pleasing.

The last conference was then taken up, the subject being, "Souls won through the Junior Societies," and Rev. W. W. Sleeper, of Stoneham, Mass., was introduced as the leader.

OPEN CONFERENCE.

SOULS WON THROUGH JUNIOR SOCIETIES.

REV. W. W. SLEEPER.

YESTERDAY at the headquarters of your entertainment committee, I discovered a young girl standing there and waiting her turn to be assigned a place of entertainment. I spoke to her and asked her if she belonged to the Junior Endeavor Society. She replied that she did, and that she came from this State of Minnesota. I suppose there are many Junior Endeavorers scattered throughout this great audience; only for reason of the multitude we cannot see them. But they are the advance guard of a mighty host of children who are being mobilized for this great work we have undertaken. Yesterday we were interested by a reference to the Crusades. Now there is in progress a new crusade of children. You remember something of the disastrous history of the Children's Crusade in the middle ages. You know how they went forward with their banners and their songs, only to meet defeat, only to meet discouragement and slavery and death. But, thanks be to God, our Junior Endeavor movement, which is our children's crusade, is going to march onward to victory. It goes with banner and song and triumph because it goes forward for Christ and for the church. But some ask, What is the need for a Junior Society of Christian Endeavor? Because our senior societies are so full of enthusiasm for the work of winning their own companions to Christ, the older boys and girls, the young men and the young women, that the little ones, the younger boys and girls, are almost of necessity crowded out. I pity the poor children. They are crowded out of almost everything. They are practically crowded out of our churches. We ministers sometimes forget to break the bread for the children in our ministrations. More and more the Sunday school has come to be the children's church.

But now we Christian Endeavorers have taken it upon ourselves, with all humility, to rectify some of the mistakes of the churches to which we belong; and here is a mistake that we are bound to correct before we get through with it. We are going to find a warm place for the children; we are going to bring them back to their own true place in their church homes.

How can we organize Junior Christian Endeavor societies? The plan is very simple. Of course I cannot stop to give details, and I only speak thus at length because the Junior work is comparatively new. Have a Junior Endeavor committee appointed by your local society. Let that committee select the very best person in all your church for superintendent. Then summon the children to a meeting. Have the announcement read from the pulpit and in the Sunday school that all boys and girls from fourteen years downwards, who are interested in the principles of Christian Endeavor, are invited to meet with the superintendent and committee at such a time. If your experience is like mine, you will have a large number of children present, for they are interested in every effort to do them good. Then read to them the admirable constitution that our United Society has prepared, and by no means leave out, as you undertake to manufacture Christian Endeavorers out of the boys and girls, the backbone of their structural anatomy — the pledge. Then you can organize and appoint your committees, and you will find that the children will enter with great heartiness and enthusiasm into this work.

What can the Junior Endeavor Society do? Why, Junior societies of Christian Endeavor have proved soul winners, very many of them; and we expect to hear testimonies here from enthusiastic workers among the children to this effect. In a society in Massachusetts, after a single year's work among the children, seven went forward and met the august committee of the church without fear and trembling, and were received into the church. I have just received word from New Hampshire that a similar experience was enjoyed there in Manchester, seven children coming forward and uniting with the church, while they were yet Junior Endeavorers — little boys and girls, yet none the less faithful and precious to Christ. After they graduated into the senior society, still others came forward and united with the church. I have also had a remarkable testimony from Minneapolis. I understand that a society in this city, numbering only 15 members, has received ten members into the church, and these ten have gone to work to bring others in. Dare we say that children are not important factors in the great work of building up the kingdom of God?

One other thing these societies can do: they can develop Christian character in the boys and girls. To my mind, that is the most important thing of all; because if these little children are rebels from God, they have not rebelled very greatly. If they have wandered somewhat from the path of righteousness, they have not wandered very far. As one Christian Endeavor worker for children says, they are God's lambs, and what they want is to be fed — fed regularly and frequently.

If time allowed, I should like to go on and mention some of the interesting incidents in this work for children; but as I look into your faces I find there great interest. You, I am sure, are lovers of children; and now we will have some testimonies from the audience. Let there be a little electricity brought into this meeting on this topic. I want to have a spark from all of you who love children and who know anything about work for children. Who will speak first?

A Delegate from Massachusetts: Eight years ago Dr. Clark was called to Phillips Church, South Boston. He immediately organized — not a Junior society, for that name was not then known, but he organized a society that has since taken the Junior name. During these last seven years every single one of the first fifty members of that Junior society has become a member of Phillips Church and is an earnest, active, faithful worker in our church or in some other church. [*Applause.*]

A Delegate: From one Junior society, one year old, eight members have come into the church.

A DELEGATE FROM TORONTO, CAN.: Last winter we formed a Junior section, the first in Toronto. The outcome has been that 35 of those Junior members have been received into the church, and the outcome still further has been that one of the most blessed revivals that Toronto has ever seen came through the formation of this Junior section of the Christian Endeavor work. We have only one member of our society between ten and fourteen that is not converted, and I expect to hear before I get back that that one is now a Christian. [*Applause.*]

DELEGATE FROM IOWA: The lady who organized the first Junior society in the country is here and we should be glad to hear from her.

MRS. E. H. SLOCUM OF IOWA: I am happy to say that, as far as is known, I organized the first Junior society. In Iowa at the present time we have sixty-four societies, with a large number of members. The first society that was formed started with five members and grew to eighty-five. Out of that eighty-five, more than seventy-five are members in our churches today and all in young people's societies. In addition to our regular work, we in Iowa lately have been forming a society for the boys — a boys' brigade. They meet together in the week time for a military drill , three quarters of an hour, followed by religious exercises.

A DELEGATE FROM PHILADELPHIA: We have a Junior society of forty active members and seventeen associate members. During the last year six of the parents have been converted and brought into the church through the work of these children. Let us stand together for the children. By the time this Convention meets again, they will roll up 100,000 new members; and when Philadelphia's banner comes before the next Convention we hope to report a Junior society in every church in the city. [*Applause.*]

DELEGATE FROM NASHVILLE, TENN.: We have a Junior society, and at a late special meeting fifteen out of thirty-five joined the church. They are more active outside of the church than the senior society.

A DELEGATE FROM PENNSYLVANIA: From the St. Louis Convention last year I went home thoroughly enthused with the idea of Junior Endeavor work. In October I organized a Junior society of twenty-five members; it now numbers a hundred and sixty-seven. Last winter we had a blessed work of grace in our church with over one hundred conversions, and among that number were nineteen or twenty from the Junior society. They passed an excellent examination and they do not cause me, their pastor, nearly so much anxiety as do the older persons who joined at that time.

A DELEGATE FROM MASSACHUSETTS: Our Junior society equals the senior society in all respects. Five joined the church in March. Those members of the senior society who have graduated from the Junior society are the best members in it.

A JUNIOR DELEGATE FROM GALESBURG, ILL.: Our Junior society was organized a year ago. There are now about twenty-one active members, ten of whom have joined the church through our efforts, and we expect many more to do so.

A DELEGATE FROM ST. LOUIS: We have a Junior Endeavor society of over sixty members; and if you will come down to us we will teach you older Christians how to keep your church covenants; we will teach you how to pray in such a way that your prayers will be answered and a wonderful work will be done for the Lord Jesus Christ in saving souls. [*Applause.*]

A DELEGATE FROM KANSAS CITY: Our society organized with ten members; we now have sixty-seven. I heard the pastor say that there were at least thirty-two of those members that he was not afraid to call upon at any time in public service to lead in prayer.

A DELEGATE FROM MASSACHUSETTS: Berkeley Temple, Boston, has a Live Junior society consisting of forty members. It has been in existence six months. Two particular points have been found helpful in our organization. The first is that no boy or girl is allowed to join the active list until he or she has been known to us for at least eight weeks. Our society is advised by two very efficient workers in the church, our assistant pastor, who is also our Sunday-school superintendent, and our Sunday-school lady worker. These two make it a point to know every child who comes to our Junior society meeting,—knowing him at home, in the school, and by personal interviews. After eight weeks this child passes to an interview in which he is thoroughly made to understand his pledge and to understand more of the love of Christ, after which, if he so decides, he is admitted as a member of the society. The presence of these two advisers in each meeting is very helpful to our society.

A DELEGATE FROM SOUTH DAKOTA: Our society is senior in name, but the terrible drouth has made it a Junior society practically. At first we had hard work to make the children take part; but by using sentence prayers each one can now pray and pray earnestly.

A DELEGATE FROM WHEELING, WEST VIRGINIA: We have just organized the first Junior society in the city, perhaps the first in the State. We cannot tell the results as yet, but we know that it is catching the boys who are beginning to think they are old enough to quit Sunday school. We organized it, first, because we needed it, and second because the children were asking for it.

A DELEGATE FROM CHICAGO: I find that we have more active members among our Juniors than we have among our seniors. We are training the children to repeat sentence prayers so that they will become accustomed to praying in public. We have them pray also for our associate members.

A DELEGATE FROM ILLINOIS: For four years our church has had a Bohemian mission, and not until a Junior society was organized have any of the members of that school joined our church. At the last communion two girls came before the session. They said it was through the efforts of the Junior society that they were led to take this step.

A DELEGATE FROM KANSAS: Among the best results of our Junior society's work is the bringing of many of the little ones into the fold of Christ. At a recent anniversary they recited the books of the Bible in their order and also the shorter catechism.

MR. SLEEPER: I propose the following recommendation to be adopted here this afternoon:

RECOMMENDED, that since a wide and most promising field for Christian Endeavor is right at hand among the children, every Christian Endeavorer should do all he can to encourage the formation, and foster the development of Junior societies.

SECRETARY BAER: I think the best way for us all to take part in this service in which we have been so much interested is by showing emphatically, without the least shadow of doubt, that we believe in this Junior movement as one of the greatest features in the work of winning souls for Jesus Christ. If you approve of this, if you mean it from the bottom of your hearts and it is no mere sentimentality or enthusiasm, and if you mean to go home and see that your children and the children of others are early brought into the Sunday school and into these Junior societies, will you show it definitely by rising to your feet. [*The whole congregation rose.*]

This closed the conferences, and a brief prayer service followed led by Mr. Trafford N. Jayne, president of the St. Paul Union. The hymn "Nearer my God to Thee," was then sung.

Rev. H. H. French, of Minneapolis, requested all members of Methodist churches present to meet in front of the platform at the close of the session to act upon certain resolutions which had been prepared, memorializing the Methodist General Conference with respect to the status of Christian Endeavor societies in the Methodist churches.

President Clark: Three weeks ago Monday, my dear friend Mr. Dickinson and myself got back to Boston from a five weeks' Christian Endeavor campaign in England. I am very glad that he is going to tell you something about this in a few moments this afternoon — Rev. C. A. Dickinson, pastor of Berkeley Temple, Boston. [*Applause.*]

ADDRESS OF REV. C. A. DICKINSON.

I WAS struck last night by Secretary Baer's repetition of the word inter. He repeated it, you remember, three times — inter, inter, interdenominational. That word seems to be at the front in this Convention, and to my mind the fact is deeply significant. It is one of the many signs that the Christian Endeavor movement is designed of God to fit into the mould of these present times and to meet a universal need of the world. Christian Endeavor is interdenominational, interurban, interstate, international, and if it be true that there be other worlds than this, I think we shall find that it is interplanetary, [*applause*] simply because it is based upon God's universal law of progress through self-denying endeavor and ministration.

The English campaign has demonstrated that there is the same need existing in the churches of Great Britain as in America, and the same readiness to adopt any method which has in it a reasonable promise of meeting that need.

Three years ago Dr. Clark visited England, and in response to the request of several men prominent in the churches there, spoke in London and elsewhere upon the work for young people. As a result an interest was aroused which led to the formation of several societies. The Sunday School Union of Great Britain, one of the most efficient and aggressive religious organizations in the country, became sponsor for the new movement, and through a special committee, whose leading spirit is Charles Waters, and its official organ the *Sunday School Chronicle*, urged the churches to adopt it.

Last winter the Sunday School Union sent over the urgent request that the president and several of the trustees of the Society should visit England and carry on a thoroughly organized Christian Endeavor campaign throughout the country. Accordingly, Dr. Clark and I sailed for England in April, and were able to address several of the great May Sunday school and guild meetings in London, and the first national Christian Endeavor convention at Crewe. We were afterwards joined by Rev. J. L. Hill and Rev. N. Boynton, two other trustees of the United Society, and together we addressed between forty and fifty audiences in nearly all of the large cities and towns throughout England.

Our experiences with English audiences were everywhere delightful. As a rule we found the Christian public hospitable to the Christian Endeavor idea and eager to know all about the workings of the Society. While Christians in England are much like Christians in America, there are some marked differences which will doubtless affect somewhat the introduction and development of the Christian Endeavor methods in the churches. The overshadowing influence of the state church which tends to drive dissenters of all denominations into a closer fellowship than that which exists away from the denominations of this country, the natural conservatism of the English character which hesitates a good while before adopting a new thing, and the English horror of anything which seems to encourage youthful precocity or priggishness, must all be taken into account in planning for a great aggressive work among the young. Yet we have this testimony given again and again by clergymen and laymen all over England: "We have tried many things and have failed. We have reached out after our young people in many ways, but they have drawn back and have refused to come with us. Nothing has appealed so strongly to our common sense as Christian Endeavor; nothing has succeeded so well among us after a brief trial. We want it; we mean to have it."

The objections there are the same in general as here. All that is needed to do away with them is to meet them courteously and let on the light. One brother in one of the London meetings asked if the tendency of the Society was not to foster a premature sobriety, and another was somewhat afraid that the movement would result in introducing into England that rushing, pushing spirit of "Young America," which he had heard a good deal about, and which, for one, he was not at all in sympathy with. These brethren, however, were soon answered by a half score of testimonies from the floor, which seemed to satisfy them that the Society was not a monastery or a nunnery on the one hand, nor a hot house for forcing precocious Christians on the other.

The first national convention of the British section of Christian Endeavor was held in Crewe, a large manufacturing city in the west of England, on May 16. It was an enthusiastic gathering, and comprised more delegates than were present at either the first or second anniversary of the United Society in this country. The mayor of the city presided, and there were many interesting addresses from pastors and from the young people. To sum up the state of things in England at the close of our campaign, I would say there are now over 120 societies, with a membership of 6,000 or 7,000. The churches are deeply interested and are inquiring much about the work. The various denominations are equally hospitable to the idea and see in it a basis for a grand united advance against the strongholds of evil. The leaders of the movement there are sanguine and hopeful, and the probabilities are that in a few years some silver-tongued Dr. Wells will come over to us from England as he has come this year from Canada, and capture the great world's Convention of Christian Endeavor for London. [*Applause.*]

At the close of Mr. Dickinson's address there came another string of announcements, after which the audience joined in singing, "Hide me."

President Clark: Now we shall have the pleasure of listening to Rev. L. W. Munhall, the evangelist, whom so many of you know, who will speak of the Society as a Missionary and Evangelistic Force. [*Applause.*]

ADDRESS OF EVANGELIST MUNHALL.

Mr. Chairman: God has stamped His creation with an intelligent design, and it is well for us, as those who are called to be laborers together with God, to understand His plan. Concerning Israel it was made known in the covenant and promise spoken to Abraham, though this was dimly outlined in all preceding history. He told Israel that if she loved Him and obeyed Him, He would give

her unnumbered and unmeasured blessings; but if she forgot Him and wandered from Him, she should be scattered among all the nations of the earth. She forsook God, she rejected Jesus Christ and desired a murderer and robber instead and said, "Let His blood be on us and on our children," and poor Israel has been murdered and robbed ever since. But God's purposes in grace concerning His ancient people are eternal; and it is well for you and me to pray for the peace of Jerusalem; for there is a promise that they that love her shall prosper, and we are told that all Israel shall be saved and she who is the bride of God will return from her wanderings and she shall be honored as no people of the earth have been or shall be honored. But Israel's rejection of Jesus Christ has turned out to our account, because we are told that in this dispensation of the Spirit, God is now choosing a people that were no people for His name, and in the eleventh chapter of Romans we have outlined to us what I should like to speak upon at this time but can only suggest to your minds.

I see it plainly set forth in the fifteenth of Acts what God's plan is concerning the nations of the earth besides poor Israel. In the fourteenth verse of the fifteenth chapter: "Simeon hath declared how God at the first did visit the Gentiles to take out of them a people for His name; and to this agree the words of the prophets, as it is written, After this I will return and will rebuild again the tabernacle of David which is fallen down, and I will build again the ruins thereof, and I will set it up; that the residue of men might seek after the Lord, and all the Gentiles, upon whom my name is called, saith the Lord, who doeth all these things." So that when poor Israel shall be gathered, the kingdom shall be established and the residue of the Gentiles shall come to God, and the kingdom shall be built and the king shall reign from the river unto the ends of the earth, when the islands of the sea shall be given Him for an inheritance and the uttermost parts of the earth for a possession, and He shall reign over all the earth as King of kings and Lord of lords.

Now, then, with this plan thus briefly outlined in your minds, will you just contemplate for a few moments the purposes of God concerning the sons and daughters of men? Do you know, as touching the redemption of men in the gospel of Jesus Christ, that I am a universalist out and out, because I am told in the ninth verse of the second chapter of Hebrews: "We see Jesus, who was made a little lower than the angels for the suffering of death, crowned with glory and honor; that he by the grace of God should taste death for every man." And in 1 John 2: 2 we read: "He is the propitiation for our sins: and not for ours only, but also for the sins of the whole world." 2 Cor. 5: 14, 15: "The love of Christ constraineth us: because we thus judge, that if one died for all, then were all dead; and that he died for all, that they which live should not henceforth live unto themselves, but unto him which died for them, and rose again." So you see by these Scriptures that Jesus Christ by the grace of God tasted death for every man and therefore every man is redeemed, and therefore does the word of God say, "Ye are not your own; ye are bought with a price; therefore glorify God in your body."

A second thing that I want you to see, is that God desires the salvation of all men. Ezek. 33: 11: "Say unto them, as I live, saith the Lord, I have no pleasure in the death of the wicked; but that the wicked turn from his way and live: turn ye, turn ye from your evil ways; for why will ye die, O house of Israel?" That refers to the Jews. Matt. 11: 28, 29 and 30: "Come unto me all ye that labor and are heavy laden, and I will give you rest. Take my yoke upon you and learn of me: for I am meek and lowly in heart: and ye shall find rest unto your souls. For my yoke is easy and my burden is light." 2 Pet.

3: 10: "The Lord is not slack concerning his promise, as some men count slackness, but is long-suffering to us-ward, not willing that any should perish, but that all should come to repentance." 1 Tim. 2: 4: "Who willeth all men to be saved, and to come unto the knowledge of the truth." Therefore, we see that Christ has not only died for all, but God desires the salvation of all; and you and I are to go out and tell the message of redemption and God's gracious willingness to save. So that while I am a universalist as touching the doctrine of redemption, I am not a Universalist as touching the doctrine of salvation. We use those terms interchangeably, and they ought not so to be used. Redemption is what Christ did when He offered himself once for all for the sins of the world upon Calvary's cross. Salvation is what God will do through the energy of the Holy Spirit for those who repent of their sins and believe on the Lord Jesus Christ that they may be saved. So that while all men are redeemed, not all men are saved; for there are those that will not come to Him that they might have life, and they will not have this Man to reign over them. Our consenting to the truth in repentance toward God and faith in the Lord Jesus Christ are reckoned to be as certainly elements in the procuring cause of our salvation, as the redemptive work of Jesus Christ upon the cross for us. Therefore we are to repent and to believe in order that redemption may be made efficacious in our behalf, to save us from the guilt of sin in justification, from the power and domination of sin in sanctification, and from the ultimate consequences of sin in glorification when Jesus Christ shall come again to be glorified in His saints.

I notice next the condition of the field. God's word tells me that "the whole world lieth in the wicked one." We are in the habit of talking about home missions and foreign missions. The Bible does not do so. There is just one kind of missionary work to be done, and that is to preach the gospel to every creature. The commission of the church of God is to go into all the world and preach the gospel to every creature,—to the Indians upon the frontiers of our land as well as the Indians in the far East or in the Islands of the Sea or the other continents south of us; to the Chinaman in the rice fields of his native land, among the mountains of Japan or in the heart of Africa, as really as in our elegant churches in our large cities in this land of civilization, and the adjoining lands that are civilized. God knows no difference between an unsaved man in China and an unsaved man in Minneapolis or St. Paul. [*Applause.*] It is just as much the business of the church of God to evangelize what we call the heathen nations as any in these cities of the civilized nations.

Now, I do believe that there are mistaken notions in the minds of many people respecting the amount of work that is to be done. There are approximately 1,500,000,000 of souls upon this round earth of ours today. I do not believe that there are 100,000,000 of them saved. I know we hear about 450,000,000 Christians: but 200,000,000 of those are Roman Catholics, and 90,000,000 are Greek Catholics, and you know how many of the rest belong to the Armenians and the Copts and the ritualistic wings of the churches of the old countries. And then you know that a great many people in our own churches are not fully saved; they have a name to live and are dead; they have a form of godliness but are without the power. And this great mass of the world's population is the class that you and I, as members of the household of faith, are commanded to go and tell that Jesus Christ died for them and that He is waiting to be gracious. Therefore we need to gird ourselves for the conflict, that we may push the battle to the gates of the wicked.

A word with regard to what is necessary in order that we may rightly qualify ourselves for the work. There is an idea that the ordained minister is to do all the preaching, and that is a mischievous idea wherever it obtains. If only the ordained ministers are to preach the gospel, two-thirds at least of the population of the United States and Canada and Great Britain and the Colonies and the Maritime Provinces will never hear the gospel of the grace of God. Now it is true, in the economy of the church, that certain men are set apart to feed the flock of God over whom God has given them charge, and they are appointed and ordained to that office and work. But you, my friends, who have not been appointed and ordained to that office and work, are commanded and fore-ordained of God to preach the gospel to every creature. Sixty-three years after the Head of the church ascended to the throne, He sent back this message: "Let him that heareth say, Come;" and whoever has heard the gospel of the grace of God is thereby commanded and commissioned to tell it out to somebody else and to everybody else whom he can reach. I remember when I resided in the city of Indianapolis, as I did before I moved to Philadelphia, that pleasant place of residence, I used to go out and organize mission schools in the schoolhouses twenty-five years ago. They could n't get any preachers, and so I used to try to preach to them. I remember the first place that we organized a mission school. There was no church down in that part of the city; it was where the rolling mills were. The people said, "Why can't we have preaching services here?" I said, "There is no ordained minister to be had." "Well, why can't you preach for us?" "I never tried it." "Suppose you try it." So I did. I got a couple of brethren to go along with me. I took the sixteenth verse of the third chapter of John, which is the gospel in miniature, as Martin Luther once said, for I knew we could not go astray on that text if we kept to the truth. I gave to one brother a certain point to elucidate and to another, another, and I said, "I will try and bring the thing together syllogistically and make the application." It was n't much of a sermon, but we had a houseful and God blessed the word. After the service the people came up and said it was good, but as they had never had any preaching before they did n't know what good preaching was. It was hard on them but it was a good thing for us. There are many talents buried that might be used in that way to the glory and praise of God, and God would give great increase to them if rightly used. Well, there came to me one day a good old Presbyterian elder, and he said, "Brother Munhall, I understand you are preaching." "Yes, sir." "Well, have n't you been ordained?" "No, sir,"—at least, I was not at that time. "Well," said he, "you ought not to preach if you are not ordained." "But," I replied, "I have been *fore-ordained* to do it and that ought to be just as good with a Presbyterian elder." [*Laughter and applause.*] Of course he could not doubt it, and he agreed that it was all right and said I might go on with his approval.

Now, while it is true that you young people who sit here today, with the flush of health upon your cheeks, with the vigor and strength of youth in your bones and with immeasurable possibilities in your life for the propagation of the gospel of the blessed God, have not been ordained to feed the flock of God, yet, according to the word of the great Head of the church, you have been foreordained to tell it out to the ends of the earth wherever dying men can hear and will hear the word of truth. [*Applause.*]

Now, certain things are necessary. It is not necessary that you should go to a theological seminary, though that might help you—and it might spoil you, too. [*Laughter.*] That is, for the work you are called to, I mean. But there are certain things necessary to qualify you, and the first is consecration—consecration not to the work of the societies of Christian Endeavor, not to the work of the church; because if you are consecrated to the work to which God has called you, when the work goes smoothly you will be encouraged and when it goes otherwise you will be discouraged. You will be full of enthusiasm in this magnificent gathering, but when you go back to your own church and see the empty pews that your minister has to preach to and the very few of the church members at the mid-week prayer meeting—and you ought to be there, no matter how many other prayer meetings you have—you will get discouraged. Your consecration ought to be to Jesus Christ, [*responses: "Amen, amen"*] and then it does not matter how the work will go so far as you are concerned. It is none of your business how it goes; it is your business to give yourself to Him that He may work through you to will and to work of His good pleasure, and then He will take care of the results, for He has promised to do that and more.

Then it is necessary for you to get down to systematic Bible study. I want to give you a text, among all the mottoes you have received. I want it to stay with you until you meet at New York next year. 2 Tim. 2: 15: "Study to show thyself approved unto God, a workman that needeth not to be ashamed, rightly dividing the word of truth." That should be your motto and that should be your aim, that you may each one be a workman that needeth not to be ashamed, rightly dividing the word of truth. God has not promised to bless anything to the conviction and salvation of men but His own Holy Word, [*Loud applause*] absolutely nothing but that. "These words," said Jesus, "that I speak unto you, they are spirit and they are life;" and when they are told out into the ears of the dying, the Holy Ghost will always accompany them to quicken those that are willing to receive them with meekness, the engrafted word which is able to save their souls into an apprehension of their condition and need and of the truth as it is in Jesus Christ, that they may be saved by the washing of regeneration and the renewing of the Holy Ghost. Make up your minds to get a Bible of your own and to search it daily whether these things are so, proving all things and holding fast that which is good. You yourselves will grow in grace correspondingly; for we never grow any faster in grace than we do in the knowledge of our Lord Jesus Christ, and you will attain thereby unto the perfect stature of men and women in Christ Jesus.

Another thing: personal work. Consecrated to Jesus Christ, diligently studying the Bible in order that you may rightly use it and wisely divide it, you are to give yourselves up personally to do personal work,— to influence your classmate, your roommate, your shopmate, the young friends that are all about you, to bring them to the church on Sunday morning to hear your pastor, to induce them if possible to come to the mid-week prayer meeting, anyhow to get them into the Sunday school and the society meeting proper, and by every means personally to influence them to come to Jesus Christ. Now I am going to tell you an open secret, and some of you won't say amen to it,— that is, I don't suppose you will, even if you are Methodists, for they don't say amen any more. [*Laughter.*] You will never have any personal influence to win your comrades and friends to Jesus Christ if you go to your meeting on Tuesday night and then to a card party or a dance or the theatre the next night. [*Loud applause and a chorus of "Amens."*] I say to you, my friends, I have travelled over many lands and have been engaged in the work which I now represent these sixteen years past. I see things pretty nearly as they are. I have mingled with all classes of people. I have seen quite 100,000 people publicly avow their faith in Jesus the Saviour Divine in meetings which I have had the pleasure of laboring in. But I have never yet met a person who was not a Christian who, brought under the convicting power of the Holy Spirit, wanted any one, even his most intimate friend, that was engaged in these worldly pastimes and pleasures to point out to him the way of salvation. Such persons have no confidence in the religious professions of the man or the woman who is given over to worldliness. I have never found an exception to that statement. I lay special emphasis upon it because of its importance. Therefore, personally united to Christ in consecration, yielding yourselves wholly to Him as alive from the dead, living so as to adorn the doctrine of God your Saviour in your life; and studying to show yourselves approved unto God, workmen that need not to be ashamed, rightly dividing the word of truth, go right forward, using your personal influence with all the fervor and all the enthusiasm of youth and all the power of God through the energy of the Holy Spirit in the soul. I am an enthusiast; but I am not a bit more enthusiastic in this Convention than I am at home. The word enthusiasm is from the Greek, *en theos*, as most of you, if not all of you, know, and it literally means, "God in you." You want to have God so in you by the power of the Holy Spirit, so filling you, so thrilling you, so dominating you, that you will be full of holy zeal and enthusiastic at all times and everywhere for God.

And then who can estimate the power and influence of these thousands of societies thus qualified, thus consecrated, thus devoted? The church never in its history had so bright and hopeful an outlook — never. Oh, if only you young people will thus yield yourselves to God as alive from the dead, what wonderful things may we not see in the next decade of years in the churches throughout this and all other lands of the earth!

I have just this thought in closing. You remember I called your attention to the millions who are perishing in India, in China, in South America, in Africa, in the Islands of the Sea, here in our own land, in Minneapolis, in St. Paul, in Philadelphia, in Boston, in Montreal, in all the cities of the earth—perishing, going swiftly down to eternal ruin as fast as time, with his muffled footfall and resistless energy, can bear them. And you and I are living in this generation, and not in the next, and you and I are to labor for this generation as God works through us to will and work of His good pleasure, not in the next, except as we shall project ourselves into the time to come, but all about us are the multitudes perishing. The storm of God's wrath against sin is waxing hot; the mystery of lawlessness is already at work and will manifest itself by and by in the anti-Christ, and there are storms ahead. "Watchman, what of the night?" "The morning cometh"—praise the Lord for that,—but also the night, to try you and test you and see what is your faith and boasting and confidence. We are here upon this mountain today, but at the foot of this mountain are those possessed of demons, and without the power of God and the thrilling touch of the divine compassion we shall not be able to dispossess these who are under their power and who are brought down enslaved to the chambers of death.

A storm swept the Atlantic and hurled the billows upon the coast of England yonder and a ship was thrown on the rocks. The night fell dark and lowering. The storm rose higher as the night deepened. Fires were kindled all along the shore, if by any means to help those who were needing help. The lifeboat was manned. Out through the breakers and into the storm they went to the rescue. By and by they came back with all on board save one man; and John Holden, who stood upon the shore, cried, "Have you all the ship's company?" They answered, "All but one man." "Why did you not get him?" "Well, our strength was well nigh gone, and if we had tarried long enough to rescue him we should all have been engulfed in the pitiless sea." Then John Holden said, "These men who have been to the rescue are well nigh exhausted. Who is there who will go with me to rescue the one man?" and six sturdy fellows came forward promptly. Then John Holden's mother threw her arms about his neck and said, "John, don't you go! Your father was swallowed up by the angry ocean, and your brother William two years ago went out upon the sea, and I fear that he is lost, too, for we have not heard of him since. You are the stay of my life and my only dependence. Who will care for me if the sea swallows you also?" Then John Holden, with his firm, strong grasp, took those arms in which he had reposed in innocent infancy and removed them from his neck; and then he said, as he pushed his mother gently aside, "There is a man there drowning, and I must go, mother. If the sea should swallow me, God will take care of you; I'm sure He will." Kissing her furrowed cheek, he turned and stepped into the life-boat which was already manned. They pushed out into the breakers and to the wreck. They found the man still clinging to the rigging, and getting him into the boat they pulled back to the shore. As the boat neared the shore, some one shouted, "Have you found the man?" "Yes," answered John Holden, "and rescued him; and say to my old mother that it is my brother William!" [*Applause and much emotion.*]

I say to you, my friends, that these millions of this present generation who are going down amid the wreck of eternal night, the billows of sin sweeping over them, bound and enslaved by the chains of passion, you and I are commanded to man the lifeboat, with the help and blessing of God, and go to their rescue; for every one of them is your brother and my brother, whether he is black or yellow, whether he is savage or semi-civilized or moves through the streets of our beautiful cities. He is your brother and mine. Let us all to the rescue! [*Loud applause.*]

Mr. Munhall's closing words made a profound impression upon the audience, and as appropriate to the incident described, Mr. Sankey sang the hymn, "Throw out the Life Line," the audience joining in the chorus with marked earnestness.

The benediction was pronounced by ex-President Rev. Geo. F. Magoun, D.D., of Iowa College.

At the close of the afternoon session, in response to the request of Rev. H. H. French, pastor of the Centenary M. E. Church, of Minneapolis, there assembled in front of the platform between four and five hundred of the Methodist delegates present. Mr. French called the meeting to order and introduced Mr. W. S. Ferguson, of Philadelphia, who read the following resolutions, memorializing the Methodist General Conference, which had been prepared at a preliminary meeting held at Centenary Church during the noon adjournment:

To the General Conference of the Methodist Episcopal Church, Omaha, Neb., U. S. A.

DEAR FATHERS AND BRETHREN:—We pastors and members of the Methodist Episcopal Church, and also members of "The Young People's Society of Christian Endeavor," do hereby respectfully memorialize your honorable body with reference to the existence of said Society in the Methodist Episcopal Church.

We set forth:

First: That since its organization (February 2, 1881), this Society has provided an inspiration of holy consecration to the activities of the younger life of the church.

Second: That during these years the existence, methods and work of this Society have been in full view of two General Conferences of the Methodist Episcopal Church.

Third: That the silence of the General Conference, interpreted to be a tacit indorsement of the Society, has given encouragement to the pastors and congregations to organize their young people into these societies.

Fourth: That under the influence of such encouragement there are now over 2,000 societies of Christian Endeavor in the Methodist Episcopal Church with a membership of 124,000 young people, consecrated to Christ and to the church.

Fifth: That these societies have become an essential factor to the growth and development of the congregations with which they are identified.

Wherefore we earnestly pray:

First: That there be no legislation of the Church that will disturb the present status of these societies, now organized within the Methodist Episcopal Church.

Second: That by special act of yours, this Society be accorded the right of way or the privileges of existence, within the Methodist Episcopal Church, equally with other young people's societies of the Church.

After some little discussion the resolutions as above were unanimously adopted and Rev. H. H. French, of Minneapolis, Rev. H. R. Bender, D. D., pastor Eighth Avenue M. E. Church, Altoona, Penn., and Mr. William S. Ferguson, of Philadelphia, Penn., were appointed a committee to secure signatures on behalf of the various Christian Endeavor societies in the Methodist Episcopal Church.

FRIDAY EVENING.

The weather was somewhat threatening Friday evening, but this did not deter another immense audience from gathering at the usual hour and filling every part of the great auditorium. First there came a delightful song service of half an hour, led by Mr. Lindsay. The introductory exercises consisted of Scripture reading, by Rev. W. F. McCauley, president of the Ohio State Union, prayer by Rev. E. R. Burkhalter, D. D., of Cedar Rapids, Iowa, and singing of the hymns "Holy Ghost with light divine," and "Hide me."

President Clark: I have great pleasure in introducing to you as our first speaker this evening, Rev. S. J. McPherson, D. D., of Chicago, Ill., who will speak on "Heroism in Common Life." [*Applause.*]

ADDRESS OF REV. S. J. MCPHERSON, D. D.

Mr. President and Friends, Fellow-Endeavorers:—First of all let us clear our minds of the fallacy that heroism is the monopoly of worldliness. As Carlyle himself said, the greatest of all heroes is our Lord Jesus. The Son of man is not a mere abstraction, dry as summer's dust, but our veritable human Brother, of genuine blood and breath, winning life's battle as He enables us to do, and realizing the loftiest possibilities of our nature.

Likewise the Son of God, He had no limitation, but such holy insight and loving power that He flung aside temptation as driftwood is tossed ashore by the swelling sea; and He trampled sin to death without once looking down. The longer I study His career the more imperative do I find it to say with a reverent modern sceptic: "Hero-worship, heartfelt, prostrate admiration, submission, burning, boundless, for a noblest God-like form of man—is not that a germ of Christianity itself?"

But Christ's heroism is no isolated exhibition of what He alone could accomplish. Object lesson He certainly is; yet He is also the pledge and first-fruits of what we ourselves may become by His grace. Downward from His lofty, lowly Calvary flows the increasing stream of His cleansing blood upon all Calvary's outlying foot-hills,—Hymettus, the Apennines, yonder Alleghanies, these adjacent Rockies.

Joseph of Arimathæa's broken tomb is mankind's open door, the little hill of Bethany is humanity's stepping-stone to that highest throne where our representative Hero sitteth king forever. Because He was lifted up we can never be the same again. He draws us to His own supernal level, and if we will we may, like Enoch, step horizontally into heaven.

Never, for example, was there a more heroic epoch than we find in the romance of modern missions. Our boys need turn no longer to demi-gods or knights errant to catch the ennobling contagion of chivalry. Theseus certainly was no more godlike a figure than the shoemaker, Carey, who disdained the paltry selfishness of his day and set out, singlehanded, to win the world back to God. Godfrey de Bouillon never won a greater battle in behalf of the holy sepulchre than Henry Martyn, who left country and culture and home and even sweetheart behind forever, and offered his feeble frame in a crusade of vicarious suffering for dying India and Persia. If ever you feel the blight of cynicism, go follow Adoniram Judson from the historic haystack down into the new Gethsemane of his Burmese prison and thence past his unknown grave in the Indian Ocean up to the welcoming throne of Christ. Whenever you are tempted to mistrust that the sordid love of money is a canker on all civilized life, look upon the lion-hearted Livingstone, descending, a volunteer sacrifice, from the dear household in old Scotia to that African hovel, where in the name of the Crucified, he died alone, upon his knees, to "heal the open sore of the world." [*Applause.*] Thank God, heroic ambition can never perish from the earth while such ideal courage and love reflect upon the awestruck eyes of men the peerless Prince of the kings of the earth.

The old idea that every hero is of divine birth or is a deified man has indeed an element of truth, for the Christian is always born from above, a child of God. Our heroism must not tolerate the low and commonplace. If you meet your "old man" of sin, in the street, the parlor, or even the closet, snub him, cut him dead. Keep company only with your "new man" created after God in righteousness and holiness of truth — the heroic mould. Yet do not imagine that heroism is the exclusive endowment of a few classic demi-gods, or feudal lords, or high-caste Brahmins. It is the common achievement of all true Christians. He who does not follow Jesus Christ will be ordinary enough. Our Model is altogether unique in this fallen world, and we shall be sufficiently unworldly and singular and heroic if we keep ourselves in His footprints.

Moreover, unlike the notions of Plutarch's "Lives" and Tennyson's "Idyls," the sphere of Christian heroism is not found on remote Olympus or the tournament pageants, but in the average daily life of man. No one is rendered heroic by strutting over some Field of the Cloth of Gold, or by tilting his lance against windmills like the absurd Don Quixote. Jesus was never the creature, but always the creator, of great occasions. His exalted mien made every homespun action great. He was as heroic in the little group of apostles, or in the domestic circle of Bethany, or amidst the solitudes of the mountain or the sea as when He was transfigured on Mt. Hermon, when He faced universal enemies in Pilate's judgment hall, or when He silently burst open the sealed doors of death. The worldly are hoodwinked into thinking that heroism is confined to scenes of parade and pomp. We need not wonder at them, for their thoughts are absorbed with the material and hackneyed; current fashion is their standard; they choke their aspirations with matters of flesh and sense. But true Christian heroism is everywhere possible. It does not tarry for flattery and applause. It meets all circumstances as they come. Its materials and opportunities are found in every-day experience. Little things, which are but tests and rehearsals of great things, are its native air; for little things, instead of waiting upon vanity and pride, disclose our constitutional attitude, our inner spirit and habit and character. Commend me at least to the hero of the farm or store or kitchen — the hero who can be trusted out of sight.

Suppose we note a few working principles of this Christian Heroism.

I. One of them is found in cherishing a high personal ideal, which belongs to the very essence of a hero. But if we do cherish such an ideal, we may as well prepare ourselves beforehand to encounter the contempt of many that call themselves practical; for the word, "practical," is often misused as a synonym of what is really superficial or gross. Such minds may confuse a high ideal with the chimera of a mere visionary. Just here is often heard the sneering cry, "Hell is paved with good intentions." How shall we answer? Shall we reply with the brothers Hare, "Pluck up the stones, ye sluggards, and break the devil's head with them"? Rather, to collective mediocrity let the same idealist retort: Much of hell may be paved with bad performances, but most of it is the bottomless pit of low or lost endeavors. No man can rise above his own best intention. To hit the mark, we may not aim below it; and the aim will infallibly mould the character. The great peril of life is lest we waste a rare ideal or keep a low one. The lordliest ideal may emerge in the lowliest things; and without such an ideal man surely degenerates into a brute, a mechanism, a clod.

What we often call realism makes an easy appeal to carnal hearts, because it is coarse; while idealism may seem remote and thin and unearthly, because it is spiritual. But what if to the upper, divinely imaged half of manhood, the ideal, after all, be the only real? A dog, a hawk, even an insect, can eclipse the keenest man in its power to see with the bodily eye. We shall rise above the beasts only as we exercise the high moral vision which is wholly absent from their economy. The bestial man is he who uses only his fleshly organs and who fills his eyes with the shadowy phantasmagoria of sense. But the human hero is the man who, like Moses, chooses to be known as the son of God rather than of Pharaoh's daughter, and who endures as seeing Him who is invisible. All true heroes are heroes of faith. Opening the inner eye of the soul, as the eleventh chapter of Hebrews shows, they prove the things not seen and live on the things eternal. Doubt is negative, a temporary makeshift, paralyzing; faith is creative, a permanent regulator, vitalizing. Doubt may break down error or expose vice, but to build up enthusiasm and power, faith is needed. For it is always more fruitful to say yes to the good than to thunder many neutralizing noes to the evil. It is better to possess the smallest mustard-seed of faith in God and man than to fill the air with poisonous upas forests of doubt towards man and devil. [*Applause.*] Young men come to me proclaiming myriad shrivelling difficulties about the Old Testament, about miracles, about the future world. I hear patiently the catalogue of their doubts, and then ask them to name the few things that they actually see and believe. Tell me what you thoroughly believe in, and I will tell you what, and how large, you are, or are sure to become.

Moreover, a man can cherish an uplifting ideal and walk by faith, only as he speaketh the truth in his heart. As Carlyle demands, it is a hero's primary characteristic to be sincere. There must be no squint in his vision of the ideal. The deadliest thing in life, as well as the meanest, is a lie. It expels all generations, like the first, from Paradise. It converts the universe into a mobilized enemy, for nature was organized to maintain truth and to ride down falsehood. It works us out of all right relations with our fellow-men. A liar soon ceases to believe himself. His memory, his imagination, his hopes, his very conscience, will play taunting tricks upon him. The Bible's list of those who are finally shut out of heaven finds its bitter climax in "whosoever loveth and maketh a lie." Like conversion, which is really its beginning, heroism keeps its back to the father of lies and joins hands with Him who is the truth.

Where will the eye of faith and the heart of truth find its ideal incarnate if not in our Lord Christ? He is the goal that satisfies. He fulfils Iole's description of Hercules, as suggested by our American Montaigne: "O Iole, how did you know that Hercules was a god?" "I knew it," answered Iole, "because my heart was content the moment my eyes fastened upon him." Let a man but know Jesus Christ and the heart within will instinctively attest Him. Truly, of Jesus we may say, only never merely "In Memoriam:"

"Thou seemest human and divine,
The highest, holiest manhood, Thou;
Our wills are ours, we know not how;
Our wills are ours, to make them Thine."

II. Another essential of heroism is courage. The present evil world is always a battle-field, even to the gentlest hero. His ideal and his faith are not congenial to it, for they reproach and shame it. He must fight the good fight of faith, or sink to the world's poor level.

What we need, however, under the name of courage, is not the empty bravado of a mouthing Falstaff, not the brute force of a pugilistic Sullivan, whom an army mule could master on equal terms [*Laughter*], not the cowardly ferocity of a tiger which flies before the stronger foe, but the calm and considerate superiority of Charles XII., of Sweden. Swedenborg is quoted as saying that he did not know what that was which others call danger, nor what that spurious daring which is inspired by inebriating draughts, for he never tasted any liquid but pure water. Of him we may say that he lived a life more remote from death, and in fact lived more than any other man. We need courage which is affectionate as well as strong, dauntless in its struggles against all sin, yet most tender in its compassion toward all sinners. We must stand ready as heroes, to do that which both we and others are afraid to do, because we alone see that it is worth doing, not from ignorance or levity, but from devotion to a noble cause. In short, we need to emulate the quiet stout-heartedness of Pilate's great Prisoner. Emulate His face-to-face denunciation of the pragmatic Pharisees, the leading shams of His time. Emulate His high-minded gentleness to little children, whom He ever welcomed most winsomely, as Homer's old Greek soldier doffed his iron helmet to kiss the shy young lad. Emulate His unpretentious faithfulness, alike under the slow tortures of the cross and the alluring glories of the resurrection and ascension. "The greatest truths are the simplest, and so are the greatest men."

You remember how the brave monk Telemachus emulated our Master. After Rome had been nominally Christian for a century, her favorite general, Stilicho, once more conquered the Goths in battle, and Rome must celebrate the victory with the brutal gladiatorial games. Let Canon Farrar repeat the old story: "The games begin; the tall, strong men enter the arena; the tragic cry echoes through the amphitheatre: 'Hail, Cæsar, we who are about to die, salute thee;' the swords are drawn, and at an instant's signal will be bathed in friendly blood. But at that very moment down leaps the rude, solitary Telemachus. 'The gladiators shall not fight,' he cries, 'are ye going to praise God by shedding innocent blood?' A hush falls, and then the inevitable yell of execration from 80,000 throats: 'Who is this impudent wretch that dares to question what we do? Away with him.' He is thrust through and falls dead. His body is kicked aside. The games go on, and the people, Christians and all, shout applause. Ay, the games go on, and the people shout, but for the last time. Shame stops forever the massacre of gladiators. Because one poor old solitary Christian has heroic and soldierly courage in his veins, one more habitual crime is wiped from the annals of the world." Emulate the courage of the monk Telemachus. [*Applause.*]

III. One other, and only one other, essential of heroism I will tarry to mention,—self-sacrifice. And by self-sacrifice I do not mean Stoicism, blind surrender to despair as a necessity; nor do I mean suffering pain for its own sake,—a useless waste; nor do I mean monasticism,—solitary selfishness for the benefit of the monk alone, a personal untransferable ticket of admission to the Celestial City, on which, if any soul ever did enter heaven, he ought not to feel at home there; he ought to feel ashamed to go absolutely alone to heaven. [*Applause.*] I mean self-sacrifice in this sense, the true sense,—devotion to a noble cause for a sufficient reason, the magnanimity of a great soul poured out for the sake of others. In this sense, brethren, self-sacrifice is not the exception; it is the inflexible rule of the Christian life. "That which thou sowest is not quickened except it die," is a universal truth. "He that loveth his life shall lose it," is a fact and not merely an exhortation. "He that loseth his life"—as Jesus did—"shall save it" forever. Jesus Christ is not simply the great substitute for dying sinners. He is also, in addition to that, the final prototype of living Christians and heroes who would put away selfishness. No man can be content—no man certainly can be noble—if he seeks to secure for himself his own private interests alone.

Now we are inclined to fancy, sometimes, that it is only selfishness that pays; but we know better. You can test the matter, not by your opinion of yourself, perhaps, but by your opinion of others. Here, for example, was young Brokaw, down on the Jersey coast the other day. Sitting on the lawn before his father's cottage, he suddenly observed some women struggling in the water, fighting for their lives against the undertow. Brokaw was a college athlete; but he was infinitely more; he was a heroic man. Without stopping a moment to count the cost to himself, without stopping to consider what the personal result would be, he plunged into the water for their rescue. He did save one or helped to save her, but the other two seized him in their frenzy, and he was drowned with them.

Pathetic, was it not? Ah, me, how pathetic it was, after his heroism, to see that fair young life sacrificed! You lament it here, 1500 miles away, and so do I. But I dare defy any one of you not to reverence and exult over his martyrdom. Why is it that you think rather of him than of the other two who lost their lives, if you and I do not revere the self-sacrifice of heroism? If he were my son my heart would swell with pride even while it ached with bereavement. No; selfishness is known and felt to be vile, even while we are continually practising it; but love, the love which will not stoop to count the small change of cost, is heroic, because it is ideal in its far-seeing vision, because it is courageous in its helpful and hopeful struggles, and because it is large and self-sacrificing in its gifts,— because, in one word, it is Christlike.

Christian Endeavorers, the unheroic man lives in meanness and dies with self-contempt. The Christian alone finds life worth living. Whatever it may cost, say what you will of it, the commonplace, craven, selfish career is a libel on humanity and an offence against God. But Florence Nightingale, rising like an angel of mercy above routine indifference and even black insinuation, to realize her ideal by ministering to homeless sufferers; John Milton, daunted by no calamity, checked by no affront, serenely recompensed even for his sightless eyes by "the conscience to have lost them, o'erplied in liberty's defence;" the "uncouth, stern-souled Baptist, facing in solitary hunger the sun-scorched desert of rock and sand," because he would herald the coming King, or silently awaiting in a malefactor's dungeon a malefactor's death, because he would be the champion of purity; nay, He whose name is above every name; His vision of faith shining in the darkness which He could not as yet comprehend; His heart untroubled and tranquil, because hope showed its beacon before; His life laid down in love that the world might never die; these surely teach us that to illustrate ideal courage and self-sacrifice in common life is at once to hold the home-field of heroism, and to bring humanity back to its birthplace in the heart of God. [*Loud applause.*]

As a fitting echo of Dr. McPherson's stirring address, the audience united in singing the hymn, "Onward, Christian Soldiers," and it is safe to say that never before was this inspiring Christian war-song so magnificently given. The building seemed almost to tremble with the power of its melody.

Then came a long series of announcements, after which President Clark stated that Mr. Sankey would sing "The Model Church." Mr. Sankey prefaced his singing with the following story:—

Mr. Sankey:—A man was going by a church not long since, who had been away from the house of God for fifteen years. There are many such men in this city and in every city in this land, and we want to reach them with kindness. This man, wandering along the street, heard the tones of the old church bell as it rang out the invitation to the house of God, and he said to himself, "I think I will go to church,—haven't been for fifteen years. I will go in and see what they are doing." Entering through the open door, he took a seat very near the front, way down the main aisle of the church. By and by the people began to pour into the church and fill up the pews. A man with his wife and six children came and took the pew in front of him. In a moment more a man with another large family took the pew behind him. The poor stranger began to feel, "Well, I have got into the wrong place. If a man comes with six children to take this pew, I will have to go out." But he sat still and waited. No one came. By and by the minister commenced to preach, and after he had got well started, the door opened and an austere looking man came walking down to this pew. Stopping at the end of the pew, in the middle of the aisle, he looked the poor fellow all over, as if to see what kind of man it was that had dared to sit down in his pew, and the poor fellow began to tremble lest he should be ordered out. The austere man sat down in the end of the pew next the aisle, and taking out his pencil he wrote on a piece of paper these words: "I pay for this pew," and handed it to the stranger. Now, my friends, that is the spirit which, if it gets into any of our churches, will keep out the people more than any preacher can bring them in. If you or I had been in the place of this stranger, I presume we would have risen and gone out, never to cross the threshold of that church again. But this man was not like that; he was a Massachusetts man; and he wrote right under what the other man had written, "How much do you pay for it?" [*Laughter.*] The man wrote again, "I pay $100," and the Yankee wrote in reply, "It is a pretty good pew and well worth $100." [*Laughter.*] Let this story teach us, friends, that we should be kind to people,— give them an opportunity to come into our churches and invite them into our pews to hear our minister and to become members of the church of Jesus Christ.

Mr. Sankey then sang the hymn announced; and when, in the course of his song-story, he came to a familiar hymn, the audience joined in singing it.

President Clark:— We shall now have the pleasure of listening to Rev. Isaac J. Lansing, of Worcester, Mass., who speaks on the subject, "A Revival of Generosity." [*Applause.*]

ADDRESS OF REV. ISAAC J. LANSING.

Mr. President and Christian Friends:— If Dr. McPherson had had time I am sure he would have said that generosity is a characteristic of all heroic souls. The heroic man is the man who does more than we expect him to do, who, when he undertakes his task, does not ask what measure men put on his duty or his conduct, but lavishes himself upon duty and accomplishes his purpose by the most generous expenditure of his powers. There never was a time when generosity and heroism alike, the generosity that is heroic and the heroism that is generous, were more needed than now. While every age has afforded abundant opportunity for heroism and generosity, no age ever offered opportunities like ours. Have you ever thanked God that you were living in the grandest century since the world began? Have you thanked God within the year 1891 that you were living in the grandest decade of the most glorious century that ever dawned in history? Now when Japan has a constitution, and Australasia a confederation, and China revolution, and India evangelization; when Italy repudiates the Pope, and the German Emperor sanctions the Lord's Day, and France banishes the Jesuit, and England and America have a hand-shaking and settle their differences by arbitration, it is the time to have a great convention like this and sing the triumphs of an early millennium. [*Applause.*]

All great revivals have induced the spirit of generosity. Pentecost broke forth from heaven, and men in Jerusalem divided their goods to every man as he had need. For my own part, I would rather be in Minneapolis and in this place, at this hour, than to have been in Jerusalem and in the upper room at Pentecost. [*Applause.*] And reverently I would say that I see no reason why we should not have a Pentecost here tonight that should go down into history as more glorious than the initial one of the Christian era. [*Applause.*] The conditions are present. We are with one accord in one place waiting and believing. I would to God that the accumulated glories and momentum of nineteen splendid and culminating centuries might burst upon us here tonight with "tongues of fire and hearts of love, to preach the reconciling word."

The *calls for a revival of generosity*, the *conditions favorable to it* and the *results of such a revival* constitute a very simple outline of a very practical theme; and I assure you that if I can reach you with my voice, I will get as near to the last man of you as I can and tell you something that you can do when you go home, besides praise and pray.

The calls for generosity are first from the field. Where is there a place that does not need gifts of money to further God's work? This is an age of enterprise, and the Christian church is not behind in enterprise. All forms of service for God and man have sprung up under the inspiration of His Spirit. On home fields, in densely populated cities, on sparsely peopled frontiers, in lines of evangelization, of education, of relief, the church is practising everywhere all sorts of philanthropy; while in foreign lands our heroes are working under every sky and in almost every province of the world. From all these fields I hear one common call, Give us more money and more men. I know of no treasury but what is more than half empty, no mission field that has men enough. Their call for help is incessant. I might have a representative from some one of these fields in my pulpit every Sunday during the year, and I wish I could have it so, and have money for them all. The fields are white for the harvest, all the harvesters praying for help.

Then the next call that we have is from the workers who are in those fields. There are men and women in this work who have gone where we do not dare to go. They are away out on the skirmish line of the Christian church. They are our representatives there. What is their voice as we listen to their report? Why, they are saying, "The lines in front of us are breaking everywhere; send forward the ammunition and the regiments." There never was such a glorious sight on any battle-field as this advanced guard of Christianity seeing everything giving way before them and only needing more money and more men to complete the splendid work of the evangelization of the world.

Then there is another call. I hear it when I put my ear to the ground and listen to the tremendous rumblings which anticipate possible upheavals. A general sentiment has swept through this world, coming up as a great ground-swell, causing men to ask, Is it right for a few to have all the wealth of the world? Is it just? Is it safe? Is it wise? Is it best for government and best for society? It is not only the socialist who is asking this question, but it comes from every political economist, every student of society, every philanthropist, every man who loves his fellow-man. These are asking, Ought any one man to have $150,000,000 while 150,000,000 men have scarcely a dollar apiece? Ought one man to have $100,000,000 and control it selfishly without regard to others' welfare? What is our answer to this question? I would say no man has a right to $150,000,000 or $100,000,000 or $50,000,000 or $1,000,000 or $500,000 or $5,000 unless he uses it for the welfare of others. [*Applause.*] You can never legislate in any land under heaven and tell a man how much he shall get control of, whether of money or of brains, or of any other talent: but God has already legislated and ordered that no man shall have a right to anything to be selfishly held or selfishly used; and the sentiment that those who are possessed of plenty should use it for God is a thoroughly Christian sentiment, whether it comes from the poor workman or from the throne of the ever-living God. This is a call to generosity which has a very ominous alternative.

There is another call which is in the nature of a challenge. It comes from the marvellous generosity of men like those who have made these Twin Cities, in investing their money in all sorts of promising enterprises, — a million dollars for a factory, a million dollars for a great warehouse, a hundred million dollars for a railroad. Everywhere these men thus show their faith in the great enterprises that they have undertaken. And when I see them doing thus and think of the wealth of the church of God, I feel as though we were challenged by the business faith of men to show how much faith we have in the gospel of the Lord Jesus Christ.

Ah, says some one, but their expenditure is not giving; they are simply investing. That is just what I ask you to do, and I am to speak of generosity tonight from that standpoint — as an investment, as putting in your money in order to take money out, putting it into the gospel as men put it into these great buildings or into these magnificent railroads, so you may draw rich dividends.

When I listen for the call from the skies, I hear the voice of Jesus, speaking to us words of eternal truth, and saying, "Give, and it shall be given unto you; good measure, pressed down, and shaken together and running over, shall men give into your bosom." What does He mean? He means that common intelligence and self-care and prudence and foresight and "looking out for number one" would lead us all to give freely and generously for God's work in order that we might get returns as munificently as God knows how to give. You say that is generosity on a low plane? It is on a low plane; it is on a plane low enough to strike the common sense of every person here and every person in the world. [*Applause.*] It suggests a practical religion like the practical warfare of the commander of the American troops at Bunker Hill, who said, "Wait until you see the whites of their eyes and aim low." So would I put the matter of generosity on the ground of an investment that will bring money; and I desire the men who want to become rich to hear me while I plead, even on that basis.

I have voiced some of the calls. What are the conditions? The conditions are marvellously favorable for a revival of generosity immediately. I suppose that Pentecost came when it did, because those who were there felt that they could not wait any longer; and I suppose a revival of generosity will come when men take their pocketbooks out and put their money down for God on the spot. So I say the conditions are pre-eminently favorable for giving generously to God this very day, this very hour.

There is a vast amount of wealth furnished to give. We are very few of us afflicted with poverty. The wealth of the country is about $60,000,000,000; and the Christian church members, as nearly as we can find out, number about one-fifth of the population. So wise men judge that they have at least one-fifth of the wealth of this country, that is, $12,000,000,000. Now, we have never so strained ourselves in giving but that this immense wealth remains very largely intact. Do you know how much we give? How large a percentage of this hoarded wealth, do you suppose, was given for home and foreign missions in the year 1886? Some of you may say we ought to have given a tenth. Some of you will say a hundredth. That is a good deal more than was given. Some may say a thousandth. That is more than was given. How much was given by the church of the Lord Jesus Christ in America, including all denominations, for missions in the year 1886? About three-tenths of one mill out of every dollar they possessed. I do not think that the world will be converted or that our duty will be accomplished unless we do a great deal more than that. But, strange to say, the proportion of our wealth that we are giving for this work is growing smaller every year. The aggregate is growing larger, the percentage smaller. It is said by an eminent minister in the last *Missionary Review of the World* that in the last year there was given for foreign missions by the Christians of America an average of twenty-five cents a member; but the converted Chinese in China gave an average of a dollar a member, while the Moravians—God bless them forever!—gave an average of twelve dollars a member. [*Applause.*] Why, if the church of Christ in America would stand up alongside of these gallant Moravian leaders, in their efforts for the conquest of the world to Christ—I speak not as a prophet, but only as a reasoner—the millennium would come before the Chicago Exposition. [*Laughter.*]

Not only have we a vast amount of wealth that hitherto has not been touched; but it is the duty of every man to increase that wealth, and principally for the purpose of making it available for God. I think it is a glorious ambition for any young man to purpose making money for God in a godlike way; for the world needs it, just as much as it needs any other good thing. For my part, I wish that you were all richer than you are, that all men had higher wages, greater profits, more comforts and luxuries. So I am going to show you how it can be done.

There are many appropriate and laudable ways of making wealth. Every man who works with his hands in an honest industry makes wealth, as you know. The man who digs the ditch for the street water-main, so as to get the city water into your house, makes your house more valuable, and so adds to your wealth and gets something for himself. So, also, men make wealth by their thoughts as well as by their hands. A Morse dreams of telegraphic communication, and his thought materializes in hundreds of millions of value in telegraph stocks. A Stevenson dreams of locomotive traction, and we have thousands of millions of dollars in railroads. An Edison conceives of speaking by a wire, and we have millions upon millions of wealth in telephones created by his thought. What, do you ask, does thought make money? Yes, I say, the thoughts of these and other thinkers create actual money values. So you see that the thoughts of men make wealth as well as the work of their hands.

But if it is true that thought makes wealth, much more manifestly does the cutting off of vices make wealth. As soon as vice is cut off and its waste stopped, then plenty comes in its place. Do you know how expensive it is to be wicked and how much expense it makes for the community? Let me give you a single concrete illustration. Some years ago, in the State of New York, there was a poor little outcast girl by the name of Mag, just like any one of myriads in all the country round about,—a friendless, parentless, wretched, neglected little girl. How much do you suppose it would have taken to have saved her? How much money? How much human service? It was not extended. She sank into vice. Seventy years passed, and somebody who knew that Mag went to the bad tried to find out what had been some of the results of her badness. They found she had had — oh, pitiful story! — 1,200 descendants in the seventy years. They found that, as far as known, 280 of these were paupers and 148 were criminals. They found positive proof that her descendants, by their vices, had cost the State $1,308,000. If she had been saved, with an expenditure of ten, twenty-five or a hundred dollars, do not you think it would have been good economy financially? Was there ever greater folly from a financial standpoint than to let Mag go down to the devil? And if that is true of one little Mag, it is equally true of millions of others. Nothing costs us like vice. Does the church? Does education? Oh no: for our laziness and our penuriousness we are paying in the costs of vice ten thousand per cent.

But further than this, positive virtue increases wealth immediately and visibly. Suppose a man buys a stove instead of a bottle of rum; is not that a gain to the community commercially? Suppose he buys a carpet instead of a pack of cards; which is the best for the community to make and for him to buy, from a financial standpoint? The truth is, as soon as a man becomes virtuous, he has new wants; he goes about to satisfy those wants. You have ten thousand wants where not long ago your ancestors had, perhaps, ten. The more wants you have, the more you will work to satisfy them. This makes civilization. Your work makes wealth; that wealth makes commerce; that commerce makes additional wealth. There is nothing that creates wealth like virtue. Nay, there is. What makes wealth? What makes virtue? What cuts off vice? What is, therefore the grandest of all agencies for making riches in this world? We answer, The gospel of the Lord Jesus Christ. [*Applause.*] I speak of it as a political economist. Give the gospel to men, they become better and immediately create wealth. They want things they did not have before. They make the effort to get them. That is industry, and industry is wealth. I say to all men who want money, You cannot make money a thousandth part as fast in any other way as you can by making men. Make manhood and you make wealth. This, certainly, is one of the conditions which favor a revival of generosity.

But after the money is made, whose is it? That is a fair question. I know what men naturally say. Some of you have made it and you say, "I made it and it is mine; it is my very own; I won every dollar of it." I knew some persons who called on a man worth millions of dollars to get help for a Young Men's Christian Association, and he called them beggars and treated them most unhandsomely. He assumed that they had no right to his wealth. So the man who has made his money says, "It is all mine; I own it, every cent of it; I do not want you to come begging for it." That is what people are saying all over this country in answer to God's calls. But is their statement true? It is theirs? Let us see.

While this man has settled himself in the belief "I made this money and it is mine," along comes a tax-gatherer, a representative of the government, and says to him, "Sir, I want a part of your wealth." "You can't have it." "Oh, but I must have it." "No, you can't have it. I made it and it is mine." "Well, sir, in the name of the government I say to you that I will have it." "How much of it are you going to take?" "All we please." "Well, but that is too much." "You cannot be consulted as to what is too much. The government, which has been your partner in making every dollar that you have, wants a share and must have it." "How much?" "Well, sir, in times of war, for the national defence, we will take every dollar you have and yourself into the bargain." "Is that fair?" "Yes, that is fair; it has always been done and will be done again." By this time your selfish man says, "I suppose I must submit. What are you going to do with my money?" "We have not fully decided." "Are you going to get police with it?" "Perhaps we will." "I don't need any police; I can take care of myself." "It does not make any difference; we will have police if we think best." "Are you going to spend it on education?" "Yes, sir, a lot of it." "I have not any children to educate." "You are very unfortunate not to have any children, but we shall spend it as we think best to educate other men's children."

So the government, as a partner, having a right to do just what it pleases with the money that it takes, takes just as much of your money as it pleases, and everybody says that is proper and right. Is it right? Certainly it is right; and if you do not think it is best to share with the government of this country, you may sell what you have to a man who is willing to pay the taxes, and migrate to Central Africa, where you can live without taxes. You can do it if you prefer to. [*Applause.*]

But if the civil government, that is, the people at large, possess such an absolute and conceded right over the property of men, I ask you — and I am appealing to your financial common sense — if the government of God has not helped you more and done more for you, and consequently has it not a better and more absolute right to what you have than any civil government can possibly have? And if the government of God has that right in all property, and you do not pay your taxes, you are a defaulter, and your goods will have to be sold for taxes for all that I can see. [*Applause.*] And if they are, it will go hard with many of us who have had our portion in this life, and in the life to come are going to be portionless.

Then it is perfectly clear that there is an obligation to the government of God resting upon every one of us to be — shall I say generous? Oh, brethren, that claim seems presumptuous. Can we be generous to this government of the United States, which some of you supported in battle with your lives? Can we be generous to the government of God, which gives us life and breath and all things? No, I will not use so unreasonable a term, so contrary to the intelligence of these Christian people, as to talk about being "generous" with God. Give Him all. Then we are in His debt forever, taking what He gives us back out of His infinite mercy with humble gratitude.

But now, what are the reasons, in addition to those already given, why we should be generous for the cause of Christ? One of these is a business reason. I say that because I mean exactly what I say. We should do our business with sufficient intelligence so that we are generous with the church of the Lord Jesus Christ. Let me illustrate precisely what I mean. Down in the southern part of the United States are a multitude of colored people who are exceedingly poor. They are doing remarkably well, but they are very, very poor. Many of them live in houses of one room, have no carpet on the floor, no table or chairs, no decent furniture of any sort, and no clothing fit to wear. Suppose that all the Christians of this country should send to the poor five millions of dollars a year to be used in Christian education, to open to them the Bible and the spelling-book, to furnish schoolhouses and training institutions and to teach them pure and undefiled religion. I verily believe that the wants which that amount of money so spent would create in them, would come back to our markets every year in demands for four times as much as we gave. They would want better houses, better furniture, better everything, and as a matter of business they would get it and you would make it for them and sell it to them; and so doing you would make in profits vastly more than you ever gave to them. Christian missions pay back in money far more than they cost.

But some one may say, That seems a kind of fanciful method of investment. Not so; that is investing in real estate. You say there are properties that are sure real estate. I would like to have you tell me what was ever surer than the ships of England and her great India warehouses, which for a hundred years had been bringing the treasures of India around the Cape of Good Hope. The English had uncounted millions of dollars invested in the India trade. But when De Lesseps cut his Suez canal through, one of the greatest economists of this country says that it destroyed about a thousand million dollars' worth of English property at a stroke. Ships were no longer needed for the passage around the Cape; warehouses were no longer wanted for the storage of goods. So when railroads were built, the same thing was true; other means of transportation depreciated in value, as also in the case of steamships. I tell you, you have not a dollar invested on earth but what by some improvement or invention may be depreciated or taken away at any time. But when our investments are in men, their value never passes away. [*Applause.*] Their glory and their excellence continue forever. Make a man out of a brute, make a Christian out of a heathen, make a civilized and godly person out of a type of which we have so many needing to be born again, and no invention, no discovery, no calamity, no catastrophe, not even the trumpet of the archangel and the rending of the skies, can make his value any less. A man in God's image is always valuable, worth a hundred per cent. in the markets of the world and in the courts of heaven; that is real estate! [*Applause.*]

Now, as to the matter of investment, I beg you to notice that investing in making men is what we have got to come to, anyhow. This is the order of God. I remember when United States bonds were worth seven and three-tenths per cent.; now they are worth two. By and by they will not be worth anything, that is, the government will get all the money it wants without paying any interest at all, simply for taking care they get it; and the question is going to be, Where shall we make our investments in order to get good percentages? The church of God is the natural leader of the world, and the world wants the leadership. When the world says to the church, "Lead us," they want to be led in the right way. The time is coming—I say it confidently—when the rich men of this world, just to save their money, will go about the work of making men in order that they may make more money and protect what they have. It is the ultimate necessity of thought, of civilization, of Christianization, of wealth, of commerce, of industry and of the church. Ay, and they have begun to do it already.

One other reason and I am done. It is a glorious reason why we should be generous with the church of God here and today. Our country, it is said, is the richest among the nations of the earth. Per capita, for every man, woman and child, we have more wealth than any other land on the face of the earth; and we are going to have more rather than less. Now, this wealth which is so desirable is coveted by men of other countries, and they are coming from all parts of the world to get a part of it. There is not a minute of the twenty-four hours, from the first day of the year to the last, but what the mighty propellers of loaded ships are churning the ocean and bringing the poor of all countries to share the wealth of America. The same thing that sent the Persians to Greece, the Vandals to Rome, the Goths to Gaul, the Danes to England, is sending people here,—to get a portion of our wealth. The man getting fifty cents a day over there wants eighty; he wants to be better off, and I confess I am very much in sympathy with him. But these persons who come are not from the best classes of those lands. They will lower wages by competition, they will diminish wealth by their vices; they will, through political demagogues and the ballot, pull down our institutions. They are foreordained of heaven to do it unless we do our best to keep them from it. What can we do?

Can we shut them out? Can we make an anti-European law and an anti-Asiatic law to keep them out? No, it probably cannot be done. "Oh, well," says some one, "I have no fears on account of immigration; our country is rich." So was Egypt rich. "Our country is great." So was India great, and Assyria and Babylonia. All this is true; but our country will not be saved by its wealth nor by its acres nor by its institutions. There is only one thing that will save it; let the foreigner come, but meet him with the gospel of the Lord Jesus Christ. Open the Bible to him; make a man of him; and when you have done that, you have made increased wealth for America for a thousand years, if America shall stand so long. [*Applause.*] Come, brothers of the far-off climes; come from Italy where the papacy has so long robbed you; come from Poland and Bohemia; come, Hungarians, out of whom may be made Kossuths; come, Germans, who have the fire of Luther in your hearts. Come; but when you come, let the church of the Lord Jesus Christ, in order to save America by saving you, pour out its wealth to save its wealth, pour out its treasure to save its treasure, pour out its obligation to God to save itself for God.

There is another reason that I will give but will not argue. You have all said, Why have you spoken on so low a plane? I have told you why. At the same time, — let all hear this, it is the best thing I have to say about generosity, — "Ye know the grace of our Lord Jesus Christ, that, though He was rich, yet for your sakes He became poor, that ye through His poverty might be rich." That is the supreme, controlling reason for generosity in this convention of Christians. All the rest are inferior arguments. That is reason sufficient. If you know that grace, take out your pocketbooks; if you believe in the security, pour out your wealth. [*Applause.*]

The wealth of the church of God must increase faster than its outlay. In giving, it is in competition with God. The beneficence of the church can never catch up with the beneficence of God. He will give us millions for thousands; He will give us dollars for pennies. He has said He would open the windows of heaven if we only brought in our tithes, and pour us out a blessing so that there should not be room enough to receive it. What shall we do with such a blessing? Build the new Jerusalem. It was coming down from God, out of heaven to earth, when John saw it, in the vision of Patmos. Let it come. We will have wealth enough, if we are generous, to produce on earth for Christ, all that John saw. We will build its foundations of precious stones, its walls of sapphire, its gates of pearl, and its streets of gold. We have enough: only give it to God and let Him use it. The interest He pays will build the city. Then His kingdom shall come, and the glory that we call heavenly will be spread throughout the earth. [*Applause.*]

At the conclusion of Mr. Lansing's address, quite a number in the audience rose to leave, on account of the rain, which had already begun to fall. Dr. Clark, however, quickly restored order and announced that Rev. John H. Barrows, D.D., of Chicago, had an important statement to make on behalf of the Trustees.

DR. BARROWS: I have been requested — nay, I was ungenerously forced by the Trustees of the United Society — to announce to this Convention the decision at which the Trustees, after long and prayerful deliberation, have arrived regarding the best place for the meeting of the next International Christian Endeavor Convention. I do not know why they selected me for this service, — a bashful Chicago preacher [*laughter*]; for I feel that Mark Twain spoke the truth when he said that the citizens of my city had some splendid virtues, but they had one great fault; they were lacking in self-confidence. [*Laughter.*] After the announcement was made to me as to my duty tonight, my brain was somewhat in the condition of the well-known young man who went from Vermont to Arizona and met his death there. When his parents asked that his remains should be sent back to the East, they got the reply by telegraph: "There were no remains; he was kicked by a mule." [*Laughter.*] Yesterday afternoon the Trustees listened to able and persuasive addresses from our Canadian brethren, urging reasons why the next International Convention should go to that City of the Royal Mount, whose splendid orator captured our hearts and dazzled our imaginations yesterday afternoon. [*Applause.*] Today we listened to able and persuasive addresses from Christian gentlemen from Denver, Omaha, and Kansas City, those three rival cities combining for once, urging that the Convention of '93 — not that for next year — should go to the heart of the continent, to the city of Denver. [*Applause.*] And we also heard this afternoon delightful addresses from Christian men and women from Ohio, and especially from Cleveland, urging us that in 1893 the Convention should go to the beautiful city of Cleveland. [*Applause.*] This afternoon we also listened to able gentlemen, ministers and others, from New York and Brooklyn, urging what they deemed strong reasons why the next Christian Endeavor Convention should be held on the island of Manhattan, which Hudson bought from the Indians for a chunk of meat, but which is rapidly becoming the central metropolitan city of the world. Dr. Deems said to us this morning that he believed that the New York delegation who came over the "Soo" railroad were Christians — they had the spirit of Polycarp and Perpetua and the martyrs. [*Laughter.*] Let me say to you that from what we heard this afternoon, we are convinced that the gentlemen of the New York and Brooklyn delegation are eminently Christian in their spirit, and that they desire, first of all and above all, that which shall most magnify the name of Jesus Christ. I, a Chicago man, who naturally rejoices that my own city, the Queen of the Lakes, captured from the Empire City the crown of the Columbian Exposition, now announce that the Empire City has captured the Convention of '92. [Great applause, the New York delegation rising and giving three cheers for Canada.] The resolution, which was passed without any apparent dissent, was in substance this: That the next Convention go to the city of New York, and that we affectionately entreat our brethren from Montreal that they give us in 1893 a Christian and Canadian welcome. [*Loud applause.*]

New York makes magnificent promises for 1892 and she will fulfil them. She will give us the influence of her metropolitan press, and she tells us that the Convention will be held in the Madison Square Garden, a beautiful building, capable of seating 18,000 people; and I understand that Secretary Baer and Father Endeavor Clark are already expanding their lungs, hoping to fill that building in July, 1892. [*Laughter.*] We believe that the interests of Christ which we represent are to be served by this decision. We believe that the holding of this Convention in New York will strengthen us at this time, especially in the interdenominational and international aspects of our work that are so prominent; and we certainly believe that the going of this Convention to New York next year will have a magnificent influence there. We believe that it will strengthen the hearts of that splendid band of Christian men and women who have, in the midst of much discouragement and much indifference and some opposition, been working for the cause which is so dear to us. They will make ready for our coming, just as Chicago is cleaning her streets in preparation for the Columbian Exposition. [*Laughter.*] Perhaps a year from now New York City will have as many Christian Endeavor societies as Philadelphia, and may be as politically pure as Chicago herself. [*Laughter and applause.*]

Now all rivalries and jealousies are buried. Our dear friend, Dr. Wells of Montreal, is soon to say "Amen" to what I have said. [*Applause.*] I was present many years ago at an international flower-show in the city of Florence, Italy, — a city whose name is floral, whose shield bears a lily, and whose chief architectural ornament, Giotto's tower, is a blossom in stone. There I saw the great Italian cities which had once slandered each other's names and assailed each other's walls now trying to see which could outblossom the others. There was Genoa the noble, Bologna the learned, Naples the gay, Florence the mother of great men, and Rome herself, venerable queen, new-crowned with hope and joy, blessing them all, — each striving to outshine the others, each pelting the others with the holy lilies of Valdarno and roses from the valleys of the Apennines, looking as if just dropped from the gardens of the Lord. To such splendid Christian rivalries we are henceforth summoned, to show forth the various flowers of the Christian graces, the virtues that adorn the doctrine of God our Saviour. Christian Endeavor makes men magnanimous. "One is your Master, even Christ; and all ye" — Boston. Cleveland, Montreal, Denver, Chicago, New York — are sisters. [*Loud applause, with cheers from Montreal and New York.*]

Dr. Barrows's remarks were followed by considerable enthusiasm, particularly on the part of the New York delegation. As Rev. Geo. H. Wells, D. D. of Montreal, came forward to "say amen" to Dr. Barrows's statement, the thunder-storm which had been gathering all the evening broke, and the rain fell heavily on the roof of the building.

Dr. Wells: I suppose, friends, the heavens sympathize with us and weep in pity for our disappointment and defeat! [*Laughter and applause.*]

Just at this point in Dr. Wells's remarks there occurred one of the most thrilling incidents of the whole Convention. A sharp clap of thunder was followed by the extinguishing of all the electric lights in the building, leaving the entire audience in absolute darkness. There was no commotion and everybody sat perfectly still. A few in the audience lighted matches or pocket lamps, but at Secretary Baer's request they were promptly extinguished. Then some one started the hymn, "Blest be the tie that binds," and although many people felt decidedly nervous, the hymn was sung with great enthusiasm. It was a profoundly impressive incident, and will never be forgotten by those who were present. After two verses had been sung, the electric lights again blazed forth and Dr. Wells resumed his speech.

Yesterday, when I had the honor of standing upon this platform, I said that a heavy though pleasant task had been assigned to me. Tonight I am in a far worse fix. A heavier task by far has been given to me, and it is not at all pleasant. [*Laughter.*] I remember once, when I was but a child, that I was taken very ill. My fond mother hastily summoned the family physician. He was an allopathist of the good old heroic and wholesale school; and as soon as he had felt my pulse and looked at my tongue, he mixed at once a hideous draught of castor oil and rhubarb, and proceeded to administer it to me, and compelled me to take it on the spot. But tonight I meet with even worse treatment than that [*laughter*], for he did not require me to smack my lips and say that it was good! [*Great laughter and applause.*] After all, I admit a little mingled feeling in this; for while your papers compliment me by speaking of me as a native Canadian — and I would consider it a compliment if it were true — yet it is the truth that I was born in the Empire State. [*Applause.*] Now, I suppose if a man has got to be whipped, it is some consolation to have it done by his own mother. [*Great laughter and applause.*] He can, at least, by some power of imagination and stretch of faith, believe that it is given in kindness and is meant for his good. And so tonight, while I as a Canadian feel sore and disappointed, and while my heart throbs in sympathy with the gallant and loyal band that sit yonder in the gallery [referring to the Canadian delegation], I remember — and I have no doubt that I can speak for them as well as for myself — that one of the chiefest boasts of our nationality is that we are loyal. [*Applause.*] We are loyal [here the electric lights again went entirely out and Dr. Wells spoke in the dark for a moment] not to any mere sentiment, but from conviction and reason, from gratitude for the goodness of the past, from confidence in the excellence of our government, and from hope and assurance in the future that all will yet be right. [*Applause.*] And so, for myself, while I regret the decision that has been reached, and while I say only a qualified "Amen" to my brother Barrows's speech in some respects, yet I say here that I am a loyal Christian Endeavorer. [*Loud applause.*] I respect the conscientiousness and am thankful for the kindness of the Board of Trustees, and I more deeply feel than I have ever done before the high honor and privilege that has been conferred upon me in being associated with such men and brethren.

Now as to the request — for they have sugar-coated the pill as far as they were able — that the Society makes, namely, that we shall welcome and entertain the Convention in 1893, so far as I can personally say tonight, and I think I can carry my brethren and sisters with me, — is it so, Canadians? [*loud applause from Canada*] — so far as we are concerned, while we must consult our societies and our unions, while we must look around the ruins and see what is left to us to reconstruct the future, though cast down we are not destroyed, and we do not mean to give in as yet. There are some consolations in defeat, as you will recognize when I assure you that the most weighty argument that carried the day for New York was that of the wickedness and the weakness of the Imperial City. [*Laughter and applause.*] We, at any rate, may feel the left-handed compliment that is paid to our excellence and strength, and knowing that we will trail our banner before the Imperial City of the Western Continent. We have also had worthy competitors whom we have distanced and left behind in this race for the Christian Endeavor Convention, — such worthy and splendid rivals as the fair Forest City that sits beside the lakes, almost at the exact centre of population of the United States, and that represents that magnificent State of Ohio, which in modern times has become the mother of presidents. And even so ancient a place and so conservative, as you are apt to think, as ours has also left behind the young and ambitious giants of the West that have been named here. While we have some compensation and consolation in our defeat, at any rate, we say, God bless and increase the Christian Endeavor Society a thousandfold! May it have grown so large before 1893 shall come that our hospitality will be taxed to the utmost, if we shall be honored in your reception and entertainment. Wherever it goes or meets, may the blessing of God go with it and forever rest upon it! [*Loud applause and the Chautauqua salute.*]

Following close upon Dr. Wells's speech, the choir sang a new hymn, or parting song, entitled, "Friends, good bye." The words of the refrain were: "At New York, at New York we'll meet you another year." These words were changed in the last verse as follows: "At Montreal, at Montreal, we'll meet you in Ninety-three." With the singing of the last chorus every member of the choir displayed a small Union Jack and waved it in time to the music. The effect was very beautiful and was received with hearty applause.

The benediction was pronounced by Rev. R. W. Brokaw, of Springfield, Mass.

At the close of the evening's exercises, the various State delegations were entertained by the churches to whose care they had respectively been assigned; and though the hour was late and the storm kept many away, the receptions were in general well attended. Most of the churches had provided interesting souvenirs which they gave to the visiting delegates. Music, speeches, and light refreshments constituted the programme in most cases.

SATURDAY FORENOON.

After the storm of the preceding evening, favorable weather again greeted the delegates; and the three or four thousand who attended the early morning prayer meeting enjoyed a delightful season of communion and prayer. The meeting was led by Miss Grace Livingston, of Winter Park, Fla., who took for the subject of the meeting, "Following Christ." Brief testimonies as to the good received through the Christian Endeavor movement were given in great number, and there were many sentence prayers. The spirit of the meeting was very earnest, and those who attended pronounced it one of the best among all the sessions of the Convention.

The song service preceding the principal session of the morning contained one novelty, — a song composed, both words and music, by Director Lindsay and dedicated to the Committee of '91. The music was lively and the words were an expression of gratitude for the many good things received at "this blessed Convention."

The regular exercises opened at 9.15 o'clock with the hymn, "At the cross," and devotional services.

After another hymn, "Hear us, O Saviour," Dr. Clark announced that Secretary Baer would not be present during the day, owing to illness which confined him to his hotel. Continuing he said:

Since Mr. Baer is not here, I want to say a word here in this State of Minnesota that I could not say were he present, and that is, to express my love for him and my gratitude to God that he was sent to help us in this work and by his executive ability so largely to do what he has done for the promotion of the work during the past year. Minnesota, you have reason to be proud that you have given to the United Society such a splendid general secretary as Mr. Baer. [*Applause.*] I congratulate you, and I especially congratulate the local union of Rochester, from which he came; and I am sure that every one of us who belongs to the Christian Endeavor ranks has reason to thank God that he was raised up and brought to us at just the juncture that he was.

In Mr. Baer's absence, Mr. William Shaw, the Treasurer of the United Society, will conduct the next hour, in which we shall hear reports from the world-wide field.

REPORTS FROM THE FIELD.

Mr. Shaw: I am very sure, dear friends, that those of you who were present at the Convention in St. Louis last year will appreciate the position in which I am placed this morning, in trying to fill the place of Secretary Baer. I had not expected to do it, and I ask your sympathy and your help, that in some measure we may fill out this hour and make it profitable to us all.

ALABAMA.

REV. E. HORACE PORTER: In the land of the mocking-bird we have something of his happy art of imitation. We have heard the notes of the Christian Endeavor hymn, we have caught them up, and they are today a part of our sacred praises. We have in the past year formed a State union of Christian Endeavor societies, although not without tribulation and hindrance. Some who began with us have gone back to other societies and hindered us very much. Our State secretary has found himself without a society in which to work, his pastor opposing the Christian Endeavor movement. But we have made progress and have increased the number of our societies many fold. Several of our societies are among our black brethren. [*Applause.*] We hope to report large progress from time to time, and trust that some day this convention will meet the demand of the day upon it and lift higher its banners by its own magnificent presence in the very heart of the great growing Southland. [*Applause.*]

TREASURER SHAW.

ARKANSAS.

MR. R. W. PORTER: At the St. Louis Convention last year the Arkansas State Union was organized. We there reported eighteen societies. We now have eighty-three, with about 2,500 members. At our State reunion yesterday we adopted resolutions condemning the opening of the World's Fair on Sunday, and all of our delegates promised to go home and work with more zeal and more earnestness for the Saviour than we have ever manifested before. [*Applause.*]

COLORADO.

MR. S. B. BRADLEY: The Centennial State ranks second to none in patriotic loyalty. She is not second to any in loyalty to "Christ and the church." The mountains are the home of freedom, and the very air seems to breathe the spirit of loyalty and consecration. Visions of towering peaks and eternal snows foster hardihood and fidelity. Our mining camps are world-famous for hospitality and good fellowship. So that nature herself and our social conditions encourage the prime qualities of Christian Endeavor fidelity and fellowship. Our people come trained from the older Eastern States, and we are receiving thousands of recruits annually, fresh from the strongholds of Christian Endeavor. Sitting at the gateway of the continent, we are blessed with the transient visits of trained workers from the East on their western tours. "Quality and not quantity" is our motto; and while we have but 3,000 active and 1,000 associate members, we pride ourselves that they are as loyal and true as any regiment in the Christian Endeavor army, and at least 200 have been won for Christ and the church. Our third State convention at Pueblo was a great success. Flourishing local unions exist in Denver, Pueblo, Colorado Springs and other cities of our State.

CONNECTICUT.

REV. C. S. NASH: We have been pushing along in Connecticut over the same line upon which we reported one year ago, namely, the evangelistic and missionary line. We have gained about seventy-five new societies with a membership of about 5,000, having in all our societies now 30,000. Our Junior societies have doubled; our benevolent contributions have increased something like forty per cent.; our additions to the church have increased thirty per cent. One in four of our associate members during the year has been converted. We are working steadily in this outside aggressive work. Our State convention last October emphasized particularly this one line of work and the convention this year will do the same. We are constantly looking out into the regions beyond.

DISTRICT OF COLUMBIA.

MR. W. H. LEWIS: When we met at St. Louis last year, we did not expect to win the banner, but we went home and did all we could. We organized societies in all our Congregational churches, in all but three of our Presbyterian churches, in nearly all our Baptist churches, and so on through all the denominations. We have n't churches enough tc organize more, or we would have them. [*Applause.*] Two of the societies organized in the past year have been the means of organizing churches. That is the way we do; we first start a Sunday school, then a Christian Endeavor society, and then follows the church.

FLORIDA.

MRS. V. S. BARBER: Florida young people, hitherto comparatively out of sight, with the pastors in the rear, in this Endeavor movement, are now very much encouraged, for the pastors are stepping forward and shaking hands with the Endeavorers and joining in their work. They ask your prayers. Their prayers are with this Convention. [*Applause.*]

GEORGIA.

MR. A. B. CARRIER: The first society of Christian Endeavor in Georgia was organized in January, 1889. In February, we organized a State union of fourteen societies. Last year we sent one delegate to St. Louis. At our last State convention we had fifty societies represented. Today we have ninety-eight societies. We have come here through great trials and tribulations, the same as New York; but we are here because we got ahead of our difficulties.

ILLINOIS.

MR. C. B. HOLDREGE: Owing to a change in the office of our secretary last month, I have not the latest information, but I can give you these figures. Number of societies, 1,202, an increase over last year of 149; number of members, 53,000, an increase of over fifty per cent.; 1,500 united with the church; we have thirty-five local unions, thirty-one district unions, twenty-one denominations represented, 122 Junior societies, 4,000 *Golden Rules* taken, and we have 1,500 delegates at this Convention. There has been a marked growth in interest in special work, in missionary zeal in Bible study and in loyalty to church and pastor. [*Applause.*]

INDIANA.

REV. A. C. HATHAWAY: Indiana is a small State and has no large cities. We represent 520 societies, an increase of thirty-three per cent. during the year. Twenty-four of these societies are Junior societies. We have fifteen local unions and have divided the State into twenty-one districts. In all of these districts except five, district conventions have been held, and these five will have their conventions before our next State convention in November. The work is progressing and we feel encouraged with the hearty support we have from the pastors and churches in general through the State. [*Applause.*]

IOWA.

REV. J. K. FOWLER, D. D.: Pardon our adulation, friends; charge it to an excusable pride. Iowa is here 800 strong — a jump of 600 over our delegation a year ago. [*Applause.*] With no overshadowing city to pour out its throng, that army of 800 speaks for itself. The rolling prairies of Iowa, the fairest fields God's sun shines upon, have emptied their enthusiastic Endeavorers upon Minneapolis. Christian Endeavor harmonizes with the Iowa environment. As we promised a year ago, the evil spirits in "original packages" have been fired out of the State [*loud applause*], and thousands of spiritual packages have been fired with the flames of Christian love. This banner State in freedom from illiteracy and all that is bad does not knowingly take steps backward. Her face is firmly forward in every moral conflict. With unflinching hope and courage she faces the enemy that has, in succession, downed Pennsylvania,

Michigan, and Nebraska; and despite the mightiest combination of wealth and wickedness ever massed against Mansoul, Iowa's Great Heart this fall is to give the liquor power another stunning blow. As she hates the saloon, so she loves Christian Endeavor. The first State beyond the Mississippi to welcome it and the first in the Union to establish the Junior branch, she has grown from 450 societies a year ago to some 700 today. We have not won the banner for actual increase of societies, but in proportion to population and churches, we might justly be rated first. And even as it is, to stand third, with Pennsylvania and New York only in the lead, is surely ground to thank God and take courage. Enthusiastic meetings have been held in the twelve districts of the State, and four societies have issued in full-grown churches. Forward steps have been taken in more careful organization. Never was there more good will for Christian Endeavor in the State, and we look for the next year to distance all the past in our Endeavor work. [*Applause.*]

KANSAS.

REV. S. F. WILSON: Kansas, the native soil of freedom, grasps hands with Iowa on the liquor and the educational question. [*Applause.*] With an inefficient president [the speaker] during the last two years, we have not made the progress that we ought. We did not try to win the banner, but we did try to strengthen the things that remained and we did add to our church membership. We had ninety-three Bible classes reported at our State Convention, with a membership of 878. We had 278 societies during last year. One hundred and twenty-six societies report 1,026 having joined the church from the societies. One hundred and seventy-two societies contributed $639.15 to the cause of missions. We have thirty-two Junior societies with an active membership of 643. Attention is also being given to the rural work. We hope soon to have a man in the field giving his whole time to this work. [*Applause.*]

KENTUCKY.

REV. G. B. OVERTON, D. D.: You think of Kentucky, perhaps, as a land where her pure air is darkened with the smoke of the distilleries and the hand of violence makes bloody her soil. But we have inexhaustible resources of gold and iron, the fairest blue grass fields on the earth, the fattest cattle, the fastest horses and the prettiest women in the world—except Minneapolis. [*Laughter.*] And we have 200,000 Baptists, more than 130,000 Methodists, 100,000 of the Church of the Disciples, a gallant army officered and equipped, of Presbyterians, Episcopalians and Lutherans, and last but not least, more than 100 Christian Endeavor societies that will change this fair land and make it the home of peace and security, and the smoke of every distillery shall be stopped in that land [*Applause.*] Kentucky shall be redeemed and joined with Iowa, as the land where even "original packages" shall not be sold against the law. Our work has increased more than eighty per cent. in the past year. We are organized now, divided into districts, and we intend to push this work until Kentucky shall be one of the most glorious lands in all the earth. [*Applause.*]

MAINE.

MR. F. A. HAMLEN: Christian Endeavor work in Maine is moving forward steadily and surely, if not rapidly. The celebration of the tenth anniversary of the foundation of this Society last February has given a great impetus to the work. We were told yesterday that the most important work of the Christian Endeavor Society does not lie in statistics but is of such nature that it cannot be reported. This is true of ou societies in Maine. The first society and many of the earlier ones were founded in Maine, and they are illustrating the doctrine of the perseverance of the saints. As the oldest child of this movement we intend to be ever worthy of our position. [*Applause.*]

MARYLAND.

REV. O. F. GREGORY, D. D.: Maryland was organized as a State union last December, with forty-seven societies. Notwithstanding the fact that some of tne Methodist Episcopal societies have withdrawn in order to unite with the

Epworth league, we have today 100 societies. Nineteen delegates were present at St. Louis; forty are present here. We expect to carry 300 to New York next year. Maryland, by its very name, has been — and those who are in power are endeavoring to make it still more so — Mary's land; but we hope, through the united prayers and endeavors of the young people of Maryland to make it Jesus Christ's land. [*Applause.*]

MASSACHUSETTS.

REV. R. W. BROKAW: Let it suffice to say for New England's greatest Commonwealth that over 900 societies are seeing to it that every young man and woman in the State is being personally invited to be a Christian; that systematic giving is being impressed upon the young people as a duty; that every young man is being made to feel his personal responsibility for spreading the gospel by giving his lifework to it. There are over sixteen young men from one county who are now in preparatory schools fitting themselves for this direct work. Who can tell what the harvest will be by and by? "We shall come rejoicing, bringing in the sheaves." [*Applause.*]

MICHIGAN.

REV. C. H. IRVING: Michigan is not going to be left behind in this great movement. Since March we have formed fifty-six societies. We have 562 societies associated in union work in Michigan, with a membership of 34, 844. And besides that, we have stimulated the Methodists so that they have 350 societies with a membership of 19,000, and the Baptists, also, with a membership of 5,000. [*Applause.*]

MINNESOTA.

REV. W. P. LANDON: At the State convention last fall one of our delegates said that she saw, all through that convention, before our motto, the word "Souls." If Minnesota were to add one word to our motto, she would say, "Souls for Christ and the Church." This great Convention is not the most important one in the history of Christian Endeavor. The one of the most vital power was when the movement was born in the meeting between Dr. Clark and the Holy Spirit. The prayer of Minnesota is that even now, here, the Holy Spirit may witness in each heart a complete dedication of ourselves to the Master's service. Inspired by that idea, Minnesota has doubled her membership during the past year, has stood among the first five States in establishing Junior societies, and has added an unusually large percentage of her associate membership to the ranks of the church. She stands represented here today by 1,500 delegates, outside of the Twin Cities. [*Applause.*] The Endeavorers of the Twin Cities are too modest to speak for themselves, and leave their guests to speak for them. [*Applause.*]

MISSOURI.

MR. G. B. GRAFF: Last year it was my privilege to report for Missouri 280 societies of Christian Endeavor. Today it gives me pleasure to report 527 societies, with a membership of 19,448. [*Applause.*] You will be glad to know that 1,610 have become members of the church from the ranks of the societies. I feel, however, that statistics are very poor to express what we have done in Missouri. Never has the standard of work been so high; never has there been so much real, direct, Christian evangelistic work done for the Master as during the past year. One society alone has held, in addition to their regular meetings, seventy-seven extra meetings, at which over thirty persons became Christians. Still another, a very small society, has held extra meetings at which twenty became converted. Stil. another society is rejoicing in the fact that every active member has brought at least one soul during the year to Christ. [*Applause.*] Still another society in a large city is carrying on a mission school and reading-room in a destitute part of that city. They keep it open every night and support a missionary to look after the enterprise at a cost to the society of $750 a year. Our societies in Missouri are doing what they can to bring about our State motto, "Missouri for Christ." [*Applause.*]

NEW HAMPSHIRE.

MR. F. W. FARNSWORTH: The little old Granite State, where Webster said men and women were made, sends greetings to this Convention from 7,000 Christian Endeavorers. We have made up our mind that if that is where men and women are made, and we must send them West, we will send them Christianized and Endeavorized. [*Applause.*]

NORTH CAROLINA.

REV. J. J. HALL, D.D.: Three years ago last May I left the beautiful city of Minneapolis for North Carolina and the sunny South. I realized the need of Christian Endeavor there and soon a society was born in my church at Raleigh. Today we can speak of twenty-five Christian Endeavor societies, with a membership of 300. I rejoice greatly in the progress of the Christian Endeavor movement in the South, because there it has no dark chasm to cross; it has no bitter feelings to allay; its face is toward the rising sun and not the setting day. [*Applause.*]

NORTH DAKOTA.

MR. R. M. CAROTHERS: North Dakota, the State of blizzards and No. 1 hard wheat, and the first State to come into the Union with constitutional prohibition [*applause*], is not in the lead, but, thank God, she is in the procession. [*Applause.*] Our State union was organized last November with fifteen societies. There are now in the State twenty-eight societies. Seventeen report 350 active members and 130 associate members. We have two Junior societies.

OHIO.

REV. W. F. MCCAULEY: I bring you greetings from the largest Christian convention ever held in the State of Ohio. That was the Christian Endeavor convention which met in Toledo last week, where we had present 1,300 delegates from outside the city that entertained the convention. The last convention before that was about as large as all previous Christian Endeavor conventions put together, and this was as large as all the rest, the last one included. Last year we had a good delegation at St. Louis. This year, I may say, you have doubled the distance to the Convention and we have doubled our delegation. [*Applause.*] Now I would like to ask all the Ohio people who think Christian Endeavor is the biggest thing in Ohio and will pledge themselves to better effort in the future, to rise. [A large number scattered through the audience rose.]

OREGON.

MISS STRONG: In April, 1890, we had a visit from Dr. Clark. At that time we had but twenty-two societies and no State organization. Since then we have organized, and we held our first State convention last October with thirty-three societies and 1,294 members. Now we have ninety-six societies and I don't know how many members. Oregon is not a veteran, but she is marching on with the rest to the victory that we believe is ours if we are faithful. [*Applause.*]

RHODE ISLAND.

MR. W. H. BAILEY: Rhode Island is not dead in Christian Endeavor, and most of you know what a live baby means. We have about seventy-five societies in the State, and they are doing much as church auxiliaries to strengthen the hearts of the pastors and much in mission and Sunday-school work. I am sure that there is a great deal of interest in "Little Rhody," and yet I wish it was stronger. [*Applause.*]

SOUTH DAKOTA.

MISS E. A. CLARK: Last year, at St. Louis, there were six from South Dakota present. Today we have 106. [*Applause.*] I thank God for that, and I hope great things for South Dakota because of the inspiration of this Convention. We cannot report great progress in numbers, but we do wish to bring ourselves in line with the other States, and we now have this word:

"Our State for Christ we sing,
Our hearts to him we bring
And trust His word.
With His dear cross in view,
Each Christian grace renew,
And make endeavor true
For Christ our Lord." [*Applause.*]

TENNESSEE.

MR. E. P. LOOSE: Please remember two things in regard to Tennessee: (1) We are in the South, where the work is so discouraging, and (2) Tennessee is the headquarters of the great Methodist Episcopal Church South, and you all know what that means. Yet I believe that Tennessee stands at the head of the Southern States in three things: in numbers, in organization, and in increase during the past year. We had at St. Louis last year, sixty-three; we have here today 120—almost double. We had 2,500 members last year; today we have 4,950—an increase of 2,450. There united with the church last year through our efforts 680. We have, what I believe no other State in the South has, a State superintendent of Junior work, with an assistant secretary for that department. [*Applause.*] . We have raised our State fund always without difficulty.

TEXAS.

MR. E. F. GROENE: Texas, the Lone Star State, bids fair eventually to rival even New York State. It does more than that now in territory, and we expect some day to outstrip New York in Christian Endeavor.

We have increased over fifty per cent. during the year, and we expect in the coming year to double, if not treble, that increase.

SOUTH CAROLINA.

REV. R. P. WATSON (a colored delegate, received with great enthusiasm): I regret very much that I cannot give the statistics for South Carolina. Mr. Wilson, whom I expected to be here, is not here; but I desire to say that South Carolina has felt the inspiration of this movement, and that at your next meeting you will hear from South Carolina in full. [*Applause.*] South Carolina is a fertile field. We feel today that the upper lights are burning, and we want to have the lower lights hung over South Carolina, that the people of that State may be raised to a sense of their duty and join hearts and hands with the United States and Canada in winning the world for Christ. [*Loud applause.*]

UTAH.

MISS MARY H. NUTTING: Utah is a little one, but she shall become a thousand. Our first Christian Endeavor society in Salt Lake City was formed five years ago, although there was one society in the Territory before that. At our convention at Ogden last March, twenty-three societies, with a total membership of 725 were reported. Every society was represented, and the attendance of members was over 350. Our president, Rev. J. B. Thrall, is tireless in his work with us and for us. God is blessing us and making us blessings to others. Pray for us, that we may "approve things that are excellent; that" we "may be sincere and without offence till the day of Christ: being filled with the fruits of righteousness . . . unto the glory and praise of God." [*Applause.*]

VERMONT.

REV. P. MCMILLAN: Vermont—a grand State to go from [*laughter*] to Minneapolis; a better State to go back to with all the enthusiasm of this Convention of Christian Endeavor. [*Applause.*] Vermont—not wide, but built high up to the skies. It was from the eyrie of the Green Mountains that the eagle eye of Mr. W. J. Van Patten saw this grand Convention ten years before it occurred. Father Endeavor Clark told me that the first man who saw what was in this Christian Endeavor movement was the man whose name I have mentioned, and who for two years presided over the National Convention. Vermont, green to the summit of her mountains, is fertile in Christian Endeavor societies and in Christian Endeavor enthusiasm. Today we report an increase fully up to that of any year. Vermont is solid for Christian Endeavor. As her hills reach to the core of the earth, so the hearts of her young people reach to the very core of this young people's movement.

VIRGINIA.

REV. W. E. JUDKINS, D.D.: I come to bring fraternal greetings and offer the hand of Christian friendship to this august body of Christian Endeavorers, sorry that I am the sole representative of the grand old historic State of Virginia, and her capital city, Richmond. We have but about forty-five societies in our State, representing five different denominations. Five of those societies are in Richmond, and one belongs to my own pastoral charge. I have been exceedingly gratified to hear the thrilling reports from the daughters of my old mother State, Kentucky and Ohio. As a Virginian, I extend to the daughters of my mother a brother's hand of welcome today. I have heard much, sir, since I have been here about the word "loyal." Let me say that we are loyal in Richmond — second to no city in our orderly observance of the Sabbath, in the large proportion of our people who attend upon the service of God in our sanctuaries; and, so far as our people and our societies are concerned, we claim to be loyal to truth, loyal to duty, loyal to God, and, as Endeavorers, loyal to Christ and the Church. [*Applause.*]

WASHINGTON.

MR. H. WILLIS CARR: Washington, one of the last on the list and one of the last to fall into line; but we think she is not the least. Our Washington Union was organized last November at Spokane. This first meeting was a local one and simply for organization. Our first convention was held at Seattle last May, where 135 delegates represented thirty-five societies out of seventy which are in existence. At this convention our State was districted into thirteen districts, for which secretaries have already been appointed. For our State secretary, we have an old New York secretary, Mr. H. L. Sizer.

WISCONSIN.

REV. W. O. CARRIER: Wisconsin is a very modest State. We are in conspicuous for our position, for we have Lake Michigan on the east, Lake Superior on the north, the Twin Cities on the west, and Chicago on the south. [*Laughter.*] Some people here seem to think that all that Wisconsin amounts to is as a good bedroom to sleep in while they go rolling across the country from one city to the other. But we are a great State, with great enterprises and great agricultural resources. We have fine forests, mines of ores,— copper, silver, and gold, but no brass. But the greatest enterprise is the Christian Endeavor movement, and it is needed. After the fashion of some, we are called a progressive State. We have repealed that Bennett law; our supreme courts have led all others in ruling the Bible out of the schools; we have breweries enough to supply the whole nation with beer if we did not drink so much at home. But the Christian Endeavor Society has taken up the challenge that has been thrown down, and we have inscribed on our banners and on the walls of our churches and engraven on our hearts the motto, "Wisconsin for Christ." [*Applause.*] Our State's Prison Society is one of the wonders of the age. With about 500 prisoners, we have 116 members in the Christian Endeavor society. We are grappling with the problem of prison reform. [*Applause.*]

ONTARIO.

MR. R. J. COLVILLE: Ontario, the leading Province of the Dominion of Canada, brings greetings to this great Convention. Last year we reported 225 societies; this year we have the joy and privilege of reporting 514 [*applause*], with a membership of 18,000. We have taken hold of this Epworth League question, and by God's grace and His guidance we have got it settled and hence you will find Epworth Leagues of Christian Endeavor. We are all brethren over in Ontario. [*Applause.*]

BRITISH COLUMBIA.

REV. THOMAS ROGERS: Last year at St. Louis I had the honor of coming from the rocky Atlantic coast to represent the Province of Nova Scotia. Today I come from the far west, from the Pacific coast, to represent British Columbia. And I may say that I come from one of the finest Provinces of the great Dominion of Canada,—a Province that is being opened up on every side by capital and is yet destined to be the home of millions. In that Province the Christian Endeavor idea has taken a strong hold. We came within one of capturing the banner for this year, and next year I have no doubt whatever that our numbers will be very largely increased. We left Vancouver last Friday afternoon, over one of the finest roads in America and arrived here on schedule time on Thursday morning. So you can see what a long ride we have had. We spent one day in the Rocky Mountains. The Canadian Pacific railroad kindly switched off our car, allowing us to spend Sunday in the Rockies, where we held a Christian Endeavor meeting and encouraged the people to form a Christian Endeavor society. [*Applause.*] We say today, "British Columbia for Christ; British Columbia for Christian Endeavor."

MANITOBA.

MR. J. W. C. SWAN: This is the first time that you have heard from Manitoba. Manitoba is in Canada. It is not the land of "No. 1 hard" wheat, but it is the land of "No. 1 hard" Christian Endeavorers. Though having a different governing body, yet we have the same sovereign over us, Jesus Christ. As to what we are doing, I can tell you that Manitoba is on fire with this Christian Endeavor movement. Pastors all over the land want to know about it, and those who were formerly against it now want it put into their churches to help them. We have at present thirty-five societies. The movement started in 1889 with only three. When we go back, arrangements have been made for forming three local and three district unions of Christian Endeavor, and in September next we hold our first convention.

PENNSYLVANIA.

MR. J. HOWARD BREED: It was expected that our president, Rev. Mr. Stewart, of Harrisburg, would respond this morning, but he is not present. It falls to me to say that Pennsylvania, the Keystone State, looks out from her position at the top of the arch on to the other States, glorying in the fact that we are all in the one arch, that we are all working together for Christ; and it was but fitting that she should win the banner for gaining during the past year the largest number of societies. If she had accomplished anything less than that, she would not have done her duty. And no one need expect that we are going to continue with any less degree of enthusiasm in our work. We have in our State organization, in our Philadelphia local union, and in all the unions throughout the State, this one idea: that it is the business of the State union and the local unions to put new societies wherever they can as quickly as possible, because the individual society is the one to attend to the spiritual work of the young people of our State. It is therefore with increased enthusiasm and with increased instruction in our hearts that we shall go back from this place with the purpose to do better than ever before in pushing this grand movement, not only among the Baptists and Presbyterians, but among the Methodists also and every other denomination. In every county we have good working district secretaries, and in almost all of them the work is being grandly done. [*Applause.*]

NEBRASKA.

MR. S. R. BOYD: Nebraska came here to get something, and I tell you we are getting it. Last year we reported 150 societies in our State; this year I am happy to report 274,—151 in the State union, ninety-three non-union. Last year we reported no Junior societies, this year thirty. Our membership throughout the State is over 9,000. We do not like to brag of figures, but we do want to say one thing: that the influence of the Christian Endeavor organization is telling upon each and every member of every society. Bible classes are being formed throughout the whole State, and prayer circles are being organized, and these together are working wonders upon the hearts of our young people.

WEST VIRGINIA.

REV. J. A. HOPKINS: I come from the little Mountain State, but I want you to know that West Virginia is for Christ and Christian Endeavor. We are yet but young in the work, the first society being organized less than three years ago in Clarksburg. A little more than a year ago we organized the first society in Wheeling; we have now six societies there, one among our colored brethren. Our first annual State convention was held last February at Salem, and so great was the enthusiasm, that we appointed the next one to be held the last week in this month, so that we have two annual conventions in one year. [*Applause.*]

CALIFORNIA.

REV. E. R. DILLE, D.D.: I bring a Pacific greeting from the Golden Gate. The State that raises big trees, has big mountains, big valleys, big cataracts, big fruits and vegetables, has an equally splendid type of Christian Endeavor. The State officers have just placed in my hands a brief report: Out of 330 societies we have only reports from 160, and these report 5,745 active members, 1,719 associate members—7,464 in all. Doubtless we have a round 10,000 of Christian Endeavor members in California. There have been added to the church during the year 354 active and 176 associate members of the societies reported. There are 609 members in nineteen Junior societies. We hope to welcome the International Convention in '94 at the earliest, and as you gave us a pyrotechnic display last night to show us the beauties of your climate, if you come to us we will show you an earthquake—a Christian Endeavor earthquake. [*Applause.*]

NEW JERSEY.

MR. E. POMEROY: New Jersey is small, but she gets there. Our societies and membership have been increasing all the year. Our societies number 454, an increase of 140 over last year. Of the associate members, 1,554 have joined the church from societies reporting. We have forty-six Junior societies with a membership of 1,487. We sent eleven delegates to St. Louis last year; we have sixty-five present here. Next year we shall send 500. We intend to increase this year the number of our societies, the number of their members, their spirit and enthusiasm, and above all the Christ-life of every one whom we can reach.

AFRICA.

REV. THOMAS L. JOHNSON: [*Tumultuous applause and waving of handkerchiefs as Mr. Johnson, a colored delegate, came forward.*] My dear friends, this hearty welcome makes the color come to my cheeks! [*Great laughter and renewed applause.*] I feel very happy this morning because I represent a very popular country, from every standpoint,—a country that has hitherto been called "the Dark Continent," but I claim this morning that it is certainly the twilight continent. It is a country where there are over 300,000,000 of people, and there are hosts of weary hearts there waiting for the dawn. Now we have not a Christian Endeavor society there that I know of; certainly there was none when I was in Africa. My health has been broken down, but, thank God, in answer to my prayer, my health is better; and I am going back to Liberia and hope to co-operate with the brethren in establishing a chain of stations from

Liberia to the Soudan, where there are from seventy to ninety millions of people, and, I suppose, not twenty missionaries. I pray you to give a thought to Africa under the burning sun, where those people have been bowing to their idols, and where there are millions today crying out for help. I ask an interest in your prayers that God will bless me in this great work. Our motto is, "Africa for Christ," and I hope to establish Christian Endeavor societies in Monrovia and all through that country, so that by another year you shall hear of the prosperous work there. I pray God that every Christian Endeavor society in this country, and all the Christian churches in this country, that seem vieing with each other to see who can do the most for Africa, will consider this one point: that Africa must be reclaimed by Africans, and mainly by her sons and daughters in this country. I believe that is God's plan. There are a million in this country who want to go back to Africa; and if we make Liberia the centre of the work, in twenty-five years we will do more good in Central Africa for my poor, long-benighted people than all other societies can do in fifty years. [*Loud applause.*]

[By request, Mr. Johnson sang the hymn, "Come to Jesus," in the Duali language, and also repeated John 3 : 16 in the same.]

OKLAHOMA.

MR. WILLIAM BLINCOE; "Oklahoma for Christ"—by this sign we conquer. We started to win immortal souls for Christ, and we won the banner. We went to Oklahoma as boomers, and by the help of God we will turn from boomers for land into boomers for Christ. We have in Oklahoma a Y. P. S. C. E. gospel wagon. Four young men forming a quartette go around through the country and hold meetings, singing and preaching and organizing Christian Endeavor societies. Last year at the St. Louis Convention we had one society; now we have fourteen, making 1,300 per cent. increase. Next year if you want the banner away from us you will have to make 500 per cent. increase—for we propose to have every town and village in Oklahoma represented by a Christian Endeavor society. [*Applause.*]

ENGLAND.

Cablegram from London: "British Section to Minneapolis Convention. Hearty greetings and good wishes. God speed the work. Ephesians 3 : 16—19." [*Loud applause.*]

JAPAN.

Cablegram: "Kobe, Japan. Ephesians 2 : 18, 19." [*Loud applause.*]

MR. SHAW: Our time is up, but I must report for the Floating Societies of Christian Endeavor. We are getting into the men-of-war; we expect to touch the merchant service, and we hope to make the sailors and those who do business on the great deep missionaries for the Lord Jesus Christ. Pray for the members of our Floating Societies of Christian Endeavor. [*Applause.*]

The following reports were written for this occasion but were not read:—

IDAHO.

REV. J. H. BARTON: Number of societies, thirteen; active members, 129; associate, seventy; added to the church from these societies during the year, sixteen. Eight societies have been organized since Sept. 1, 1890. These figures are only approximate as there are several societies from which I have no recent report.

INDIAN TERRITORY.

MR. HARRY C. WILLIAMS: To all Christian Endeavorers, I would say Courage. We of the Indian Territory are coming on in the work. Although our report is not a glowing one, yet it is one of which we feel that we can be proud when you remember that we were completely forgotten in the preparation. Upon speaking with one of the committee as to where the delegates from the Indian Territory should sit, he replied, "Why, I never so much as thought of any one coming from there." Since the starting of the Christian Endeavor work in the Indian Territory, two years and a half ago, in one society of eight members, we now have twelve societies, the membership of each society ranging from thirty to sixty. The Muskogee society, from which I am a delegate, has a membership of fifty-nine,— forty of whom, at least, are Indians. The Endeavor societies have accomplished untold good among the Indians, both in building up the membership and attendance of the church and in aiding young Christians to stand firm for Christ. We hope to double the number of societies the coming year.

MONTANA.

MRS. F. N. SMITH: We are weak in numbers but strong in faith, hope and love for Christ and the church. We have been unable to hear from all the Christian Endeavor societies of the State, but as near as we can ascertain the numbers are as follows: three societies in the Church of the Disciples, one Baptist, two Presbyterian, six Congregational and one Methodist, making a total of thirteen societies with about 600 members. We have no State organization because of the sparse population and the long distances. The nearest are one hundred miles apart. We have city unions and are working for a State union. We are but infants in the work. Our oldest church is but nine years old. The best society is at Livingston, and their president, Miss M. E. Wolcott, formerly of Minneapolis, sends greeting in Col. 2: 5. As a large part of our churches are home missionary churches and some without church buildings, the efforts of the societies are directed towards the improving of the church buildings, making up the minister's salary, carrying on Sunday schools, etc. We feel that we are growing in grace and love for our Master; and now may the Lord bless you and cause His face to shine upon you.

NEW YORK.

HENRY D. JACKSON: New York has added in the past year 550 new societies and now has over 2,300 local societies with a membership of 125,000. I rejoice in reporting conversions to the number of 7,200 in the past year. New York State is divided into fifty-five districts, forty-five of which have held helpful conferences. Perfect harmony exists, as it always has, within our borders, and at present an unusual interest is being manifested throughout the whole State. While we have experienced our usual increase in membership, perhaps not as great effort has been put forth in this direction as in emphasizing the need of thorough Christian Endeavor principles in all of our organizations. More attention has been paid to the quality of our membership than its growth; and the present indications point to a rich harvest in the coming month's work.

Following the State reports, Bishop Samuel Fallows, D.D., of Chicago took the chair and the congregation united in singing, "Onward, Christian soldiers." A brief prayer service was then led by Mr. W. H. McClain, of St. Louis, chairman of the Committee of '90. A few moments of silent prayer were followed by one verse of the hymn, "Sweet hour of prayer." Mr. Mason of Missouri led in prayer for the spread of the world-wide movement and Rev. B. B. Tyler of New York for the coming of Christ's kingdom. The service closed with singing the last verse of "Sweet hour of prayer."

Bishop Fallows then announced that the Pastors' Hour would be conducted by Rev. J. S. Black, D.D., of Minneapolis.

PASTORS' HOUR.

DR. BLACK: I do not quite understand how it is that I am received in such solemn silence. You just now received one black man with thunders of applause: why not another? [*Laughter.*] I do not know to what circumstance I am indebted for this great honor, unless it so happens that I am the pastor of the First Presbyterian Church of this city, one of the earliest pioneers in this great Northwest, herself the mother of churches. We have fifteen ministers on the programme. I have already received the names of three more; and as there are thirty divisions and subdivisions of the Christian church represented in the Y. P. S. C. E., it follows that we may receive other names; and therefore, in order that we may all be treated alike, we are to ring the clergy down every three minutes. And let me tell you that, being long-winded by nature and also by grace, this will be more of a trial to them than it was to those Christian Endeavorers who gave such brief and admirable reports yesterday and today.

After all, this is perhaps the most appropriate hour of this Convention. This is a ministers' movement. There are 16,200 societies of Christian Endeavor: that means 16,200 ministers in living connection with this movement. Think of it! Were they here, even this vast auditorium would not hold them. It is not possible at this stage for us ministers to give such experience as we may in the days that are to come. Even Dr. Clark himself has only ten years' experience to look back upon; most of us have only four or five or six or seven years. When it comes to 1910, at that Convention ministers may be able to say with more definiteness what has been done by the Y. P. S. C. E. It is a solemn and inspiring thought that the ministers of the future, the office-bearers of our churches of the future, are today receiving their training in the ranks of the Y. P. S. C. E. And when it comes to 1991, such of us as are here a century after this may be able to speak of still larger experience; and I hope by that time that we will be able to speak of the men who have taken the lessons and the consecration of the Y. P. S. C. E. with them into the White House, into our halls of legislature, and on to the judge's bench. [*Applause.*] For my own part, and to give my own testimony, I heartily say God speed to these societies of Christian Endeavor. Why? In the first place, I have found them a missing link—and this is what religious science is seeking for as well as physical—between the Sunday school and the church. And I find that in my church the young people of both sexes, more especially the young men, do not stay away from the Sunday school as they used to do. I value it because it is a training in parliamentary practice to the young men in religious things. [*The bell rings.*] But I am rung down [*laughter*], and if I don't obey the bell how can I insist on the other fellows doing so?

It is most appropriate that, after the many requests for silence in the hall that we have had, I should first call upon that denomination of Christians who are the apostles and the expounders of silence and the might of the silent hour,—the Friends,—who will be represented by Rev. Alfred C. Hathaway of Richmond, Ind. [*Applause.*]

REV. ALFRED C. HATHAWAY, RICHMOND, IND. (FRIENDS): Dr. Haines, of Indianapolis, is responsible for the anecdote of a man who, when asked to define the difference between a Friend and a Methodist, replied, "A Friend is a Quaker, and a Methodist is an earth-quaker." [*Laughter.*] However this may be, we will leave the authorities to decide; but I am here this morning to represent the Friends, and as a Friend to say to you that the Friends are staunch friends of Christian Endeavor. [*Applause.*] That their friendship is of a very substantial and a very satisfactory kind, I hope you will find; for it is of that sort which William Penn had for the Indians, which has lasted among his descendants to this day and is continually remembered by the Indians. The Friends have always held strong convictions. They have become accustomed to holding convictions and positions which have not been popular; consequently their strength of conviction in maintaining their positions. And so I say to you that though they have been a little slow in accepting Christian Endeavor, they are doing it most heartily, and in doing so they have done it for reasons. In the first place, they have accepted Christian Endeavor because they believe they shall get something out of it; and in the second place, because they believe that Christian Endeavor will get something out of them. For, as you know, and as has been said from this platform, the Friends have been the practisers and exponents of silence. It was so especially a generation ago; but now many of the Friends are noisy, as I am trying to prove to you at this moment. [*Laughter.*] The Friends find that Christian Endeavor supplies a place which has long been vacant. Their young people have not been properly employed, and they find that this has helped them not only to recognize, but to utilize, the strength of their young people. The fact that they desired to run elsewhere was no doubt due to the very cause which Pharaoh assigned to the desire of the children of Israel to depart from Egypt: "Ye are idle." Inasmuch as through the instrumentality of the Christian Endeavor Society the Friends have set their young people to work, they have not only come to be able to hold their young people but are gathering others. [*Applause.*]

REV. J. L. PARSONS, ST. LOUIS, MO. (CHRISTIANS [DISCIPLES]): Your beloved secretary who is now quite ill from overwork has kindly invited me to express to you the attitude towards the Christian Endeavor movement of the people who choose to wear the name common to all followers of the Master, "Christians." These people have no denominational organization. They are not an organized ecclesiastical body. They have no authoritative council, conference, or assembly; and yet they are one people. They are bound together by the strong but common tie of faith in our Lord Jesus Christ, and this is their only tie. They have but one test of fellowship, and that is obedience unto the authority of our only Lord Jesus Christ. Standing upon this broad and high ground these people do most cordially and earnestly receive and encourage the Christian Endeavor movement, chiefly because its pledge is, "Trusting in the Lord Jesus Christ, I promise Him that I will strive to do whatever He would have me do." It is a fundamental principle with us that we are to receive and encourage every man who receives and acknowledges the authority of the Lord Jesus Christ. Said one Christian man to another, "Can you do this for Christ?" "No," said he, "I am under promise to my church." To another man he said, "Can you do this for Christ?" "No, I am under promise to my minister." Then said the first man, "I want to find a man who is under promise to Christ," and we find that man in the Christian Endeavor movement. [*Applause.*]

REV. C. B. WILCOX, ST. PAUL, MINN. (METHODIST EPISCOPAL): I belong to that denomination whose purpose it is to make the earth quake, and we want the Christian Endeavor to assist us in that work. As a pastor in the Methodist Episcopal Church, I have found the Y. P. S. C. E. a strong arm of power. In the church which I served immediately preceding my present pastorate, there were six young men in this organization licensed to preach. Two of them are travelling evangelists, and during the last three years no less than three thousand persons have professed Christ through their instrumentality. Four of the six are pastors in the Methodist Episcopal Church and two of them are giving promise of very large usefulness. In the church which I am now serving, there is a mission supported by the Christian Endeavor society in one of the most neglected portions of the city, and that society is the only society that always has money in its treasury. My prayer meetings would be slimly attended were it not for the Christian Endeavor society. I find it loyal to the Sunday school, loyal to the public services. I state these facts in order that you may know that the Christian Endeavor Society is loyal to the local churches in Methodism. [*Loud applause.*] There are in the Methodist Episcopal Church, 5,000 chapters of the Epworth League, with a membership of 350,000. There are 2,208 Christian Endeavor societies, with a membership of perhaps 150,000, making over 7,000 young people's societies with a total membership of 500,000. I wish they were all members of the Christian Endeavor Society. [*Applause.*] In a certain sense they are, but I would that they were as we are here today, and I trust the time will come when they will be. Those Methodists present here have taken steps towards memorializing our next General Conference in the interests of this movement. [*Applause.*] Methodism is a child of providence. It has been defined as Christianity in earnest. Its history and its results fully declare that it is a child of providence. As such it cannot afford to ignore other children of providence. The Christian Endeavor Society is such a child. It was said of the apostles when they came to a certain place, "These that have turned the world upside down are come hither also." That is true of the Y. P. S. C. E., and we propose to go on turning the world upside down until it gets right side up. [*Loud applause.*]

REV. W. W. DAWLEY, ST. PAUL, MINN. (BAPTIST): Co-workers in redeeming this world for Jesus Christ, I am glad to greet you and bring you congratulations this morning from the Baptists. The seed of Christian Endeavor has found good ground among the Baptists of America. Father Endeavor Clark planted the seed; we have watered it [*laughter*], and God has given the increase. We rejoice with you today, fellow-Endeavorers, that this little seed is a grain of mustard-seed, which, planted in that Williston Church, has today become a mighty tree in whose wide-spreading and fruit-laden branches all nations and all denominations are fast finding shelter and food. It has been of untold value to us as Baptists. It has made many of our Baptist young people better and more intelligent Baptists. [*Applause.*] It has stimulated loyalty to Jesus Christ, and it thereby has stimulated loyalty to the principles that we love. I hail it as God's manna sent from heaven, though a Congregationalist brought it to us; and we are feeding upon it, and with nearly 2,400 societies we are finding that even our Baptist muscle is being developed on that kind of food.

REV. J. F. COWAN, PITTSBURG, PENN. (METHODIST PROTESTANT): I have heard of an Irishman who was assistant in a chemical laboratory. One day the experiment was to make air of oxygen and nitrogen, and the Irishman handled the flasks. On the next day the experiment was to make water of gases, and the Irishman was told to hand over the oxygen flask. "Faith," said Pat, "and it is mesilf that is larnin' that I make water of wind by putting in a little more juice." [*Laughter.*] Now, Christian Endeavor is Methodism with a little more juice in it. The essential elements of Methodism are spiritual enthusiasm and methods for applying it. The vital principles of Christian Endeavor are covenanted consecrated zeal for Christ and channels for it to flow through. I care not if some one says, After all, this is nothing but a Methodist class-meeting changed and under a different name; for just as Methodism was but a revival of primitive Christianity under a different name, so Christian Endeavor is a revival of the spirit of Methodism under a different name and with a broader application, and we Methodists all believe in a second blessing. [*Applause.*] If it is Methodism, then we welcome more Methodism. If our bread is buttered on one side, we are willing to have it buttered upon the other. I welcome Christian Endeavor as a representative of a branch of the Methodist church because of its broad fellowship. I want to say here today that young Methodist Protestants are not close communion Methodists; we want no denominational fences, and we shall not have them. [*Loud applause.*] Our young people come of a stock that has protested against being lorded over in matters of faith; and for fifty years this motto of the Christian Endeavor Society has stood as the keystone of our polity, "One is your Master, even Christ; and all ye are brethren." [*Applause.*]

REV. M. F. MCKIRAHAN, TOPEKA, KAN. (UNITED PRESBYTERIAN): The United Presbyterian Church of North America has always manifested a very great interest in the spiritual and moral welfare of her youth, believing that if you train up a child in the way in which he should go, in after years he will not depart from it; and she has been trying for all these years of her history to furnish this training. She has in some good degree succeeded in indoctrinating her young people, in the home, in the Sabbath school and in the church, in the doctrines of the word of God, believing that the Scriptures of the Old and New Testaments are the infallible and only rule of faith and practice. She has made development to some degree; but when this brilliant idea came along, she believed it was a good thing, and she appropriated it and is trying to train up a generation to become active workers in the Master's vineyard. Christian Endeavor has so far proven a great blessing to us; and we have not forgotten the children, either, for we lay great stress upon the Junior work. We have already almost trained a generation of Juniors and have inaugurated still another work behind the Juniors, which we call the Primary Society of Christian Endeavor. So we have the three branches, and all along the line we are following this great movement, until we shall have a whole generation of Christian Endeavorers ready for every good work. [*Applause.*]

REV. SMITH BAKER, D.D., MINNEAPOLIS (CONGREGATIONAL): Several years ago a couple came from the country to me to be married. When I said to the young man, "Do you take this woman to be your lawful wedded wife?" "Of course," said he, "what do you suppose I came here for?" [*Laughter.*] Now, I represent the primitive, apostolic, Plymouth Rock, high-church Congregationalists [*laughter*], and that is just what we have come here for: to indorse this Christian Endeavor movement. As a mother takes her nursing child, looking into its laughing eyes, and kisses it, so each of our churches takes this Christian Endeavor Society, folds it to her heart and kisses it as her most hopeful child. [*Applause.*] Now we Congregationalists, you know,—we modern, primitive Congregationalists, without any "new departure" or "higher criticism," —believe somewhat in the Presbyterian doctrine and the Baptist individuality stirred up with a Methodist stick [*laughter*], and the Christian Endeavor movement comes as near crystallizing this thing as anything that God has given us. We have not the advantage or disadvantage of some of you, in having bishops over us,—though we are all bishops, you know,—or great assemblies to govern us; and hence, if we have any power, it must be in the developed individuality of our members. Therefore we have hailed—and do still—the developing, organizing power of the Y. P. S. C. E. as our hope in this democratic country in which we live. So then, we take this newest child of providence in church history, this third great marked evolution of this century, and hug it to our hearts and say, From this are to come the leaders of our churches, the leaders of our political destiny, the leaders of our commercial and educational destiny in the years to come. [*Loud applause.*]

REV. GEO. B. OVERTON, D.D., LOUISVILLE, KY. (METHODIST EPISCOPAL, SOUTH): I am glad today to represent the Methodist Episcopal Church South in this august presence. I hail from the city where the Methodist Episcopal Church South was organized in 1845, and yet we are an integral part of the Methodist Episcopal Church in America. The Methodist Episcopal Church South accepted heartily the results of the war, [*applause*] and we are loyal today to the American flag. [*Applause.*] We are proud that the last shackle has been stricken from the slave and that this country is one and indissoluble. [*Applause.*] We glory in the fact that at the time when the war closed there were 200,000 Christians of our brethren in black that had been brought to Christ through our church; and today we have missionaries in China and Japan and Mexico, and we have sent Dr. Deems to New York to help christianize that great city. [*Laughter.*] Out into this great Northwest we are sending faithful missionaries to help bring this country to the Lord Jesus. We accept the Bible as God's word, and we believe it all. Not only so, but we are loyal Methodists, of the Pauline-Wesleyan type, and our first men came from Maine, where the Christian Endeavor Society comes from. We expect to try this Christian Endeavor Society and find it better than the Epworth League, and then we will be Epworth League Christian Endeavorers throughout our entire church. [*Applause.*]

REV. R. L. SWAIN, WESTERVILLE, O. (UNITED BRETHREN): The name in full of the church which I represent is The United Brethren in Christ; and we expect that, if we cannot realize church union in this world, in the next, at least, we shall all be united brethren in Christ. [*Applause.*] Many of you, perhaps, do not even know of us, partly because, for many years, we were wholly a German-speaking people. But today we are 200,000 strong, and during the last twelve months we have received into our communion 20,000 persons on the two simple and yet wonderful affirmations: first, "I believe the Bible to be the word of God," and second, "I have found the Lord Jesus Christ in my life." If you do not know of us, friends, we know of you, and we love you. If the United Brethren Church should go back on Christian Endeavor, she would go back on everything which has characterized the United Brethren Church. The United Brethren Church existed in this country for thirty-five years without an organization, and for twenty-five years without a name, being simply a fraternal relation of brethren who met and recognized each other as being brethren in the Lord Jesus Christ. And so upon this one brotherhood we have lived unto the present time. United Brethrenism has had a Christian Endeavor society for fifteen years, pure and simple, with the exception of the backbone; and I want to say to you that that oldest society which has existed for fifteen years in the United Brethren Church, and which has spread considerably, about one year ago was transferred to the Christian Endeavor Society. [*Applause.*] In the Tulpehocken Valley the United Brethren established in 1749 the first weekly prayer meeting in America, — a fact which the churches of America have not as yet seemingly learned. Upon these principles we are truly Christian Endeavor, — heart, soul, and body. [*Applause.*]

REV. A. DEW. MASON, BROOKLYN, N. Y. (REFORMED DUTCH): Dr. Black said that his church was the pioneer church in the Northwest. I come to bring the greetings to this Convention of the pioneer society of Christian Endeavor of the pioneer church of America, the Reformed Dutch Church, which 250 years ago planted the standard of the church of Christ upon the shores of the new world. The society which I have the honor to represent from my own church in Brooklyn was the first society to be organized in the cities of New York and Brooklyn; and we shall be very happy, in connection with our sister societies, to extend to you the right hand of fellowship in 1892. The reason the old Dutch Church loves the Christian Endeavor movement and took it up so early is because Christian Endeavor agrees with the Dutch Church. Why? Because our two main mottoes — expressing principles which all Christians must have — have been brought out and developed most perfectly in the Christian Endeavor movement. These two mottoes we cling to and love. One is in the language of the old mother church, — the language which hurled defiance at Spain and Elba and Romanism in the days of old, and which laid the foundations of civil and religious liberty for the new world: "*Eendracht maakt macht*," "In union there is strength." We of the Christian Endeavor movement have found that out; we of America have found that out. God grant that the Christian Endeavor societies of America may more and more learn that only in Christ our Lord is there strength for us. And then the second motto is in the language which ruled the world in the old days: "*Nisi Dominus frustra*," "Without God all is in vain." Yes, brethren, we have learned that in our Christian Endeavor work. We have magnificent opportunities, grand enthusiasm, wonderful organization; but without God all is in vain. God grant that we shall ever find it so! [*Applause.*]

REV. J. B. JORDAN, PAWTUCKET, R. I. (FREE BAPTIST): I represent one of the smallest denominations in the Christian church, it may be, but we have in our various churches a great many societies,—I cannot state the number of members. In the greater number of the churches in the State of Rhode Island they are almost all Christian Endeavor societies, but in common with one of the great bodies of the Christian church we have a denominational society. When I was pastor of a church in this city some years ago, we had here a Christian Endeavor society. When I went to the State of Maine, we had there a society of the Advocates of Christian Fidelity. I had the honor for two years of being the official head of that general society, with societies all over this country, some in the Provinces and some in India. I want simply to say this here today, that amid the enthusiasm and inspiration of this great gathering I have no argument to bring in favor of a distinctive denominational society. [*Applause.*] I want to take hold of this work more especially, and our church as a whole is in wonderful sympathy with organized effort among young people. These three things are impressed upon us in these organizations—this triple "C": concertion, which means to plan, to plan together; consecration, which means the giving up of the heart and life to Jesus Christ; and concentration, the devotion of all our energies to that great work which He has put before us of winning souls and bringing them into the kingdom of our Lord and Saviour, Jesus Christ. [*Applause.*]

REV. D. A. GRAHAM, MINNEAPOLIS (AFRICAN METHODIST): I am glad to have the opportunity of speaking a word of indorsement from the denomination which I represent. African Methodism hails the Christian Endeavor movement with the most hearty congratulations. We are a part of the great Methodist body of the world, over 500,000 strong, and moving on to get hold of the masses of the young people. The days of darkness which have gone by make it impossible for us to accomplish the work among the old people that we desire; but in the young people we see our hope, and they are the ones we are laying hold of and bringing to Christ. And in this Christian Endeavor movement we find that we have the greatest assistance, above that of any other movement that has been put forward in America. We hail the movement because it is, as has been so often proclaimed from this platform, interdenominational and international, and more, I am proud to say,—interracial. [*Loud and repeated applause.*] We are carrying on the grand principle that is contained in the motto of this year: "One is your Master, even Christ; and all ye are brethren." [*Applause.*]

REV. A. J. TURKLE, OMAHA, NEB. (LUTHERAN): I am glad to bring greetings from the Lutheran Church, because the Lutheran Church is learning to love Christian Endeavor. When Martin Luther began his work, he gave us the open Bible, out of which Christian Endeavorers are learning to get God's truth day after day. When he had done this, he immediately formed his young people together to train them in the Christian life. We are learning to love this Society because it is in harmony with the principle and the spirit of our church, so old and dear to us; and if old and dear and sometimes slow to give up, yet because it has brought so many young people to Christ and trained them to strong Christian lives, we love it more and more. [*Applause.*]

BISHOP SAM'L FALLOWS, D.D., CHICAGO, ILL. (REFORMED EPISCOPALIAN): You may ask what is the meaning of the word, "reformed," as applied to the church which I have the honor of representing. Just let me say, etymologically, ecclesiastically, theologically, it simply means the true Episcopal Church formed again, re-formed on the old lines [*applause*], which included all the Presbyterians in the past, all the Congregationalists like my good brother who represents Plymouth Rock principles in all their purity and power, and all the Methodists, because the Reformed Episcopal Church had its hand on John Wesley and would have kept its hand on every descendant of Wesley if circumstances and Providence had permitted. [*Laughter.*] Now, then, for this reason the Reformed Episcopal Church, as a church, is fully committed to the Christian Endeavor movement, and in almost every church of our denomination the Christian Endeavor societies are found. In my own church, as I have said before, the Christian Endeavor society is my right arm of strength. God bless it and bless all the societies. [*Applause.*]

REV. ROBERT E. CALDWELL, LOUISVILLE, KY. (SOUTHERN PRESBYTERIAN): The Y. P. S. C. E. has attracted wide attention throughout the Southern Presbyterian Church. The spirit of inquiry is abroad amongst them, and already a large number have pledged their hands and their hearts to the work for young people and for the salvation of the world through the young people of this land. It is taking hold upon our hearts in the Southern land; and if the Y. P. S. C. E. did not take hold upon us, it would be the first thing that is good that has ever approached us and made its overtures to us that has not been welcomed to our bosoms. It is said of the celebrated Rowland Hill that on one occasion he was asked if he held to the doctrines of Calvinism. "No, sir," said he, "the doctrines of Calvinism hold me." We believe that the sentiment and the principles and the ideas formulated in the Y. P. S. C. E. have in them the will of God, and that the will of God must and will take hold upon all our hearts. I do not speak in behalf of my church at large; it will speak for itself. What I say is upon my own personal responsibility; but I thank God that I am here in this vast gathering. [*Applause.*]

REV. C. J. PALMER (EPISCOPALIAN): You have noticed how all the speakers who have spoken have dwelt upon the fact that this Society has seemed to take hold providentially of their special line and special mission. This is also true of the Episcopal Church. Its distinctive characteristic is reliance on taking the young from the very first, and considering them as belonging to Jesus Christ. Now, that is precisely the idea of this Society, — to take hold of the young in the Junior department, and to encourage a continual growth, just as Jesus Christ did, who increased in wisdom and stature and, at the same time, coincident with it, in favor with God and man. In that way this Society takes hold of the essential idea of the church, of continual feeding.

DR. BLACK: A hundred years from now I hope that we shall still have the pastors' hour on the Christian Endeavor Convention programme and I hope that some of us will be there to listen. But I hope that it will not be as the representatives of thirty denominations but as the representatives of States in the universal republic of God. Meanwhile, as chairman of this meeting, and being of an inventive turn of mind, I have discovered a new church, and I want to call on the Church of the Holy Revival. Its representative here is Mr. Sankey. [*Applause.*]

MR. SANKEY: I will speak to you my sentiments in a song. We are glad to welcome to the field of Christian labor all these young hearts and voices. We believe it is the most encouraging feature of all the outlook in the world today, that these consecrated hearts should be united and go throughout all the world holding up one name, the name of Jesus Christ. And after all our conventions and all our labors, evangelistic and otherwise, are over, "We shall meet beyond the river by and by."

Mr. Sankey sang this hymn, giving to various sections of the audience and choir each one line of the refrain, "By and by." One section would sing it in full voice, then another section would echo it very softly, then the audience would join in on the final refrain, producing an impressive and beautiful effect.

DR. BLACK: Before I call upon the last speaker, let me say just one word for the ministers. Counting from the time that we started, we lack four minutes of our hour, and we have shared in that beautiful hymn as an extra. Now, to wind up this delightful hour, I will call upon one who represents himself and who also represents all the churches, Rev. Dr. Deems of New York. [*Loud applause.*]

DR. C. F. DEEMS, PASTOR OF THE CHURCH OF THE STRANGERS, NEW YORK: Dear Master, did I ever think that in the Church of the Strangers I should minister to so great a congregation of my people? Yet here they all are. All these belong to the church of the strangers, — think of that; and now you have resolved to come home next year, and I have been sitting here in mortal agony, saying, Oh, Lord, how shall I move out the walls of the Strangers' Church and take the whole church of the strangers in? But come on, brethren, come on, and see if perhaps next year we shall not have a church even as large as this for you to come into. Talk about the children of providence, — providence is the most prolific parent in all the universe. The Church of the Strangers is a child of providence. I had no doubt of it when it began. God made the Church of the Strangers in the city of New York. I have not stood for any denomination; I have not tried to belong to anybody in particular; I have simply stood there and preached the gospel of the Son of God. I love all the brethren of Christ Jesus, and it seems to me God prepared me for it. I was born in the South, educated in the Middle States; I married in the North; my father was a Methodist minister, my stepmother was a Presbyterian, I was converted in an Episcopal Sunday school, and now, by the grace of God, I am very much like the old Episcopalian lady who lost her prayer-book — I have nothing but the Lord to depend on now [*great laughter and applause*], nothing but the Lord and the societies of Christian Endeavor. [*Applause.*] As I have stood by you when you were young, I shall expect you to stand by me when I am old — if I can ever get to be old. [*Renewed laughter and applause.*]

By request of the Illinois delegation, the audience united in singing the hymn which had made such a reputation at the St. Louis Convention, "The Endeavor Band." Meanwhile the Canadian delegation unrolled and fastened to the gallery a large banner bearing the inscription, "Montreal, 1893." Dr. Clark immediately called attention to it, and his announcement was received with prolonged cheers.

Dr. Clark then introduced as the next speaker, Rev. A. A. Fulton, of Canton, China, the originator of the pledge of two cents a week to missions, who was announced to speak on "The Society for All the World." Mr. Fulton was given a most cordial reception as he came forward to make his address.

ADDRESS OF REV. A. A. FULTON.

Mr. Chairman, Christian Endeavorers: Some one said to me, "Fulton, what are you going to expect at Minneapolis?" I said, "I am going to Minneapolis for half a million dollars for missions." [*Applause.*] The assertion has been made that the Christian Endeavor Society is like a great cannon that only gives forth sound. Thank God, Christian Endeavorers *are* sound; they are going to sound out this gospel to every part of the heathen world. Now, as I have said, I came here for half a million dollars. My faith was too weak; I am going to have a million dollars for missions, and I am going to give you the reasons why we want that million dollars.

In the first place, because the command of our Lord Jesus Christ to go into all the world and preach this gospel stands today just as it stood when He was upon the earth. That command has never been abrogated, never been annulled, and can never be compromised by any speculations in theology. The second reason is this: I do not see how any man can ever be saved without hearing this gospel. Our Lord Jesus Christ has conditioned salvation upon hearing. "Faith cometh by hearing." Now, one of the great problems that the missionary has to meet is this stupendous fact. He sees millions and millions of human beings wholly given over to idolatry. I have seen five times as many people as are here in this house following along in procession after one miserable idol. And the question has come to me, Will all these people be saved if they do not hear the gospel? And then I have turned to my Bible and I have been constrained to ask, How can you yourself be saved if you do not give them the gospel? That is the second reason. Now for the third reason. I want that million of dollars from these Christian Endeavorers because of the helplessness of the heathen world without Christianity. I wish I could speak of India and Africa and Japan, but I cannot do it. Look today at China — 350 millions of human beings, and, except where Christianity has been, they know no more about the gospel of Christ than they do about the philosophy of Kant. For 2,000 years they have been stationary. Confucius was a great teacher, and he gave to the Chinese a fine ethical system; but mere human ethics can no more regenerate and elevate and purify a nation than dead machinery can force water up the side of a mountain. They are stationary, and they will be stationary until we give them the gospel. What have Confucianism and Buddhism done for women in the world? Go with me in imagination today down to Canton; go into the great provinces of China, and look upon woman's condition. Has she one shadow more of privilege, of liberty, of comfort, than she had when Jesus Christ was upon this earth? Not by a hair's breadth. The same old statutes are on the law books of China in all their meanness and repulsiveness as they were thousands of years ago. Woman is not welcomed at birth; she is sold in marriage to any man, irrespective of his moral character; she lives without the precious consolations of the gospel, and is buried with idolatrous rites. No man may deny these statements. Confucianism has made the Chinese a homogeneous people; Buddhism, with its lying superstitions, has made the Chinese an idolatrous people; Christianity alone can make them a spiritual people. The condition of China today is that of a land which sees on the right-hand side a desert and on the left-hand side a limitless ocean. Confucianism is pure agnosticism; it tells nothing about God. Buddhism is only a limitless ocean of superstition. I affirm today that the condition of the Chinese 350 millions is like that of the four lepers who sat at the gate of the city of Samaria, who said, "If we stay here we die, if we go into the city the famine is there;" and they have not a miserable chance of falling back upon the host of Syrians if perchance they may be saved.

I want that million of money in the next place because of the sufferings of the Chinese and of other heathen nations. Do you know that idolatry causes a people great bodily sufferings? When a man pays ten dollars for a garment, he gets some equivalent for his money; but when he pays twenty dollars for an idol, he is miserably defrauded. I say, on account of the sufferings of the heathen world we want that money. Notice this thing. I have been in China where I have seen women working in the rice fields under a burning sun, fourteen hours a day, for five cents. That money is taken at the end of a week and is spent in incense and idolatrous worship at some temple, and the poor woman has not enough rice to keep body and soul together. That is the condition of 150,000,000 people. I have seen thousands of people setting up a common stone for an object of worship. They are doing it today, and they will do it until we give them the gospel. Those are the five reasons why I want that money.

Now another thing. How are we going to get that money? I have a plan for you, and it is this: we are all going to give two cents a week for foreign missions. Let every member of every society of Christian Endeavor give two cents a week for foreign missions. I tell you, brethren, we can put into operation a mighty power that will shake the heathen world. Already the States of Ohio, Indiana, Minnesota, and the local unions of New York, Boston, Philadelphia, Baltimore, Harrisburg, Cleveland, Detroit, and many others, have adopted this plan, and the membership today is not far from 75,000, and that means 75,000 dollars for foreign missions. [*Applause.*]

How is this to be done? Every Christian Endeavorer is to give two cents a week for foreign missions: that is a dollar a year, and a million Christian Endeavorers is a million dollars a year. Now let me tell you how this is to be done. If you go up one of the great rivers of China, you will see a great number of water-wheels, tremendous water-wheels, and around the rim of every wheel you will see a bamboo tube. That tube holds two quarts of water. Now you will notice that at every revolution of that wheel, the united contents of those tubes are poured into great troughs and sent far and wide over the parched rice fields. That is an illustration of what Christian Endeavor is. Every society is a water-wheel: every member who gives two cents a week is one of the tubes upon the rim of that wheel; the great troughs are your denominational boards, and the fields white to the harvest are the 800,000,000 of helpless heathen. Let us all make this a plan of our life. And I say this: Put all your money into the regular denominational boards. [*Applause.*] Don't undertake independent mission work. If you give two cents a week for missions and you are a Presbyterian, send that to the Presbyterian board. If you are a Methodist, send your money to the Methodist board. If you are a Baptist, send it to the Baptist board. Don't you see that we can put this millions of dollars into the boards by all doing this work? We want to work this plan just as Nehemiah, when he went down to Jerusalem, builded the walls of the city. The people all did something at the same time, and they all did something until the wall was finished.

Now we are going to have here this afternoon four thousand pledge books, and these books are going to be distributed to all the societies. But before that is done, I want to put this pledge to all Christian Endeavorers here. Will you not give two cents a week for foreign missions, — not less than that, — and give it all your life long? I am going to ask everybody to stand up who will assent to this pledge. I want Indiana to stand up first and then Ohio, for as Ohio and Indiana go, so goes the Union. [*Laughter and applause.*]

Responding to this request, nearly the entire audience rose to its feet amid great enthusiasm.

MR. FULTON: Take these pledge books home with you, and next year when I go back to China, I will send you a cablegram: Hold fast to the two cents a week for Christ. [*Loud applause.*]

The session closed with the usual announcements and the benediction by Rev. W. H. McMillen, D.D.

SATURDAY AFTERNOON.

No session was held at the auditorium in the afternoon; instead, a grand excursion to Lake Minnetonka was the order of the programme. Arrangements had been made by the Committee of '91 with the Great Northern Railroad to transport, at a small price for the round trip, all who desired to go to the lake. It was calculated that some seven or eight thousand of the delegates availed themselves of the opportunity to visit this beautiful sheet of water, and at two o'clock the trains began leaving the Union Depot at intervals of ten or fifteen minutes. The ride to the lake proved a delightful one, occupying about forty minutes. The Hotel Lafayette was placed at the disposal of the excursionists, and its roomy parlors, wide verandas, and beautiful lawns made an ideal place for the excursion headquarters. No formal exercises were held and the delegates roamed about at will. A large number patronized the lake steamers and enjoyed a tour round the lake. Others united in State or college reunions. President Clark, with the other officers of the Society and the Trustees, held a reception in the hotel parlors which was largely attended. Many were satisfied simply to find seats on the hotel verandas and engage in social conversation, listen to the music furnished by the hotel orchestra and enjoy the landscape. Altogether it was a very pleasant time, and by seven o'clock the trains had returned all the excursionists to the city without a single mishap.

SATURDAY EVENING.

Apparently the delegates did not find the afternoon excursion so wearying but that they could come together for another session, for they were present in full force when the time arrived for the evening's exercises at the Convention hall. Rev. Wayland Hoyt, D.D., of Minneapolis, presided, and called on Rev. Leighton Williams, of New York City, to read the Scriptures. The hymn, "Stand up for Jesus," was then sung, after which Rev. J. Clement French, D.D., of Newark, N. J. led in prayer, closing with the Lord's Prayer, in which the audience joined. Some necessary announcements were then made and another hymn, "Sowing in the Morning," was sung.

DR. HOYT: Not undenominational but interdenominational; and therefore delightful and sacred spiritual fellowship is a principle of Christian Endeavor.

In Swatow, there was a Christian Chinese merchant who had on one occasion to go to Hong Kong. He could not speak the dialect of Hong Kong. When he returned to Swatow, the only missionary there asked him if he had had a pleasant time. He said he had, a delightful time. "But," he said, "you could not understand the dialect in Hong Kong; how could you have such a pleasant time?" He answered, "I went into a chapel and sat down, and an old man came in and began to talk to me. I could not understand a word he said; but when he said 'Jesus' I nodded my head. I understood that, and when I talked and I said 'Jesus' he nodded his head, and so we had a delightful time." So it is that love to the one divine Lord binds together all who love Him, whether they be separated by ecclesiastical dialect or by government or by oceans; and Christian Endeavor, without demanding that we yield a particle of our denominational convictions which are precious to us, gives us opportunity to express, as we do in this magnificent Convention, our deep spiritual unity in Jesus Christ our Lord. We are to consider that phase of our Christian Endeavor movement tonight, and the first speech will be concerning "International Fellowship," and it will be made by Rev. William Patterson, of Toronto, Canada. [*Applause.*]

ADDRESS OF REV. WILLIAM PATTERSON.

Fellow-Endeavorers: Before I say anything on the subject assigned me, I would like to tell you who I am. I am a Scotch-Irish-Canadian-American. [*Laughter.*] My forefathers were born in Scotland, that land of loyal hearts and true, and I myself was born in old Ireland, that is still the gem of the seas. My home is in Canada — that country that is bounded on the east by the noisy Atlantic, on the west by the broad Pacific, on the north by the north pole and on the south by the Great Republic. From the time when I was a boy, I always loved America. Long before I saw her shores, I had wandered in the good lands of the North, and the cotton fields of the South. Long before I had crossed the Atlantic, I had sailed up the Mississippi and gazed in wonder and astonishment at the broad and mighty Amazon. Some of the best and truest friends I have are members of this republic. And so all through. I have loved this land, and I can claim tonight that I love not only Scotland and Ireland and Canada, but this great republic.

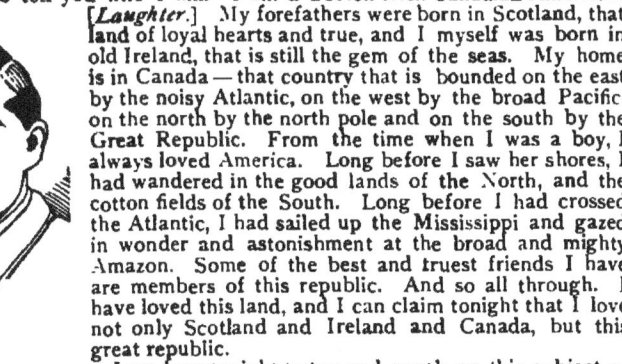

I am here tonight to try and speak on this subject of international fellowship. There are various ways of taking it up. I might try to show you how Christian Endeavor is adapted for every land and every people. I might try to show you how this Society is adapted for the metaphysical and thinking Scotch as well as for the warm-hearted Irishman and the go-ahead American. Every place that the Bible is adapted for, every place that the church is adapted for, the Christian Endeavor Society is adapted for, since it is not outside the church neither is it a wing of the church, but the very heart and core of the church. [*Applause.*] But now, since we are all wise here,— because a great many have come from the East and all the wise men come from there [*laughter*], — since we all believe that the Christian Endeavor Society is adapted for every land and community and people, it is not necessary for me to dwell upon that part of the subject. I will therefore take up another part of it and try to show you how Christian Endeavor is adapted and designed to bring together the nations of the earth and to bring about that glorious international fellowship that we long for, that we pray for, that we work for, and that we will never be satisfied until we have obtained.

With regard to this international fellowship, let me say that it exists to a great extent between Canada and this republic. We in Canada invited this Convention over to meet with us next year at Montreal. We would have given you a grand and royal reception. But it was thought better to have it in New York; and now, since you cannot come to us, we have decided to go to you. [*Applause.*] So I can tell you that next July we intend to take New York by storm. We will not take any of her forts, but we want to capture the hearts of the people. And let me say here for the Canadians, that it is the prayer of every Canadian that Almighty God will bless the Convention of '92 and make it the grandest and the greatest and the most glorious that this world has ever seen. [*Applause.*] We have fellowship between these countries and we mean to have it, notwithstanding all that wily politicians in either country may say. We are determined to love each other and work together in harmony for the glorious cause of our glorified Redeemer.

Let me also say, with regard to the old lands, that we have Christian international fellowship. Every summer the streets of our great cities abroad are crowded by Americans, and the English are always glad to see them — especially the merchants, if their purses are long and full. And let me tell you this: that there are many of the churches and many of the schools and many of the mansions in that old land that have been built by American millionnaires; and two of the greatest men in England are the greatest lovers of this republic, — I mean Mr. Gladstone and Mr. Spurgeon. [*Loud applause.*]

But while this is true with regard to the United States and Canada and the United States and England, we all know that there is not international fellowship among all the nations of the earth. We know that many of them are increasing their navies and their armies, adding regiment to regiment and man-of-war to man-of-war. Now, can Christians be satisfied that this is the right thing to do? Did God Almighty ever make the eye of man to take aim at his fellow-man? Did God ever give man faculties in order that he might invent instruments by which to murder his fellow-men? Never, we say; and it is the duty of every Christian to pray for and to work for that grand time when all the nations of the earth shall be united in true international fellowship. [*Applause.*] Statesmen see that this is necessary, and many suggestions have been made as to how this should be brought about. Let me refer to a few of these and show you how they never can accomplish that for which they are designed.

Some say that if we get the royal families to intermarry that would bring about international fellowship. Well, some of the royal families might not love each other, for one thing; and for another thing, some countries have no royal families; so that that plan would not work. Then there is another suggestion: to get the commerce of the nations so interwoven that it would be to the loss of any nation to go to war with another. But this is the very basest of motives to lead men to be at peace. They would say, "Now it will not pay to go to war," but after a time it would pay and then they would go,—like the woman with a goose laying a golden egg; some day she forgets, and off comes the head of the goose. Then there is another suggestion; namely, that these nations be connected by every nation's so increasing its armies and navies that one nation would be afraid of the other. That is one reason why we have no wars today, because one nation is afraid to go to war with another. But this will not do, because just so soon as one nation feels that she is stronger than the other, the gate is open and the way is clear to declare war. All these devices must fail because the appeal is to the baser elements in man; they do not appeal to his nobler nature.

But let me try to show you the means by which alone this international fellowship may be brought about. We must first of all find out the cause of the international strife, and then we may be able to suggest a remedy. International strife, you remember, began in the garden of Eden; it began when our first parents partook of the forbidden fruit. It was then that man began to find fault with his wife—and many a man has done that since then. You see how it was shown afterwards in the case of Cain and his brother, and in the case of Lamech who rejoiced when he had made a sword with which he could kill his fellow-man. So it kept on going year after year, until after the Flood, when we find men who had been gathered into one family going out in three different directions, forming three different peoples, and these peoples rising up against each other, tribe against tribe, nation against nation, kingdom against kingdom,—a state of things which we have had during all these six thousand years. But God designed that there should be another Adam, to come and bring about international fellowship and to destroy the international strife that the first Adam brought in. And so we find indications of this all along. We find that God would not allow the temple to be built by a man of war but by the king of peace. We find the prophets looking down through the vistas of the ages, seeing the grand time that we are speaking of, when men should beat their swords into ploughshares and their spears into pruning hooks, hanging the trumpet in the hall and ceasing to call their armies to war; when they would dwell together in unity with nothing to hurt or destroy in all the holy mountain of the Lord. And so, when Messiah came, you remember that He came in a reign of peace. You remember that when His birth was announced it was said He was to bring peace upon the earth and good will among men. You remember that when He preached His first sermon He referred in that sermon to this international fellowship in the time of Elijah and Elisha, when they were entertained by the widows, whose sons were raised from the dead. You remember that when He would show to His disciples who their brother was, it was the good Samaritan that He made to play the friend to the man who had fallen among thieves. He conversed with the woman at the well of Jacob, to the amazement of herself and His disciples; and He marvelled at the faith of the man who was a Roman centurion, when He said to the Syrophœnician woman, "Oh, great is thy faith," and at last when He was nailed to the cross and there was hung over His head that superscription written in three languages, the Latin, the Greek, and the Hebrew, representing the three great nations of the world, we have international fellowship. And so afterwards, you remember, when He gave His last command to His disciples, it was that they should go into all the earth and make disciples of all nations. You remember also the day of Pentecost, when they were all assembled together. There were men there from every nation under heaven; they had all things in common; they had common principles; they had hearts beating in loyalty to one another; they were all brought close to Him who was their head and their king, and they realized then that they were brethren. And so we find one of the grandest and the greatest of His apostles, the Apostle Paul, a man who was a Hebrew of the Hebrews, declaring, Henceforth I know no man after the flesh; he says that these walls have been broken down, that all men are just alike to him, the Jew and the Gentile, the bond and the free, the barbarian and the Scythian, the Roman and the Greek; and so his great heart goes out and takes in the whole universe, realizing that the Master came to bring about this international fellowship.

Thus we find that the only way to secure international fellowship is by bringing men to Christ; and when they are brought to Him they are brought to one another, and the closer they are brought to Him the closer they are brought to one another. We need not try to weld them together, because the nations have tried that and they have utterly failed.

And this is one of the grand things of this Convention. It is here that we have them from different countries; it is here that we have them welded together in that common brotherhood, realizing that God is our Father and that all men are our brethren. Two or three things have happened at this Convention which it would pay a man to go ten thousand miles to see and hear. There was one from a nation of people, many of whom are despised, who rose in that gallery and told us that he had put his trust in Christ and that he was going back to China to tell the same story to his friends; and this vast assembly became almost wild with enthusiasm, and every heart went out in sympathy to that young Chinese. And today on this platform there stood one from Africa, one of those who in former years was despised; but when he stood here did not every heart go out to him in love, and did we not give him the grandest reception that any man has received during this Convention? And last night, when the thunders and the lightnings were terrifying men and all the lights went out and we were in darkness,—you know how great assemblies in theatres and such places would have tumbled over one another, crushing one another to death; but we sat here singing, "Blest be the tie that binds our hearts in Christian love." I thank God for that thunder-storm. [*Loud applause.*]

Thus international fellowship is to be brought about only by bringing men to Christ and bringing them nearer to one another. And these are the two very things that Christian Endeavor has been organized for. The farther off men are from Christ, the farther they are from one another; and the nearer they are to Christ, the nearer they are to one another. The more of Christ there is in a man's heart, the less of a bigot and a sectarian he will be, for Christ will be all in all to him. His motto will no longer be one State or one Province or one country for Christ, but the world for Him,—the world which He loved and for which He gave Himself.

And then think of the possibilities of this Convention. We have been told of the difficulties that stand before us, and they are truly great. But have you thought to contrast this assembly with that which met at Pentecost. Let me tell you that this is one of the most marvellous gatherings that this world has ever seen since the day of Pentecost? Often more people have been gathered together, but when have from ten to fifteen thousand people been assembled together, not only Christians in name, but those who have gone forth as soldiers of Christ, men and women who have consecrated themselves to his service. I am confident that never before was such an assembly gathered together. And oh, brethren, think of what we could do in bringing about this international fellowship, and by so doing bring about that glorious time when He whose right it is shall reign from the river to the ends of the earth and from sea to sea. Do you remember, at Pentecost there were assembled 120 people. They were not as learned as we are; they had not one-thousandth part of the advantages that we have; they were fishermen, shepherds, farmers. Think of the difficulties they had to contend with: 120 people assembled together, 120 millions in the Roman empire. That great nation of the Greeks held the preaching of the cross as foolishness, and to the Jews, whose heart was full of enmity, it was a stumbling-block. But these 120 people went forward in the name of the Lord, and in the third century Christianity ascended the throne of the Cæsars and the cross was the emblem on its banners. Oh, if we could only realize, then, what we can do here in this vast assembly, as we go to our homes, giving our hearts to the Lord Jesus Christ, asking Him to take us and use us! For have we not the same Spirit? Have we not far greater advantages? The question with each one of us ought to be: Will we let God use us? Oh, brethren, if I could send home this thought; if I could get the men and women here to say, "Lord Jesus, take me and use me; fill me with thy Spirit and help me to bring others to thyself," then I would rejoice in coming here. Ah, brethren, there is no time for idle slumber while souls are passing into eternity. There is no time for questionable amusements; there is no time for wrangling or jangling over these differences. Let us all go forward, heart to heart, shoulder to shoulder, hand to hand, as a grand army of the Lord, whose weapons are not carnal but spiritual, to the pulling down of the strongholds of evil and to the advancement of the cause of our Lord and Master. Then the kingdoms of the world will become the kingdom of Christ. Yes, they will! That glorious day is coming. But the question is, Are you and I to have a part in bringing it about? Are we going to hasten on that glorious day when He shall reign from the river to the ends of the earth, when all nations shall be welded together, when all voices shall join in singing the grand song of redemption, "Worthy is he that hath redeemed us by his blood?" [*Applause.*]

Mr. Patterson's address was followed by a solo by Mr. Sankey, "What a wonderful Saviour is Jesus." Dr. Clark announced that on Sunday evening an outdoor meeting, for the benefit of those who could not get into the Convention hall, would be held on the tiers of seats at the west of the building, to be in charge of Dr. McKaig, of Minneapolis. The audience then united in singing, "Hear us, O Saviour."

DR. HOYT: I have now great pleasure in presenting to you the accomplished and eloquent president of Brown University, Rev. E. Benjamin Andrews, D.D., LL.D., who will speak to us of "Interdenominational Fellowship." [*Loud applause.*]

ADDRESS OF PRESIDENT E. B. ANDREWS, D.D., LL.D.

Mr. President: Some twenty years ago, the State of New York enjoyed the services of the last, I believe, of its noble old line of Dutch governors. At that time the governor's name was Bouck. He was better versed in agriculture and even in politics than he was in ecclesiastical archaeology. The last year that he was governor Archbishop Hughes, then bishop, made a visit to Rome. When he was about to return, some of the governor's political friends advised him, as a good stroke of political wisdom, to go down to Albany and welcome the bishop as he stepped off the boat. The governor took the hint and went. He stood on the wharf, and when the bishop came ashore he stepped up to him, shook his hand and said, "How do you do, Bishop Hughes? I am very glad to see you. How is Mrs. Hughes?" [*Laughter.*] The bishop did not know for a moment whether to laugh or to be indignant, but he thought it became his dignity better to be a little offended. So he looked sternly at the governor and said, "Why, governor, of course you must know that the clergy of the Catholic Church do not have wives." Whereupon the good governor threw up his hands and said, "Good Lord! How long since that began?" [*Laughter.*] Well, when I came to Minneapolis, looked upon this immense assemblage of people, and saw a building that had been dedicated to the largest purposes, commercial and political, packed from one end to the other so that there was hardly a seat that could be had, and when I remembered that the audience had gathered thus in the name of the Lord Jesus Christ and to further the ends of His religion, I said, I wonder how long since this new interest in the Christian religion began in the land I love.

Well, I think that already one of the finest things that has been accomplished by the work of this noble organization is that it has brought the different denominations of Christianity nearer together than they ever were before. If you go back to the earliest days of Christianity you find no denominations. In the writings of the New Testament the church is the great idea, and the New Testament conception of the church is not, in my belief, as has sometimes been held, that merely of a putting together of a large number of local churches; but the central thought is that of the church as a totality. The notion of unity is paramount and foremost. Our Lord declared to His disciples, and through them to all the world, that He would found a church and that the gates of hell should not prevail against it. The apostles took up that thought, and sought in every way to help their Lord carry out the purpose that He had thus expressed. You have to come down to post-Reformation times before you find anything exactly like the modern denomination. There were in the old church, of course, certain sects; but they all had the distinctive mark—and I might say the accursed consciousness—of sects, in that each one wanted to be *the* church. Each was ready to exclude all others; the people of each loved themselves; they thought that they and they alone held saving truth, and they had no satisfaction with other people, even if they regarded them as Christians at all, except in so far as they could make them willing to come over to their side. There was in those days of the church no case of groups of Christian people not excluding one another, not claiming the power of the keys, but regarding all as Christians equally with themselves and wishing each other well. There was no spectacle in the church anterior to the Reformation such as we have before us in the meetings of this Convention.

Now, the great curse of denominational life, since denominational life began, has been the tendency to drift back into the old sectarian temper, to forget the conception of catholicity, to be narrow and exclusive in our ecclesiastical life and thought. I think that the modern Protestant world takes far too little interest in the old church that was before the Reformation. I do not now refer to the sects that existed then, but to the old Catholic Church, which gave to the world Luther and Melanchthon and Calvin and Knox. We are too apt to think of that old church as something tainted and coarse. In this we err; for although there may have been—as certainly there were—grave evils in the church of those ancient days, it was after all God's church. In it was the greater part of all the virtue that was then in the world. It set going all the reforms in the interest of God and of humanity that were inaugurated then. It placed humanity in the way of putting down slavery; it built up the entire structure of international law. We ought to recognize these deeds, for they were far the greatest that had ever been done by men for humanity at that time. Again, although I speak as a Protestant,—which I am to the bottom of my heart,—I must say that

I think Protestants are often too narrow in their speech concerning the present Catholic Church. We should by all means condemn the evils, doctrinal and practical, in the Catholic Church, as we should those in our own churches; but we have no right to ignore the multitudes of faithful and godly people who regard the pope as St. Peter's successor. We wish to convert them, and the best means to that result is to show toward them the spirit of Christian charity, which is certainly not done when we assume that no Catholic can possibly be saved.

Well, then, going a little further, we still betray, I think, a very narrow spirit, to a great extent the spirit of ancient sectarianism, in our relations one with another as Christian denominations. I make a very sharp distinction between the notion of a denomination and the notion of a sect. The very words "sect" and "denomination" have a very important meaning which ought not to be left out of sight. "Sect" means a cut, a slice, something shorn off, so as to stand out independently and have nothing to do for the time being with the body from which it is cut. The word "denomination" points rather to the superficies of things. It is a nominal word; it calls attention to nominal distinctions, and thereby induces us to think beneath the surface for that glorious body of Christian faith and doctrine in which we are all united. That is to say, what unites us together is more immense, more grand, more divine, than all that separates us. What I mean to say is that although we are at heart denominations and not sects, we find that our denominational authorities and particularly the editors of our Protestant religious newspapers — I hope they are not here: if they are they will please forgive me — usually exhibit, or tend to, the spirit of sectarianism rather than that spirit of denominationalism to which I have just referred. [*Applause.*]

Now, what is the characteristic of that spirit? I will try briefly to set it forth. It is the remnant of the old papal idea of the power of the keys. It is the assumption that each denomination, after all its professions to the contrary, is continually falling into,—that somehow or other it is ordained of God to give the law to other ecclesiastical bodies; that somehow I am a little better than you. You can come and help me in my religious work, you can stand beside me in my pulpit, even; but, after all, my church is somewhat nearer to the ideal of Jesus Christ than yours, and I therefore admonish you to abjure your polity and adopt mine. One may think that some position like that is indispensable if we are to retain our denominational convictions. I do not believe it. I should like to explain, if there were time, that there is an immense distinction between my holding sacred certain convictions, differentiating me in belief, it may be quite radically, from my fellow, and the denial that that fellow with his other beliefs, so intolerable to me, is as truly a product of the divine Spirit as I am. He may seem to me all astray, and his theology may actually be so, yet the man himself may be even nearer to God and nearer the path of duty than I am or have ever been. What I desire to urge here, in all earnestness, is that we seek to carry out the strict idea of denominationalism as distinguished from sectarianism; that each name of us rid itself wholly and forever of all claim to any power of the keys. I believe it possible for each of us to develop denominationally, while laying aside all thought of lording it over God's heritage. To remember that while we have our convictions others have theirs, and that they have just as good a right to theirs as we to ours, will not hinder at all the growth of our peculiar tenets. To see that this idea is not impossible of realization one needs only to go back to that wonderfully interesting period in the history of the ancient church, the days of Cyprian, before the papacy began to get a foothold in the world. At that time every bishopric in the old Catholic Church regarded itself as having the right to develop along the lines of its own preference, subject only to the revisionary power of the general council. Now suppose that the development had gone on naturally and that the general council had been mild, never stepping in to exercise its authority except in matters vitally concerning the Christian faith: one can see that the different departments of Christendom would have developed very differently one from another. After the course of a few centuries, there would have been Baptists in one part of the Christian world, Congregationalists in another, Presbyterians, I dare say, in another, and Methodists in another; but there would have been nowhere any thought on any one's part of a right to exclude, to say, "My polity is the only one that God will or can tolerate." There would have been parties with convictions, on polity and on all else, but each would have been, in polity as elsewhere, deferential toward the convictions of all the rest.

What we want, it seems to me, is to come back to that old condition of things. The papacy, when it had the power, set us a very bad example,—the example of claiming power: and none of us have, as yet, had the grace or the wisdom entirely to rid ourselves of the influence of that pernicious example.

Let us suppose, dear friends, that by the grace of God we were enabled to lay aside all pretence of exercising the power of the keys, developing henceforth purely as so many Christian denominations, with no sectarianism any more, with no thought of exclusion any more, letting each godly man think his own thought, you still calling him a Christian; each church having its own polity and its own doctrine, while no one pronounced anathemas upon it on that account. Suppose we could come to that; let us think for one moment what some of the advantages to the Christian and social life of the world in which we live would be.

For one thing, we should instantly get a great deal nearer to one another as Christian denominations. We should understand one another better than we do. Most men seem to think that if you are going to testify in the strongest possible way to the truth which you believe, the way to do it is utterly to cast out from your fellowship or vicinage every one who differs from you. If a neighbor agrees with you, then you will fellowship him; if not, out with him! Most people suppose truth to be advanced in that way. Is any worse nonsense possible to man than that? [*Applause.*]

Of what good is a sermon favoring immersion in a church where everybody believes in immersion? Yet I have heard many such since my boyhood — good ones, splendid, in which every text of Scripture bearing on the subject of water was ably handled. Of what earthly advantage is a sermon to prove infant baptism in a congregation where everybody believes in it? I presume that many of you have listened to such, though I never did. Does it not stand to reason that if we are to reach the people whom we would gladly convert we should not thrust them off, not put them too far from us, but get ourselves as near to them as we can? In a church where a good many believed in some other form of baptism than immersion, were you to present a good gospel sermon on baptism, provided you had the right spirit in it, you might do a great deal of good. Commonly such sermons effect very little, and they sometimes do much harm.

There would come, then, a better understanding among Christian denominations with reference to each other's tenets. Unfortunately for me, I do not know very well, except out of books, what my Presbyterian brethren believe. I believe in them, God knows, for I know their works; but just why they believe as they do and just why in certain things they practise as they do, I never could find out, and I would be glad to find out. Were we nearer together I could learn. I have no doubt they could substantiate their beliefs triumphantly, as I could my own — and I tell you I could do it right well if I had time. [*Laughter.*]

Another immense advantage from the displacement of sectarianism would be a better system and order in working the larger and older communities of this country and other countries in the name of Jesus. Take any of the great cities of our country — unless it is Minneapolis, altogether the most wonderful city I was ever in — if there is in it a locality where you are certain to find gold nuggets if you excavate for a church, where you can surely rent your pews to great advantage and hire an able minister, if there is such a community as that, plenty of denominations are ready to rush right into it. In my own city we Baptists had a nice field all spied out. We were going to plant a church there as soon as we could pass around a paper and buy a piece of land. But the first thing we knew, our noble Congregationalist brethren had that same piece of land all bought. Well, God bless them; they will do a great deal of good there, and some time I am going out to preach for my brother who engineered the movement. But look at the darker places of our cities. There is not much rivalry there, is there, brethren? Ah, it is a shame upon us as Christian men that there are so many un-Christianized spots in all our great cities. There is effort enough perhaps,—though that is a doubtful proposition. There is at least a great deal of effort on the part of every true church of Christ to reach those places, but there is usually no system. The Baptists go tumbling in. They want to do some splendid work; and the Methodists, the Presbyterians, the Episcopalians, and the Congregationalists, they never take counsel of one another. One part of the field may be overworked, another part entirely deserted and not cultivated at all. Alas! alas! these desert districts are more common than the others.

Thirdly, and perhaps most important of all. If we could be genuine, simon-pure denominations, lay aside all our sectarian spirit; I mean if we could get all our friends at home to do it,—for I take it for granted that all of us in this Christian Endeavor Convention have already done it,—then we should have a power in working new fields such as has never been seen in this country or in the newer parts of any other since our Lord hung upon His cross. One of the saddest spectacles in the world you may see at present in almost any of the smaller towns on the frontier. You find there, as has been stated recently in this city, innumerable little towns of 700 people, with seven or eight churches each, most of these bearing one or another of the various evangelical names. It results that no one of those churches is really able to support a minister; that ministers are underfed, their families insufficiently clothed, and that a considerable part of the sustenance they do get comes from the older parts of the country. Meeting-houses, if they have any, are out of repair. In such a place, often, not one of the denominations is able to own a house of worship having the slightest attractions for any who are not perfectly sanctified already. If there is, in the community, one of those numerous men, lacking faith, perhaps, yet with great respect for religion, who, under other circumstances, would have a pew in the house of God and send his children to the Sunday school, occasionally attending divine service himself, that man gives all those churches a very wide berth, with the consequence that he increases in his worldliness and his children grow up heathen. It seems to me entirely practicable, without the surrender by any one of an iota of important conviction, without going very far out of our way, to carry into effect some such plan as this. Let all the evangelical denominations, say in Minnesota, elect at some of their yearly meetings two men each, one a well-known and trusted layman, the other a well-known and trusted minister, and let the brethren thus elected constitute themselves into a Religious Outlook and Advance Committee for the entire State. Then let them look over the smaller communities where this anarchy which I have described is presented, and with reference to each, publish in the local newspapers some statement like this: "It is our conviction, after careful examination and prayer, that the religious needs of this town demand that all Christian people in it should, for the time being, with their presence and their substance aid the Methodists." In that town, the Methodists would be the rallying centre till their church got stung; in another it would be the Congregationalists, in another the Presbyterians, in another I should hope that possibly the Baptists might be found worthy. [*Laughter and applause.*] Depend upon it, the working of a committee constituted like that would not be unfair; provided they deserved it, all Christian denominations would come in for their share of growth and advancement. The most energetic would grow most, and all would grow ten times faster than they now do or can.

In every town, after a time, the newcomer would find some one church at least having more than a name to live, some decent establishment, able to support a minister, with a good meeting-house and a fair looking parsonage, whose minister would not be obliged to send East every year for barrels of clothing and supplies. God bless our ministers and home missionaries who have to resort to those means; but I say before God tonight that there ought to be fewer of them, and there would be if the people of God showed more sanctified common sense in executing the great commission. [*Loud applause.*]

Just one other thing. It has fallen to my lot within the last ten or fifteen years to engage to some extent in social study. The great social problems of our time are to be solved, I believe, by the operation of the Spirit of God on the consciences of men. It seems to me that the work of this organization, in various localities where it is established, might most profitably be turned to a goodly extent in the direction of social study, toward the examination of those great questions upon the right solution of which the welfare of humanity in the immediate future seems absolutely to depend. And if we are to study them in our religious character at all, how can our studies be better conducted than by the little fraternities and gatherings of Christian Endeavorers scattered up and down the land? We need awakening to certain new aspects of the religion that we love, and to certain new dangers which confront it. It is very well to come together in a meeting like this and consecrate ourselves subjectively, because there is no good religious work done which does not depend first of all upon correct inward motives. We need the consecration we get here, and we need to hold our consecration meetings at home. But, my brethren, I do say and I do believe — and you will find it borne out by the word of God — that the continual stirring up of our religious feelings *without some corresponding activity* is not a religious exercise, and may, after a little time, lead to results positively perverse. We need to look sharply at all these facts, in our religious and social life. "New occasions," a poet has told us —

— "teach new duties: time makes ancient good uncouth;
We must upward still, and onward, who would keep abreast of Truth;
Lo, before us gleam her camp-fires! We ourselves must pilgrims be,
Launch our Mayflower, and steer boldly through the desperate winter sea,
Nor attempt the future's portal with the past's blood-rusted key."

[*Loud applause.*]

Following President Andrews's address, the popular hymn, "Throw out the life-line," was sung by Mr. Sankey as a solo, the audience joining enthusiastically in the chorus.

The report of the committee on resolutions was then presented through Rev. Howard B. Grose, of Boston.

Mr. Grose: We none of us need to be told that President Andrews is a bold man, after hearing him pay that splendid compliment to Minneapolis and stop there, without going on even so much as to make scriptural allusion to St. Paul. [*Laughter.*] I will give you a perfectly safe piece of advice. While we are gathered here we should follow the example of Abraham Lincoln. When he was President, two hat-makers of Philadelphia each tried to make the very finest silk hat that could be produced, and sent it to the President. It so happened that both of these hat-makers called upon him afterwards at the same time, and for a moment he was a little nonplussed as to what to say. But with his quick wit he turned to them and said, "Gentlemen, your hats do mutually surpass each other." [*Laughter.*] So we can say of these two cities with perfect safety: they do mutually surpass each other. [*Applause.*] Your Committee on Resolutions respectfully present the following report:—

RESOLUTIONS.

The Tenth International Convention of this Society, held in the beautiful city of Minneapolis, eclipses all previous gatherings of the hosts of Christian Endeavor.

Resolved, that the thanks of this Convention are cordially given to the Christian Endeavor Unions of the Twin Cities, and to the admirable and tireless Committee of '91, whose wisdom, foresight, kindness, and ability have contributed so largely to make this the grandest and most successful Christian assembly ever held on this continent.

Resolved, that our deep gratitude is expressed to the pastors and people of the Twin Cities who have so cordially co-operated with the indefatigable Committee; and that we thank them especially for providing a Convention Hall so perfect in its acoustic properties that 11,000 delegates could listen with delighted interest to the inspiring and masterly addresses with which we have been favored.

Resolved, that we express our gratitude to hotels for favors given, to railroads for transportation, and to the newspapers that have furnished so careful, excellent, and friendly reports of the Convention.

Resolved, that our thanks are heartily given to the grand chorus, to Mr. L. F. Lindsay, their inspiring director, and to his able assistants; and also to Mr. Ira D. Sankey, whose consecrated voice has continued for us the blessed ministry which has made him the leader of Christian song the wide world over.

Resolved, that we express again our grateful appreciation of the services of our Treasurer, Mr. William Shaw, and of the tireless and efficient labors of our Secretary, Mr. J. W. Baer, whose annual report thrilled our hearts; and that we affectionately repeat our salutations to our ever-honored President, whose masterly address on "Fidelity and Fellowship" sets forth the convictions to which we now publicly and emphatically express our renewed allegiance and devotion.

This Convention disclaims all authority over the local societies. The sole authority, under Christ, to which any Christian Endeavor society should look is the church of which it is a part. The great objects of this Convention are inspiration and fellowship. Yet such a great and representative gathering may well give voice to the accepted principles of the Christian Endeavor movement, inasmuch as one of these principles is unswerving loyalty to the church of God.

Resolved, that we recommend that all our societies adopt the so-called "revised pledge," which contains the clause: "I will make it the rule of my life . . . . . to support my own church in every way, especially by attending all her regular Sunday and mid-week services, unless prevented by some reason which I can conscientiously give to my Saviour;" and secondly, that every effort be made by our lookout committees to promote the fidelity of the members to this as well as to the other requirements of the pledge. To emphasize this underlying principle, we also recommend that each society submit important measures and proposed lists of officers to the pastor and the official members of the church for their approval.

Resolved, that, as at our Convention last year and always, we now again declare the pledge essential to a society of Christian Endeavor; and that those who in any way weaken or tamper with the principle of obligation as embodied in the covenant idea of the pledge are destroying the very foundations on which the Society rests, and cannot be recognized as true societies of Christian Endeavor.

Resolved, that, as it has been against the policy of Christian Endeavor to employ paid State secretaries or other State or local officers, we deem it unwise to depart from that policy, and would consider it equally unwise for societies to unite in employing a State evangelist or other salaried agent, on the ground that this would not be consistent with the principle that each local society exists solely in and for its own church.

Resolved, that, as from the beginning, we stand upon an evangelical basis (meaning by "evangelical," personal faith in the divine-human person and atoning work of our Lord and Saviour, Jesus Christ, as the only and sufficient source of salvation); and we recommend that, as in the United Society, only societies connected with evangelical churches be enrolled on the list of State and local unions.

Resolved, that we recognize with gratitude that the international features of Christian Endeavor are becoming more and more apparent, and that we send our fraternal salutations to Christian Endeavor societies in Great Britain, Australia, France, India, Africa, and throughout the world.

Resolved, that we welcome to the fellowship of our Conventions and unions all denominational societies which, as a guarantee of the adoption of the Christian Endeavor pledge and working methods, adopt our name in connection with any denominational name; that we heartily approve of the earnest setting forth, in the President's annual address, of the great value and inspiration of interdenominational fellowship, which not only adds joy and strength for service, but enables us to present to the world a united Christian front and a practical illustration of the Saviour's prayer, "that they all may be one."

Resolved, that we regard with great interest and hearty approval the proposition now before the Evangelical Alliance of the United States to invite the evangelical churches of America to erect on the grounds of the Columbian Exposition a Christian Temple, which shall house and shelter our Bible, Tract, Missionary, Sunday-school, Young People's and other societies, furnishing ample room for reception parlors, offices for the display of all forms of Christian literature,—such a temple to be the meeting-place of representatives of Protestant Christendom.

Resolved, that as patriotic young people, we are intensely interested in the celebration of the Columbian Exposition, and we especially rejoice that the intellectual and moral aspects and achievements of civilization are to be brought out by a series of World's Congresses on religion, education, and temperance.

Resolved, that we, the representatives of one million and eight thousand members of the Young People's Society of Christian Endeavor of this continent, in convention assembled, do reaffirm our allegiance to the sacred observance of the Sabbath Day, and hereby express our condemnation of, and strong opposition to, the opening of the Columbian Exposition on that day.

Resolved, that we urge active effort on the part of individual members' societies, local and State organizations, to prevent such opening; and to that end that all State and local gatherings appoint committees to have this special work in charge.

Since the liquor traffic is the implacable enemy of righteousness and purity, of Christ and His church,

Resolved, that we condemn intemperance in every form; that we stand for total abstinence, for the suppression of the saloon, and for the annihilation of the power of the whiskey ring in the politics of this nation.

Recognizing with devout gratitude that one blessed outcome of Christian Endeavor has been an increased love for and study of the Word of God,

Resolved, that we commend to all the societies the systematic study of the Bible according to the plan of Inductive Studies already familiar, and that we believe there is a great advantage in having these studies uniform, as are the prayer-meeting topics.

Mr. Grose: The Board of Trustees have also prepared the following Platform of Principles.

PLATFORM OF PRINCIPLES.

We reaffirm that these are the principles of the Y. P. S. C. E.:—

First and foremost, Personal devotion to our divine Lord and Saviour, Jesus Christ.

Second, Utmost loyalty to their respective denominations on the part of all Christian Endeavor societies.

Third, Steadiest personal love and service for the local church in which a society of Christian Endeavor exists. The church for each local society is the local church with which it is connected.

Fourth, Interdenominational spiritual fellowship among evangelical denominations, so setting forth their spiritual unity in Jesus Christ.

Fifth, Inasmuch as the name Christian Endeavor, by a marvellous and triumphant trial and history of ten years, has come to mean the definite pledge for the weekly prayer meeting, the monthly consecration service, and the work of the lookout committee, we earnestly urge that, in all Christian fairness, societies which adopt substantially these methods adopt also the name, Christian Endeavor, and that this name be not applied to other methods of work. We believe that Christian Endeavor has earned the exclusive right to its own name and to its own principles and methods.

Sixth, Christian Endeavor interposes no barriers to the denominational control of the young people, and rejoices when denominations suggest special lines of scriptural study, of denominational indoctrination, of denominational missionary activity, local, home and foreign.

Seventh, Christian Endeavor only desires that its fidelity to Christ and the local church, and its opportunity for delightful spiritual fellowship, be recognized and preserved.

The question on the adoption of the resolutions and platform of principles was unanimously carried, *viva voce*.

Dr. Hoyt: Christian Endeavor is a great army with banners, and there is now to be a presentation of banners nobly won. Professor W. W. Andrews, of Mt. Allison University, Sackville, New Brunswick, will make the presentation.

Prof. Andrews: A year ago I had the pleasure of taking part with Dr. Clark in a ceremony which has been known as "the marriage of the flags"—those which now repose so peacefully together at my feet. I have been called upon by the Board of Trustees to take part in a service which I regard as giving to me a higher honor. These flags tell the story of bloodshed, of war, of harrowing history—both of them. The banners which I am to present tonight to those who have won them by hard and earnest endeavor are associated with no story of cruelty, but they celebrate victories gained by regiments in this our great army who are under the command of the Prince of Peace. The banner which I now hold in my hand has been won by the State making the greatest proportionate increase during the past year,—Oklahoma. [*Loud applause.*]

This banner, I believe, contains badges which have been worn at every one of all the Conventions yet held in the history of this movement, the word "almost" has come to have a very ominous meaning to me as a Canadian [*laughter*], for let me tell you, I am a British Canadian, with the blood of Charles the First and the blood of that first American, Oliver Cromwell, also, in my veins, and sometimes the two strains of blood still get into trouble. We "almost" won next year's Convention—almost but lost. [*Laughter.*] We "almost" won this banner; for, following close upon the heels of Oklahoma was that great Switzerland and Italy combined of America, the land of gold and of grain, British Columbia,—almost but lost. [*Renewed laughter.*] We have heard the story of Oklahoma, how the people encamped upon her borders until Old Time rang out the signal of the wonderful movement, and then there was a stampede such as never was seen in the history of the world before,—the liveliest squatting of the century. But there has come another set of squatters, the host of Christian Endeavor societies now to be found in that Territory. I believe Oklahoma almost starved the first squatters; God give her grace to teach her young Christian Endeavor societies to keep the standard of obligation and faithfulness to the cast-iron pledge so strong and high that they will know how to take care of themselves. To Oklahoma let me say: All the Christian Endeavorers of this great American Union, from Hell Gate, where the Convention meets next year [*great laughter and applause*], to the Golden Gate, from Mexico to Manitoba, rejoice with you. We salute you; we give you good cheer. And Canada, which we Canadians think — and your great statesmen who have studied our institutions will bear out the statement — is the freest nation in the world [*applause from Canada*], Canada, the youngest of the self-governing federations of the world, Canada, the burliest of that grand brotherhood of colonies, to which we are proud to belong, forming the English empire, — Oklahoma, Canada salutes you, Canada rejoices in your victory. [*Applause.*] Now I shall call upon Miss Susie Griffith to receive for her State this banner. [*Loud and prolonged applause, with the Chautauqua salute, as Miss Griffith came to the front of the platform.*] Little Oklahoma, wonderful Oklahoma, [*tenderly*] beautiful Oklahoma [*great laughter and applause*], take this banner and keep it as long as you can. [*Loud applause as Miss Griffith gracefully received the banner and resumed her seat.*]

I am now to present this banner to the State which during the past year has made the greatest increase absolutely. This goes to the State of coal and iron, Pennsylvania; and here we have [*as Rev. George B. Stewart of Harrisburg, Penn., came forward*], the representative of that great State — six feet of magnificent American citizenship [*laughter*], who for his State will receive this banner. One thing William Penn was remarkable for, he knew how to get there. [*Applause.*] And now these Christian Endeavorers in this past year have proven themselves worthy sons of William Penn. God bless them in their great work. We give them this banner, that to the City of Brotherly Love, to Allegheny, to Harrisburg, to Pittsburg, they may take it and carry with them the honor which, in the name of the Christian Endeavor societies whose delegates are here assembled, it confers, feeling that in this they have won a success which may perhaps be hard to repeat, but which with anxious eyes they hope they may repeat, meanwhile ourselves making it for them as hard as possible. Pennsylvania will receive this banner. [*Loud applause.*]

REV. MR. STEWART: Mr. Speaker, "Beautiful Oklahoma" has obeyed the Scripture injunction to "let the women keep silence in the churches" [*laughter*]; but being neither beautiful nor little nor a woman, I suppose it is my privilege to speak for my compatriots standing there in the corner of the gallery, of whom I am justly proud and for whom I am glad to stand as a representative. I receive this banner, sir, of you because of its intrinsic worth and also because of what it represents. It represents to us the great ideas of our Christian Endeavor movement. First, Christian fellowship. How many societies are here represented on this banner, how many unions, how many States, all gathered together in beautiful harmony of color and beautiful harmony of purpose indicated by the words that are printed thereon! Fellowship in Christian work, fellowship in Christian discipleship is represented by this banner which you now give to us. It represents also to me — and I know it does to you — something quite as valuable as that and quite as dear; I mean the value of the individual. The separate badges on this banner are representative of individual societies; and individual societies, if they are Christian Endeavor in principle, emphasize the importance of the individual member in the society. One great aim and purpose of Christian Endeavor is to bring out the obscure and latent talent in the society. So that on this banner of badges there is brought before us the importance of the small society and of the large, of the great local union and of the small, and also the value of the individual member in the society. Opposite me, sir, is a banner [*the American flag*], and you will understand me and those whom you represent, as well as all patriots, when I say this, to me, is the most beautiful banner that floats in the breezes of God. I love it as I love my home. It represents to us great ideas, one of which this banner also represents — "E pluribus unum" [*loud applause*], "One out of many," for we are one, as we have heard over and over again in this

Christian Convention. You have been pleased, sir, to refer to Pennsylvania. Allow me to say that this banner represents growth for which I am grateful. Our rivers in Pennsylvania, as you probably know, are cut through the mountains. They do not run parallel with the valleys as in many other parts of the country. Christian Endeavor has cut down through the mountains in Pennsylvania, has broken down barriers, has removed obstacles between different denominations and between different sections of our glorious State; and now we are one, and we are glad to know that we are growing bigger,—we are already larger than six-foot-two. We have gained six hundred societies, I believe, in the past year and I hope it will be six hundred more next year. Then, sir, speaking for the union which I have the honor to represent, speaking for the band of 250 that came with us all along through Canada—to which we hope to go in a couple of years [*applause*]—speaking also for the 1,400 societies in Pennsylvania, speaking for the 70,000 Christian Endeavorers in Pennsylvania, I thank you for this trophy and hope that it may long wave over the land of coal and iron and oil and Christian Endeavor. [*Loud applause.*]

At this point the Pennsylvania delegation rose and sang together a new song, "The very same Jesus," which was received with much applause.

Dr. Hoyt: I am sure we all congratulate both Oklahoma and Pennsylvania; but it is to be understood that neither for Oklahoma nor for Pennsylvania are these banners to be permanent possessions unless they keep on doing, as they say in the Southern country, "right smart." [*Applause.*] Next year these banners will be given, one, to that State or Territory or Province which shall make the greatest absolute progress, and the other to that making the greatest relative progress.

Following the presentation ceremony, Mr. Shaw read a number of announcements and exhibited the first-fruits of Mr. Fulton's missionary appeal, $12.00 in cash collected on one of the trains returning from Minnetonka in the afternoon. "Blest be the tie" was the hymn sung in closing and Rev. W. P. McKee, of Minneapolis, pronounced the benediction.

SUNDAY FORENOON.

President Clark called the Convention to order at 8.35 o'clock.

The Scriptures were read by Mr. W. H. Pennell, of Portland, Me., the first signer of the Christian Endeavor Constitution, and Rev. C. A. Reese, of Minneapolis, led in prayer, by special request giving thanks for the prospect of a bountiful harvest, the audience joining in the Lord's Prayer at the close. The familiar hymn, "Nearer, my God, to thee," was then sung.

President Clark: It is in accordance with the fundamental principles of our Society that we love and reverence the church of God and make everything bend to the regular church services. On that account we have come together an hour earlier than we otherwise should, at a very inconvenient time of the day for our morning session, in order that this Convention need not interfere with the church services. Moreover, we desire that the Spirit of God should be poured out on all religious assemblies today in the cities of St. Paul and Minneapolis. We will be led in a brief prayer service by Rev. B. B. Tyler, of New York, remembering especially the churches, the pastors, and all who attend the churches in these two cities today.

Mr. Tyler: Let us never forget that it is "not by might nor by power," but by the Spirit of the living God that victories in the conflict in which we are engaged are to be won. When at last the battles shall have been fought and the final victory shall have been gained, we will all be constrained in humility and gratitude to say, Not unto us, not unto us, but unto thy great name, O God, be all the glory. It is as true today as it has ever been that Paul may plant and that Apollos may water, but God and He alone can give the increase. The church of Christ was formed in a prayer meeting. Open the New Testament at the first chapter of Acts and read the story of our Lord's ascension. Read how that, as His sacred form disappeared from the midst of His disciples and they stood gazing after Him as a cloud of glory enveloped Him, removing Him from their mortal vision, white-robed visitants from the other world arrested their attention by saying, "Ye men of Galilee, why stand ye gazing up into heaven? This same Jesus which is taken up from you into heaven shall so come in like manner as ye have seen Him go into heaven." I wonder if, when the Lord comes a second time, not as a sin-offering but unto the salvation of His people, it will not be on His holy day. And now these disciples turned from the mount of ascension and entering the city of Jerusalem they went into an upper room where they were all together,— Peter and John and James and Andrew and Philip and Thomas and Bartholemew and Matthew and James the son of Alphæus and Simon the Zealot and Judas the son of James. Mark now what they did during the interval between the ascension of our Lord and the outpouring of His Holy Spirit: "These all, with one accord, continued steadfastly in prayer,"— and these alone? No,— "with the women and Mary the mother of Jesus and with his brethren." Let us in like manner, that is, with one accord, wait before God this morning in prayer and let us expect a blessing. Let us ask, believing that God will hear and that He will answer and that He will abundantly bless the pastors of these Twin Cities and their congregations, the visiting messengers of the cross and the messages which they shall deliver, the Sunday-school superintendents and their teachers and pupils, and the Young People's Societies of Christian Endeavor. We wait to ask a blessing on these services this morning. Let our minds be united in this. Let us agree in this one thing, asking God for this one blessing and expect it.

A few moments were spent in silent prayer, after which was sung the hymn, "Jesus, lover of my soul." Dr. Clark then introduced President William R. Harper, of the University of Chicago.

Dr. Harper had had scattered through the audience little leaflets, giving a plan of systematic Bible study for Christian Endeavor societies and containing also the syllabus of his address which was entitled, "Nineveh's Fall: a Book Study of the Prophecy of Nahum, with Some Applications."

ADDRESS OF PRES. WM. R. HARPER.

The Old Testament prophet, you believe and I believe, was divinely sent to do for the chosen nation and for all time a special work. We believe that in some way or other this Old Testament prophet acted in his work and in his words under the influence of a higher power. We believe also that the Old Testament prophet, whoever he was, whether Isaiah or Jeremiah, was the preacher of his times. He did for his day and generation what our New Testament ministers are doing for our day and generation. The prophet stood, surrounded by men who were committing sin, and rebuked them for their sin. He stood in the midst of political combinations and directed the king how to act. The prophet was thus not only the preacher of his times, he was the orator of his times. Will you picture to yourself this man, Isaiah or Jeremiah or Nahum, standing before great audiences of men, rebuking them for their sins or comforting them in their distress, telling them of the calamity which is so soon to overtake them because of their iniquity, or promising to them a glorious future if only they will obey God and do His will?

But every Old Testament prophet had a particular work. Do you remember the story of Joel? A great invasion of locusts has come, and in addition there is the severe affliction of drought; and between the locusts and the drought it would seem that man and beast would perish from the face of the earth. Joel steps forward and calls the people to repent, to fast, to pray to God. They repent, they fast and they pray, and the prayer is answered; and there come the promises: "O men of Israel, these locusts shall be destroyed. O men of Israel, rain shall be poured out and the drought shall be removed." Then the prophet, rising from the temporal promises—you remember the story—tells them of higher promises: "Afterwards I will pour out my Spirit upon all flesh," and you know the rest of it. A little later he tells them how their enemies—God's enemies, all who have been in hostility to God—shall be utterly destroyed. This was Joel's message; and if there were time, we might almost in a word get at the particular message which each prophet brought. Nowhere for example, in Scripture, in Old Testament or in New, is the love of God more vividly or more forcibly described than in the much-neglected book of Hosea. Each prophet had his particular message and—one point more—the message in every case was for the times of the prophet first of all. Whatever may have been the deeper meaning, whatever may have been the relation of these words to future times, they had a meaning then and there—a meaning for the people who first heard them; and it is our business—you will agree with me—to find first that meaning, and all other meanings will follow closely.

If these things are true in the study of Nahum, we recognize him as divinely sent to utter words which we are to study. We understand that he was a preacher to the people who heard him; that he had a purpose in his words, a particular message, and that that message was closely connected with those times in which he lived. If this is true, we must know something of the times.

It was not in the reign of Hezekiah—the early portion of that reign, as some tell us—that Nahum spoke (712-700); nor was it in the latter part of Hezekiah's reign (701-697), as others tell us, that he spoke. It was rather in the reign of that most wicked of all kings, Manasseh, in whose reign the very streets of Jerusalem ran with the blood of those who were persecuted. It was at this time that our prophet stands before an assembled multitude and utters these words. He preaches concerning Assyria, and it is well for us to remember that for two centuries Assyria had been in contact with Israel. Two hundred years before this time, Shalmaneser II. was in conflict with Ahab and Jehu. A little later, Tiglath-pileser conquers Northern Israel and Syria. Still a little later,—you remember the sad story,—Shalmaneser laid siege to the city of Samaria, and after three years of siege, Sargon, the Assyrian king, captured the city, and the northern nation ceased to exist. A little later, Sennacherib makes an invasion into Judah and carries off 200,000 of the people. You remember the outcome of his invasion. Still later, Esar-haddon makes an invasion, and now we are in the reign of the last great king of Assyria,—the king who left us more monuments than any other of the Assyrian kings,—Asshur-bani-pal. It is in this last reign, when Assyria had reached the height of her glory and before she is about to fall, that Nahum preaches.

Did our prophet live in Judah or in Assyria? Because of the presence of some Assyrian words in the book, because we have so vivid a description of Nineveh that it would seem as if it were written by an eye-witness, because it has to do almost solely with Nineveh, some tell us that the prophet Nahum lived and preached in Nineveh. But, on the other hand, the imagery of our book is clearly that of Palestine. Moreover, the purpose of the prophet, in accordance with the purpose of all the prophets, was to assure and comfort Judah; and we may well believe that Nahum preached in Jerusalem about Nineveh in the distance.

If there were time, we might take up a minute study of the style of the book, but I may only say a word. It is exhaustive; it is vivid, as I am sure every reader of the book will testify, and it is most forcible. "There is some diminution of inward power and wealth of thought as compared with the prince of prophets, Isaiah; still there are many descriptions which are extremely vivid and truly poetic, and the art used in presenting the material is most excellent."

Will you read with me the book of Nahum? I will read, not a translation, but a free paraphrase. It is the burden of Nineveh, the sentence of the great city that has for centuries ruled the world. The prophet has in mind only Nineveh and her destruction; but with singular appropriateness, he opens with a recognition of the supreme majesty and power of the great Jehovah who rules the world. (Verse 2). "Jehovah is jealous, a jealous and avenging God,—yes, avenging and full of wrath, furious, taking vengeance on His adversaries, keeping alive His wrath to His enemies; One who may be provoked, One who kindles into anger, and who keeps that anger stirred up until vengeance is obtained." The great thought, you will see, is that of vengeance. Three times the word is repeated. And such a thought is not strange if we take into consideration the history of Israel and Assyria, and if we remember for a moment how cruel and pitiless Assyria has been toward Judah for the last two centuries. "Jehovah," the prophet tells the people who listen to his words, "Jehovah will surely inflict vengeance upon all His enemies. Jehovah is slow to anger. So says the Lord; so speaks history; so"—will you imagine the prophet addressing this great crowd of people who listen to his words?—"so we Israelites have felt. But He has been waiting, waiting. Two centuries have passed, and all this time Assyria has been inflicting injury upon Israel. Where, during these centuries, has Jehovah been? Waiting. And why has He been waiting? Not because He is weak, for He is great in power; not because He purposes to remit punishment, for He never permits wickedness to go unpunished. Calmly looking on, He permits the vast restraining power of His wrath to be accomplished until the measure is filled up and runs over."

Then (v. 3) we have a description of this mighty power of God and of the appearance of Jehovah in judgment, with all nature in commotion. "Jehovah is in the whirlwind and the storm. He moves with tempest speed and tempest power. Clouds are the dust of His feet. Although present and in power He is concealed." Then comes the representation of the scorching heat. First, the power of Jehovah is likened to the tempest, then to the scorching heat, and still again (v. 5) to the earthquake and violent rain. "The mountains quake at Him and the hills melt; the earth is upheaved at His presence—yea, the world and all that dwell therein." The tempest, the scorching heat, the earthquake, and still one more mighty figure—fiery eruption. "Who can stand before His indignation? Who can abide in the presence of His anger? His power is poured out like fire, and the rocks are rent asunder before Him."

Keep in mind the situation. Do not forget that the prophet is talking to a great crowd of people, a people who have been ground down for two centuries under the hand of this pitiless conqueror. "This God who comes as a tempest, a scorching heat, an earthquake and fiery eruption to His enemies, this God is a stronghold in the day of trouble for those who trust Him. O Judah, you need not fear if your confidence is placed on Him. But He will sweep Nineveh with an overwhelming flood and its place shall be utterly destroyed. His enemies He will chase into the darkness of hell."

Then again the prophet turns to Nineveh: "O Nineveh, what is it that you purpose against Jehovah? He will completely destroy you. No second blow on Nineveh will be needed. You may stand, O Nineveh, in phalanx as close and terrible as netted thorns. You may drink, and in your intoxication feel that no power can harm you; but Jehovah's wrath will consume you as dry stubble. Your kings have gone forth to war devising evil against Jehovah and His people. For many years you have counselled wickedness; you have been hostile. But now hear, Assyria, the message which Jehovah has for you. However many thine arms, however strong thy forces, thou shalt be cut down and perish. As for Judah, it is true that I have chastised her; but I will allow her to suffer no more from you. For, Judah, I, Jehovah, will break the Assyrian yoke from off thee; I will burst asunder his bonds. But for you, Assyria, there shall be no posterity to bear thy name. From thy temples I will destroy all idols; I will defile the site of thy ruined temples with the bones of the dead; for these temples shall be thy grave; thou art vile."

In the second chapter, with the last verse of the first, we have a description of the fall of Nineveh. You will remember that the prophet is speaking almost sixty years before the events took place. Let us not forget that we are not reading history; we are reading and studying prophecy, prediction. The prophet sees, in vision, the siege and the swift messengers coming west from the city to announce the news that the city has fallen.

"See, O Judah, see! There come over the mountains the feet of the messenger of glad tidings. Hear what the messenger says. Peace, peace, for the great oppressor, the cruel tyrant, is fallen. Keep thy feast of thanksgiving, O Judah, pay now thy vows, for the man of wickedness shall never again invade thee; Assyria is utterly cut off."

Again the scene changes. The prophet in his vision is in front of Nineveh. He addresses the city with words of irony: "O Nineveh, the hammerer, the Median king, is coming up against thee." Then comes an exhortation: "Man thy walls; guard the way; make thy loins strong; yes, fortify thyself mightily. And well you may, for it is none other than Jehovah who sends this host, and it is His purpose to restore to Israel her glory of which you, Nineveh, have robbed her, tearing off her boughs and destroying her branches."

Still again the scene changes. The prophet is on the outside of the walls. He sees the Median army preparing for battles: "The Median soldiers have shields painted red, the war color. The valiant men are clothed in scarlet." (Assyria's color was blue.) "The chariots flash like fire; the spears and spear-shafts quiver." He then reverts to the situation inside the city: "The chariots are rushing madly through the streets; they rattle wildly; they shine like fire; they flash to this part and to that like the lightning. The king inside the city is trusting to his warriors; but they stumble as they rush on, dazed as if waked from sleep. They hasten to the walls, but it is too late. The testudo has already been set against them and (v. 6) it is all over, the city is taken. The city gates, defended by broad canals from the Tigris, are pressed open and the palace sinks into ruins. The city is uncovered, she is carried away. Her handmaids beat upon their breasts and mourn with the sad voice of doves. The streams, hitherto flowing in their channels, symbols of her prosperity, now spread like a great sea. What has been her pride now becomes her destruction. Her leaders cry to the fleeing warriors, Stand, make a stand; but no one looks back."

The prophet addresses the Median soldiers as they rush to the spoiling of the city: "Take the spoil of silver, O Media, the spoil of gold; for there is no end of treasure and costly booty." And then he still further describes the vision which has been given him of Jehovah: "All in Nineveh is desolation, emptiness, ruin. The heart melts; the knees smite together; the loins tremble; the faces all grow pale. Where now is the den of lions and the feeding-place of young lions? Where is the place in which the lions and their whelps had their quarters, afraid of nothing? The lion that tore in pieces for his whelps and strangled for his lionesses and filled his cave with prey and his lairs with ravin,—where is he, O Assyria? I, Jehovah of hosts, am against thee." This explains the situation. "I will burn thy chariots in smoke; thy warriors shall be devoured with the sword. The earth henceforth shall be free from thy violence; your threatening messenger shall no more be heard."

Chapter 3. The prophet might well have stopped here, but he does not feel satisfied; his emotion will not let him close. Besides, he has not yet indicated as clearly as he desires the cause of it all, and so he resumes the description of this great catastrophe. "Woe to the city of blood, all full of lies and violence, never ceasing in its works of plunder. Hark! the cracking of whips! Hark! the rattling of wheels, the rearing of horses, the bounding of chariots, the charging of cavalry, the flashing of swords, the glittering of spears, a multitude of slain and a great heap of carcases; and there is no end of the corpses, and they stumble over the corpses. And why, why has the avenging hand of Jehovah struck down this city and all that were in it? Because of the multitude of the whoredoms of the well-favored harlot, the mistress of witchcrafts, that selleth nations even with her whoredoms and families through her witchcrafts. Why must Nineveh die and perish from upon the face of the earth? Because of her deceitful friendships, because of her crafty politics and her seducing idolatry. O Assyria, I, Jehovah of hosts, am against thee. I will lift thy skirts over thy head and I will show the nations thy nakedness and shame. I will cast abominable filth upon thee and make thee vile,—yes, I will make thee a laughing-stock, and all who look upon thee will flee from thee and say, Nineveh is laid waste. No one will bemoan you; no comforters will be found for you. Ah, Assyria, you may laugh at these words; you may think yourself strong, able to resist every attack; but do not quiet yourself with any such false confidence. Art thou better than Thebes, the great city of the solar god, better than Thebes, which was enthroned on both sides of the Nile and girdled by waters, whose rampart was the Nile, whose wall was the sea? Art thou, O Assyria, better than Thebes, whose hosts were valiant Thebans and Egyptians, whose allies were Arabs and Libyans, who, in spite of all this, has just been carried into exile and slavery, her little children dashed in pieces against the walls, her nobles sold by lot for slaves and her great men bound in chains? Art thou better than was this Thebes that today lies in ruins? Thou, too, O Assyria, shalt drink Jehovah's cup of punishment. It shall be dark, and thou shalt search for a place of protection against the enemy. Thy fortresses shall be like fig-trees with first ripe figs that need only to be shaken to fall into the hands of the enemy. Thy men in that day, O Nineveh, are nothing but women; thy gates shall be open to the enemy; fire shall devour thy bars. Use every precaution; strengthen every point; draw water and store it up in preparation for the siege; repair the fortresses; make bricks for the strongholds of thy walls and thy towers. Do all this: it will avail nothing. Fire will devour thee; sword will cut thee off. Become as many as the locusts, countless as grasshoppers; the sword will devour thee as the locust devours the leaves of the field. Thy merchants, more numerous than the stars of heaven, who have devoured the earth as do locusts, shall flee away, and thy warriors shall be like locusts, but in a different sense—locusts which lie on the hedges when it is cold, but when the sun rises they flee away and there is no sign where they have been. O king of Assyria, the shepherds of thine empire, thy princes, sleep; thy nobles slumber; thy people are scattered over the mountains and there is no one to gather them. Thy hurt is incurable; the stroke means death, and it is death mourned by none. Rather, all that hear of it shall clap their hands; for where is the nation that has not felt thy merciless power?"

Will you bring this book together very briefly and study the parts? We have had in the first part of it a representation of Jehovah as a jealous God, inflicting vengeance upon His enemies, but one who at the same time is a fortress for His people. We have had, in the second place, an announcement, over and over again, that while God would be a stronghold for Judah, He will utterly destroy Nineveh. Then came a description of the means by which Nineveh should be destroyed,—the manner and the cause of the destruction. And then the prophet has not said enough; he announces the absolute certainty of it all. Thebes could not be delivered from God, neither can Nineveh. Every effort will be in vain; no might shall save her; the doomed city shall perish. This was a sermon, or a series of sermons, delivered in public, before great crowds of people doubtless, at least fifty years, if not sixty or more, before Nineveh fell,—delivered when Nineveh seemingly was the mightiest city upon the face of the earth, delivered when there was no hope or chance from the human point of view that such a thing might happen. And perhaps that is the greatest thought of this book,—the fact that a prophet of God could and did see in the things about him that which told him that he received from God a message that this great empire was so soon to perish.

But that is not all of the book of Nahum. Will you consider the essential ideas? First, what is the conception of God which is presented in this book? The prophet represents Jehovah as a judge; he represents Him as jealous; he represents Him as a holy one, setting heaven and earth into commotion in order to fight against pride, despotism, violence, and cruelty. That is one side—Jehovah a God of justice, holy and therefore just. But there is another side He represents Jehovah as a holy one, employing His power and majesty to protect His own people whom He loves, to whom He has made promises, promises which shall be kept. Jehovah is holy and therefore He is a loving God. Both of these great sides of the character of God are presented in the conception which our prophet gives us. He tells us that Jehovah is slow to anger, patient, enduring, accepting insult upon insult, assault upon assault, waiting until the time becomes ripe,—waiting, not because He is weak, for He is great in power, able to manifest Himself in forms the most terrible; waiting. not because He will remit the punishment, for God never lets wickedness go unpunished; but calmly waiting until the period of vengeance shall have come,

Secondly, what do we learn in this book as to the purpose of the prophet? The thought has already been stated. Nahum did not stand in Assyria and preach to the Assyrians, hoping thereby to turn them from their evil ways, as did Jonah. Nahum stood in Jerusalem and preached to the inhabitants of Jerusalem concerning Nineveh. The words which he uttered probably were never heard by an inhabitant of Nineveh. They were not intended so to be heard. They were words of assurance, words of comfort, to the poor, downcast, disconsolate Hebrews who believed in God and yet feared that God had abandoned them; who could not understand why, with their faith in Jehovah, He should neglect them and allow this pitiless conqueror to crush them to the ground. This was the purpose primarily. But there was another purpose. The words were uttered not only for the people of his day, but for all time. The prophet tells us here the occasion of the downfall of every great empire that has lived and fallen. He gives us here the great principles of government. He tells us why it is that a nation that has reached the pitch of glory and power that Assyria had reached must perish; and what Nahum has said concerning Nineveh holds good of Babylon, of Rome, and of all the great empires that have lived and have ceased to be. The words contain principles that are eternal; they are not words simply for that time, though primarily for that time.

The third essential idea relates to the fulfilment of prophecy. Two or three hundred years before Nahum lived, Jonah, a prophet of Israel, stood in this same city of Nineveh and announced to them in specific terms that within forty days Nineveh would be destroyed. We remember the story, how Nineveh fasted and repented, and how the king and nobles and people of that great city put on sackcloth and ashes and turned to God. And we remember, also, how, when this had happened, God repented, Nineveh was spared, and Jonah was dissatisfied with the result. Jonah preached in Nineveh, and his sermon was successful. He preached, and, as a result of his preaching, Nineveh repented and was saved, and his prediction, though a most specific one, was not fulfilled. But the case is different with Nahum. He speaks in Jerusalem, and he speaks not to Nineveh but concerning Nineveh, and the result is different. For Nineveh has passed the point where repentance may be hoped for. Nineveh has passed beyond all bounds, and our prophet tells us that Nineveh shall fall, and Nineveh did fall. Jonah's prophecy was unfulfilled, Nahum's prophecy fulfilled to the letter.

Fourthly, is there in this book any of the Messianic element? What do you mean by the Messianic element? Do you mean a verse in Genesis or a passage in Exodus, or something in Deuteronomy or Isaiah,—passages here and there throughout the book, which refer directly to a great king, the Messiah, our Lord? If this is what you mean by the Messianic element, you will at once see that there is nothing of it in this book. But the Messianic element is something broader. The Messianic element is the whole Old Testament dispensation. For every event that occurred in the history of the chosen people, from the time they were chosen as a people, every word that was uttered by a sacred prophet or lawgiver,—all this looked forward and was preparatory to the coming of Jesus Christ; and in this broad sense the Messianic element underlies our book. For one of its great teachings, coming up again and again, is the justice of God: and another, side by side with it, is that wickedness cannot go unpunished. We have here this teaching illustrated as perhaps nowhere else in the Old Testament.

Fifthly, where does Nahum stand in history and prophecy? Think for a moment where we are, 660 years before Christ. Remember that up to this time the Hebrew nation has been in contact only with Semitic nations and with Egypt; the Hebrew nation has come in contact only with men of nations having the same blood in their veins. Up to this time the Hebrew nation and the Hebrew prophets have only dealt with men who were closely allied to them. But now that fact ceases, and with the fall of Nineveh a new empire comes forward, the Median empire, and Indo-European contact comes in. From this time forward Israel is to be brought into relations with a wider empire, with another family of the great families of the earth; and there comes, first, Media, then Persia, then Greece, then Rome—all nations of an entirely different family. And so Nahum occupies a central place in Israelitish history and Israelitish prophecy. He is the last of the old régime, and the first of the new régime.

What, then, have we done this morning in these thirty or forty minutes? Very briefly and very imperfectly we have tried to get the thought of an entire book. If we could have had a full hour we would have made the work much more perfect. Think it over once more: the character of God, a God of vengeance to those who are evil and a God of love to those who are His people; the destruction which is coming upon Nineveh because of her sins; the means, the manner, the occasion, and the certainty of it all. There you have the book of Nahum in a dozen words.

Is it wise, is it worth while, this study of a book as a book, without reference to the specific verses which it contains? Consider first, the possibility of book study. (1) It requires a comparatively short time. Such a book as Isaiah will take longer, but the minor prophets may be studied in this rapid way, in a half-hour or an hour. (2) It demands few helps. The fewer helps the better, for you must not allow yourself to be bewildered with details, with the comments of commentators. You must study the book itself, and the only help you need in such study, or nearly the only help, is a brief historical introduction and the help which God gives to all who seek Him in earnestness. (3) It consists mainly of an intelligent reading of the book. We have done nothing here this morning but read this book, and it is one of the hardest books to read. Joel is much easier. (4) Anybody, everybody, can do it. Not everybody can take a verse and do close, careful, critical work upon it. Only a few are given by God the opportunity and the possibility of doing this thing; but anybody, everybody, can study a book as a book. Think of the satisfaction there is in getting a view of a book as a book, and of getting one book and then another book and then another, until the whole sixty-six are ours. There is no reason under heaven why every one of us should not have in our possession a broad outline and a broad comprehension of every book in the Old Testament and the New. [*Applause.*]

Consider, further, the satisfaction in book study. (1) It emphasizes the historical element. Let me ask you a question. Why is it that most of you have never been interested in the Old Testament prophets? Why is it that you regard them as dry, dull reading, and never — or but seldom, if ever — read them? For this reason: because you are not acquainted with the historical element which lies back of each one. In order to study a book as a book, you must get at the historical element; and the moment you touch the historical element, the moment you come into contact with the times when these words were uttered, that moment the book becomes a thing of life and fire, and you become intensely interested in it. You must remember that these books are just as much the word of God as the books of the New Testament. (2) It furnishes something comprehensive and complete. (3) It is general rather than minute. (4) It is definite and tangible. (5) It is systematic and scientific. Some one will tell you that such rapid work is not thorough. He is right. Some one will tell you that such rapid reading is not scientific. He is wrong. It is scientific to get a knowledge of a thing as a whole, to get the broad outlines of it and then to take up the outlines one by one in the light of the whole. No other method is scientific.

Consider, thirdly, the importance of book study. (1) It is necessary to a right comprehension of any chapter or verse in the book. I say it and you cannot dispute it: no man can understand the meaning of a verse in a chapter who has not studied the chapter as a whole, and no man or woman can understand the meaning of a chapter who has not studied the book as a whole. (2) It is necessary to an appreciation of the work as a whole of a man or a period. Take Isaiah; you read half a dozen verses here and half a dozen verses there and half a dozen verses further on. Can you get any conception of the work that Isaiah did in that way — Isaiah, in his fifty or sixty years of ministry? How only can you come to a proper appreciation of Isaiah? Begin when he is a boy twenty years of age, when he stands before that Jewish audience in Jerusalem and tells them of his inaugural vision; then follow him up day after day, month after month, year after year, decade after decade, until you find him an old man with gray hair, standing before that same audience, or the descendants of that audience, and preaching with reference to the invasion of Sennacherib. In that way, by studying the book of Isaiah as a whole, you get a conception of Isaiah's work as a whole, and you are better able to appreciate any particular part of Isaiah's work which he did. (3) It is necessary to an understanding of the relation sustained by one writer or period to another. (4) It is necessary to an appreciation of the gradual growth of the divine revelation.

Finally, as to the method of book study, I refer you to the last page of the syllabus, which I will not take time to read. May I ask you, if it is possible for you to find the time — and oh, dear friends, if you cannot find time to study the Bible, what is it that you can find time for? — that you will take it up book by book, one after the other, with a definite plan, with a clear outline, and make your resolve before God and before man that this Bible, or as large a portion of it as possible, shall be yours — yours as a whole, yours for your own sake and yours for the sake of the people whom you are called to lead. [*Loud applause.*]

Dr. Clark: I wish every Christian Endeavor society might have a plan for the systematic study of the Bible along these lines. [*Applause.*] Let us have the best there is. Let us not take up a sectional plan of study since we can have something that is universal, something that is interdenominational; and here we have it in this leaflet which Professor Harper has prepared for us.

The morning session closed with singing the Doxology, and the benediction by Rev. J. B. Donaldson, D.D., of Minneapolis.

SUNDAY AFTERNOON.

The delightful weather and the absence of services in the city churches served to draw out an audience in the afternoon which more than comfortably filled the Convention hall. The exercises began with the usual song service, and soon after half-past two Rev. H. C. Farrar, D.D., of Albany, N. Y., who presided at this session, announced the hymn, "Nearer, my God, to thee," which was sung. The Scriptures were read and prayer offered by Rev. M. F. McKirahan, of Topeka, Kansas.

Dr. Farrar: Hardly a session of our Convention this year has been of intenser interest than that which gathers around the session of this afternoon. "To every man his work," is the text for the hour; and when we understand that here are speakers to address us on "The Young Man at Work," "The Young Woman at Work," "The Child at Work," and that greater question that confronts America today, the temperance question, it is evident that a mighty spiritual interest centres in this hour. I hope the prayers of every one will go up that God's blessing may crown the speakers with clearness of conception, steadiness of faith, and earnestness of utterance, that their faith may connect with our faith, and that we may catch an inspiration that shall help us in going out to work on these special lines of the topics suggested. We shall first hear, on the topic, "The Young Man at Work," from Mr. A. Alonzo Stagg, of Springfield, Mass., the well-known college athlete. Let us give him a cordial reception. [*Loud applause.*]

ADDRESS OF MR. A. ALONZO STAGG.

It is my privilege this afternoon to speak of the young man for service, or the young man at work. This is not the only situation in which the young man appears to advantage. He is interesting, for instance, most of us think, when at play. He has God-given tendencies towards play; they are natural, and therefore they are abilities to be respected and cultivated. The young man is full of animal spirits; he is surcharged with activities that must find vent. Some of us choose to let these activities, these energies, have vent in one way, some in another. Some of us like to let out our energy in mischief-making, others in boisterousness, others in sports, and still others in work. The idea of our American age is work for the young man. We see this in the rush and strife after wealth and business success. We see it in the rush and strife after professional and literary and political honors. We see it also when we look upon a young man endued with the idea of self-cultivation, of self-improvement. For instance, let a young man get into his head the idea that he wants to improve his body, and you will see him work day after day, with a persistence and with an ambition that will generally conquer. You will see him try to improve his body as a whole or in individual parts, in skill, in endurance, in symmetry. Or take a young man who is aiming to get an education, who wants to improve his mind, and you will see that young man working almost steadily from early morning until late at night, and he will work with all the spare time that he has to accomplish this end. This desire for an education, coupled with the willingness to work, is what brings so many young men to our colleges who are poor, who are willing to sacrifice their health and to endure privation and want for the sake of improving their minds and getting an education.

But we have come to a new age, an age when the young man is counted on as a factor in society and when he is reckoned as of immediate and practical value. The young man was not so reckoned formerly. Years ago, generations ago, he was looked upon merely for what he would be in the future, whether for usefulness or mischief it was not known. He was waited for; he was acted upon, or he was allowed to run loose. But times have changed, and changed for the better. The young man now has a place in society; he now has a place in organization, and the world is looking to him for better things. Behold the young man of this modern age, as he stands full of equipment for work; he stands unparalleled in strength, in ambition, in courage, in enthusiasm, and in good fellowship. I say in strength,—life's richest and fullest blood is coursing through his arteries and filling his whole being with rich and magnificent strength; his whole muscular system is quick and responsive; his mind is alert, anticipative, and original. In courage—he feels and knows the strength within him; John says, "I have written unto you, young men, because ye are strong;" to his expectant nature few things seem impossible. In ambition—the very air he breathes is filled with it; he feeds his quick imagination on the fruits of his observation, and these are moulded and fashioned into new and far-reaching ambition. In enthusiasm—he is thrilled by whatever touches his sensitive nature; he feels and feels deeply; he believes in his convictions with all his heart, and they take deep hold upon him. In good fellowship—he has learned this from boyhood up by daily companionship with his playmates, and his quick and sympathetic heart takes the whole world into his confidence. Could master-builder have finer material with which to work? Could magnificent structure have grander foundation on which to be built?

Such is the young man that comes forth to the West and puts forth his energies and builds up this magificent domain. And yet that same magnificent energy, that same fine equipment that the young man has for the work in this world, he has for the Christian work. If that equipment is valuable for work in this world, it is manifoldly more valuable for work along Christian lines, and the young man ought to shape his character for Christian service. He ought to cultivate the spirit of service. He may do that in one way by identifying himself with some Christian work that appeals to him. At least, he can do it by breathing forth the spirit of Christ as he goes about from day to day. He ought to discipline himself for service. Practise self-control, perseverance,—these all are necessary that a man may grow up a full-rounded worker for Christ.

Let me, for a moment, bring before you the way in which our blessed Master worked when he was upon earth. I have been reading lately and trying to find out just how the Master worked. I have found that He always did that which was at hand. No duty that stood beside Him passed neglected. He did not wait until He got to Jerusalem, nor did He go down into Egypt, before He began His work. He began it immediately after His baptism, and He began it there by the Jordan. And then the Master worked persistently; he worked incessantly; no time for rest for Him when there was a duty at hand. He did not, when He went away on a summer vacation, lay aside his work; but as He went around through those hills of Galilee, by those mountain streams He let fall from Him those acts of kindness and deeds of love that have been a blessing to the world. Then the Master worked with perfect humility; He gave God the glory. "I must work the works of Him that sent me," were His words, and day after day He did those works. It made no difference what sort of work it was, whether among the poor or among the rich, among the learned or among the ignorant; it was all the same to Him. And then our Master worked with prayer. Do you know the very first thing our Master did after he was baptized was to raise His eyes to heaven and His voice in prayer? "And praying, the heaven was opened, and the Holy Ghost descended in a bodily form, as a dove, upon Him." And later on, again and again, we see as we read that the Master was accustomed to go apart for prayer. How can we who expect to be Christian workers, who expect to follow in the Master's footsteps, — how can we work unless we seek our Father constantly in prayer and supplication? The Master prayed for the Holy Ghost again and again. The Scripture says that He went forth "in the Spirit." If the Lord Jesus needed to pray for the Holy Spirit, much more do we. How can we expect to do any Christian work satisfactorily or successfully if we do not pray for the Holy Spirit?

Christianity needs the young men. The church today is crying out that it cannot get hold of the young men, and the feeling is that the young men must go out after their mates and bring them in, and it is our God-given right so to do. In 1861 the young men of the South and the North rushed forth to the battle-front. They were the ones on whom the nation depended. So it is the young men of today on whom Christ is depending for His work. Did not God have the Lord Jesus wait until He was a young man before He sent Him forth to tell of the glad tidings? Did not the Lord Jesus Himself, when He was looking about for His apostles, for men who would stand by Him and work for Him—did He not pick out young men for His service? Was it not a young man, Paul, on whom the charge was laid to go and preach to the Gentiles and spread abroad the Christian church throughout the then known world? It was likewise a young man, Luther, who established Protestantism in this world. It was also a young man, Wesley, who thrilled all England by the power of the Holy Spirit working in him. It was also a young man, George Williams, who established the Young Men's Christian Association, which has now encircled the earth with its organizations and its members. It was also a young man, Francis E. Clark, who set on foot this magnificent movement, which is now stirring up the church and establishing the church for work in the future. [*Applause.*]

There is yet work for young men; it is not all done. I see some before me who are called to be apostles, who are called to be Luthers, who are called to be Wesleys, who are called to be Williamses, who are called to be Clarks. I hear the voice of the Lord calling you. Why do you wait? The Master says, "Follow me. I have work for you to do, for the harvest truly is plenteous and the laborers are few." [*Loud applause.*]

At the close of Mr. Stagg's address the audience joined in singing the hymn, "Bringing in the sheaves." Mr. Sankey followed with a solo, "We shall meet beyond the river," giving the refrain, "By and by," to different sections of the congregation. At the conclusion of the hymn, Mr. Sankey led in a brief prayer.

Dr. Farrar: We have heard of "The Young Man at Work." I am glad that God is calling the young man's sister to work, equally vigorously with himself. I have the pleasure of introducing to you Miss Margaret W. Leitch, of Ceylon, India, who will speak to us of "The Young Woman at Work," referring especially to the opportunity and the form of work in foreign fields. [*Loud applause.*]

ADDRESS OF MISS MARGARET W. LEITCH.

I am speaking this afternoon to a great army of young men and women who have signed the following pledge: "Trusting in the Lord Jesus Christ for strength, I promise Him that I will strive to do whatever He would like to have me do." Dear Christian Endeavorers, are you willing to go anywhere that Jesus Christ would like to have you go, and to do any work that He would like to have you do? If the Lord Jesus were to stand by your supper table tonight, as He stood once by the side of His disciples in Jerusalem, and if He were to say to you as He said to them, "As the Father hath sent me, even so send I you," what would you say to Him? Could you look up in His dear face and say, "Lord Jesus, I do desire to be in this world as Thou wast in the world. I do desire to live the Christ-life in this world. Make me more like Thyself." If the Lord Jesus were to speak to us, would He not say, "Lovest thou me? Feed my sheep." "And other sheep I have, which are not of this fold; them also I must bring and they shall hear my voice; and there shall be one fold and one shepherd." Your Jesus has some poor, lost, wandering sheep in India, in China, in Africa, on the dark mountains of heathenism. They have never heard of the Good Shepherd; they have never heard of the heavenly fold. If you love Christ, show how much you love Him by the way in which you strive to keep His commandments, by the way in which you go out after these lost ones until you find them. Do you realize that there are in the world today a thousand millions of heathen and Mohammedans? Only a fourth of the human race have the gospel; three-fourths are without the gospel, and two out of every three people in the world today have never heard the gospel. Here we are in this comfortable and beautiful hall, singing and talking about the gospel, and rejoicing in the gospel; but ought we not to make more earnest efforts to give the gospel to those who are without it?

Do the heathen need the gospel? I wish I could picture to you how much they need it, how great is their ignorance, how deep is their darkness. One day when I was in Ceylon, walking through one of the villages, I found a poor mother in her home, lying flat on the ground, beating her face in the dust, and weeping and wailing most piteously. She had lost her only child. It was all she had in the world, all she had to care for and to love, for the human heart is just the same all the world over, and mothers love their children. This child had been taken away by death, and she had no hope of ever seeing it again, no hope of ever taking it in her arms again and knowing it as her child; and her heart was breaking. I see in this audience many mothers. Perhaps there may be some mother here who has lost a little child. What did you do in that sad hour? You went into your closet; you looked up into the face of your Christ; you believed that He had taken your little one to His home in heaven, that He was caring for it tenderly, better than you could care for it, that it was safe and happy with Him, and that you would see it again by and by; and your heart was comforted. Is it not so? Remember, there are other human hearts that need the same comfort that comforted you in your hours of great sorrow.

Remember, the mothers in heathen lands need to know about the Lord Jesus Christ as much as you do. Our Lord Jesus came "to bind up the broken-hearted, to comfort all that mourn;" but there are millions of mourners in heathen lands who have never heard of Jesus Christ. O friends, what is it that makes life worth living to you? Is it that you have houses and lands and money in the bank? Are these the things that are precious to you? No; it is that you have heard of God, that He loves you, and that Jesus Christ is your Saviour and friend; it is that you have a glorious hope of an immortality with Christ beyond the grave. If these are the things that are precious to you, oh, then, make haste to give this precious gospel of redemption and of hope to the sinning and sorrowing millions in heathen lands who are without it.

What is the Christian church doing at the present time to give the gospel to the heathen? Out of every 5,000 church members in Christian lands only one goes as a missionary to the heathen. What is the Christian church giving to send the gospel to the heathen? The average giving of Christians in Christian lands to send the gospel to the millions in heathen lands is something like five cents a month per church member. Is this the measure of our love for Christ? The measure of our obedience is the true measure of our love to Him. It is not what we say or sing, but what we do that shows whether we love Christ or not. [*Applause.*]

Dr. Duff, that great missionary hero, used to say, "The Christian church is just playing at missions;" and it may be that we are only playing at Christianity. Some one has said that the evangelization of the world ought to be the great work of the church, and not merely a small branch of the church's work; and if it is true that it ought to be the great work of the church, then it ought to be the great work of every member of the church, and it ought to be your great work and mine. Think of what might be done if people were only in earnest. Look at what the Moravians are doing, — a poor, humble, simple people. Do they send only one missionary out of every 5,000 of their church membership? No; they send to the foreign field one out of seventy. Do they give only five cents a month per church member to the foreign missionary work? No: they give $1.25 a month, or $15.00 a year, on the average, per church member. [*Applause.*] They send to the foreign field five missionaries for every minister at home. They say that their church exists for the purpose of giving the gospel to the world. And I want to ask you, For what do your churches exist? For what does the Y. P. S. C. E. exist? For what do you and I live? The Christian has only one business in the world, — to promote the coming of Christ's kingdom. That is our great work in the world. We have been redeemed, redeemed by the precious blood of Christ, redeemed from the love of self, and the service of self, to the glorious service of our Lord Jesus Christ. Would that we might realize this, our "high calling," and go forth to the great work of our lives. St. Paul said a beautiful thing in the fourteenth verse of the sixth chapter of Galatians: "God forbid that I should glory, save in the cross of our Lord Jesus Christ, by whom the world is crucified unto me, and I unto the world." I wish we might all say that, — that the world is crucified unto us and that we are dead to the world, dead to its honors, its pleasures, its emoluments; that its praise cannot allure us and its blame cannot terrify us, — dead to the world, but alive forevermore unto Jesus Christ, alive to every cause that is near to His heart, alive to the promotion of His kingdom. If it were so with each one of us, then I am sure that a great number from this large audience would rise up and follow the Lord Jesus Christ to give the gospel to the millions and millions of our brothers and sisters in heathen lands who are without it.

If you would like to know of the work of one missionary in the foreign field, let me tell you the story of Miss Agnew. She was born in New York; and when a little girl, eight years of age, studying in a day school in New York City, her teacher taught her a lesson in geography and pointed out the heathen and Christian lands. That little girl, then and there, decided that if she grew up she would be a missionary and go and tell the heathen about Jesus. She never forgot that resolve; and in due time, when the way was open, she went to Ceylon.

She lived in Ceylon forty-three unbroken years. She had good health and strength, and she loved her work. During forty-one years she was the lady principal of the Oodooville girl's boarding-school. She taught, altogether, a thousand girls in that school. She taught the children, and in some instances the grandchildren, of her first pupils in the school. All the people loved her, and because her pupils all called her "mother," the people of the district poetically called her "the mother of a thousand daughters." She was very happy in her work, and God gave her His presence and His blessing. During those forty-one years six hundred girls from that school gave their hearts to Jesus Christ and publicly confessed him as their Saviour and Lord. Six hundred girls went out from that school to shine as lights in their homes and villages. They are now the wives of pastors and catechists, colporteurs and teachers, doctors, lawyers, merchants, and farmers. Some of them are the wives of the chief men of the district. They are scattered all over Ceylon and in Southern India, and wherever you meet them you will find them shining for Christ. A great many of them are engaged in Christian work in their churches, Sabbath schools, day schools, and villages. In northern Ceylon alone forty Bible-readers are giving their lives to evangelistic work, and are teaching the women in a thousand homes. These were nearly all trained by Miss Agnew. When we think how greatly God honored and used her, and how her life was a blessing in hundreds of homes, bringing to these homes the peace and the joy and the hope that the gospel alone can give, we cannot help thinking how precious a life consecrated to Christ may be. Perhaps many from this audience may go out and do in China, in India, or in the islands of the sea, just such a work as Miss Agnew was privileged to do.

There may be some here who will say, "I would like to go, but I am afraid that I am not good enough to go; I am afraid that I should not be successful if I should go." Dear friends, what is the secret of success? Does it depend on having a high education or possessing great talents and superior linguistic ability? No. Christ has told us the secret of success. He has said, "He that abideth in me, and I in him, the same bringeth forth much fruit." That is the secret of success,—to abide in Jesus Christ, to draw all your grace and strength and power from Him. Separate from Him you may be only a poor, weak branch, with nothing of any value in yourself; but united with Jesus Christ you cannot fail, you must succeed. "Christ Jesus . . . is made unto us wisdom and righteousness and sanctification and redemption." What you need is to be emptied of self that you may be filled with the fulness of Him who possesses all things. If you go out in his strength, you cannot fail; you must succeed.

Oh, there comes the call from all over India and all over the heathen world for more laborers. Who are there in this great audience who will respond to that call? Dr. Scudder, of the Arcot Mission in India, writes: "During my long experience in India, I have never felt that the claims of India were so urgent as now. A restless, almost feverish, spirit of inquiry pervades the whole community." The Rev. Dr. Clough, of the Telugu Mission, has come to this country after fifteen years of labor, asking for twenty-five additional missionaries for that field. He reports that during the last fifteen years that mission has enjoyed one uninterrupted revival and 40,000 converts have been added to the church fold in that one district in India alone. Bishop Thoburn, of the Methodist Episcopal Mission, writing to us a few weeks ago, said: "The condition of things in India is most hopeful. We, in our mission, could baptize a thousand persons a month if we only had a sufficient number of missionaries and native helpers to instruct those who are asking for baptism." And he says further, "I hope to live to see the time when the people of India will come to Christ, not merely by the few thousand in a year, but by the hundred thousand a year." I also hope to live to see that glorious time, and I mean to work for it, and I hope that you also will work to hasten its coming. Dr. Chamberlain, of the Arcot Mission, says that if the people of India are to hear the gospel in this generation, in addition to all the native helpers who can be employed, it is necessary that there should be, in order to superintend and direct the work, one missionary for every 50,000 people. Surely that is not an unreasonable number,—one missionary to every 50,000 of the population. Yet according to that estimate, nearly 5,000 additional missionaries are needed in India, and Dr. Chamberlain says that if the churches of Christendom should send to them 5,000 additional missionaries within five years, he believes that it would be possible to give the gospel to the people of India in this generation. If 5,000 additional missionaries are needed in India, then 5,000 additional missionaries are needed in China, and 5,000 in Africa, and 5,000 in the remainder of the heathen world. Altogether, 20,000 additional missionaries are needed within five years, if the people of heathen lands are to hear the gospel in this generation. Dear friends, who is going to give the people of heathen lands the gospel? The people of the next generation cannot give the heathen of this generation the gospel. If the heathen of this generation are to hear the gospel, the Christians now living should give them the gospel in this generation. [*Applause.*]

You have heard of the great Student Volunteer Movement for foreign missions, which has come into existence during the last few years. There are at the present time in the United States 6,000 young men and women, graduates or undergraduates of the various schools and colleges and seminaries, who have signed the followtng pledge: "I am willing and desirous, God permitting me, to become a foreign missionary." These are 6,000 of the brightest young men and young women of the land, and the motto of this Student Volunteer Movement is: "The world for Christ in this generation." My friends, I want to ring out that motto in your hearing today. I want to ask you, Will you not take it as the motto of your Y. P. S. C. E., "The world for Christ in this generation"? [*Applause.*] It can be done; it is entirely possible. Our Lord has said, 'According to your faith be it unto you." I want to inquire, What share is the Y. P. S. C. E. going to have in this great work? I have something to ask from you this afternoon. There has been a great burden on my heart ever since I was invited to come and address this meeting. I must give you a message that I believe God has given me to give to you. It is this: I want to ask for 16,000 missionaries from the Young People's Societies of Christian Endeavor and the funds to support them. You have in this great organization 16,000 societies with a million members; that is, on an average, more than sixty members for each society. Is it not possible for each society to send out one —one out of sixty, and to support that one on the foreign field? I would advise that these missionaries go out under the denominational boards of these various societies. If a missionary is selected, let that missionary apply to the denominational board of your society, and let the money for his or her support go through that denominational board. For example, if a Y. P. S. C. E. is connected with a Congregational church, let the missionary who goes out to represent that society apply to be appointed by the Congregational board, and let the money for his or her support be paid through the Congregational board. In the same way, if your Y. P. S. C. E. is connected with a Presbyterian church or a Baptist church.

What would be the result of this movement? Why, the result would be that the work of all the different missionary boards would be greatly augmented. What would be the result in heathen lands? A glorious revival in all heathen lands; and I am sure one result would be the establishing very soon of 16,000 societies of Christian Endeavor in Africa, in China, and in all the round world. Do you want that your society should be international? Make it so, then, in reality, not merely in name. Let India and China and Africa and the whole round world be full of societies of Christian Endeavor. And what would be the result here at home? I believe the result would be a great outpouring of God's Spirit in your midst. You want a blessing, an abiding blessing? How are you going to get it? You have come up here, expecting to receive a blessing, and you want to carry back a blessing with you to your society. How are you going to get it? Christ has told us the way to secure a blessing. He has said, "He that hath my commandments, and keepeth them, he it is that loveth me; and he that loveth me shall be loved of my Father, and I will love him, and will manifest myself to him." Notice that the love of God and of Jesus Christ and the manifestation of Jesus Christ, all hinges on the keeping of his commandments; and if you want to get a blessing in your own hearts, in your homes, in your societies of Christian Endeavor, go to work with heart and soul and mind to keep the commandments of Jesus Christ, and do not forget that last and great commandment: "Go ye into all the world, and preach the gospel to every creature."

Now I want to ask you, Have you a missionary committee in your Y. P. S. C. E.? If not, will you not establish one at the first meeting of your society? Have you a monthly prayer meeting in connection with the work in your society? If not, will you not arrange that the missionary committee shall have charge of a monthly missionary prayer meeting, which shall be one of your regular meetings; and that at that prayer meeting the work in foreign fields shall be systematically and earnestly studied? Have you in your community any Student Volunteers? Have these ever given an address in your church? If not, will you not ask your pastor whether he will not arrange for a meeting at which the Student Volunteers of your vicinity may present the needs of the foreign field and the great work waiting to be done in heathen lands? The next thing I want to ask is, Will you not begin at once to pray the Lord of the harvest that He will send forth to the harvest one laborer from your society? Can you not spare one young man or one young woman out of the sixty members of the average society? Will you not begin to pray immediately that God Himself will choose and send forth that one to be your representative in the foreign field? And if it should be that God should choose the best one that you have, the one upon whom you chiefly rely, the most earnest Christian worker, the most successful soul-winner, then I beseech of you, do not keep that one back; do not say, "We cannot spare you; you are too valuable; let some one else go; we need you at home." I pray you, give your best to Jesus Christ, remembering that God gave His best to you. There were a father and mother in the New England States who gave their only daughter to go as a missionary to China. At the good-bye meeting that father stood up and said to those present, "We love our daughter; she is very dear to us, but we have nothing too precious to give to the Lord Jesus Christ." I wish that every one of us here could say that,—that we love Christ, and we have nothing too precious to give to Him. Our time,—He shall have it; our talents,—they shall be devoted to Him: our money, our influence, our friendships, our entire possessions, we do lay at His feet, we do consecrate to his service.

I believe there must be many young people in this audience and in these societies who could go out at their own charges. What an honor, what a privilege, it would be for any young man to go out in connection with one of the missionary societies, but paying his own expenses! Then I believe that there must be many in this audience who could, all by themselves, support a missionary in the foreign field. There is a lady in Scotland, a teacher in one of the public schools, who receives a salary of $1,000 a year, and lives on $500, and the other $500 she gives to one of the missionary societies to support a missionary substitute in China. She has her own missionary in the foreign field. She would like to go in person, but she cannot; so she sends a substitute. If you cannot go yourself, send one in your place; have your own representative in the foreign field. Are there not many here who receive $1,000 a year who could live on $500 and give the remainder to support a foreign missionary in the field? Try it, and see whether God does not bless and reward you for the sacrifice. I would like to tell you of three sisters in Edinburgh. They said, "All of us should not stay at home. One of us ought to go to the foreign field, and the two who stay at home will support her." So one went as a missionary to Africa, and the two who remained at home said to the society under which their sister had been appointed that they would be responsible for her support. But a friend of theirs, hearing of this, said to them: "I know your circumstances. This will be a heavy task for you. Let me bear half of her support." And those two sisters, one a teacher and the other a dressmaker, are working, and earning, and saving, and are paying, year by year, half of the support of their sister who is in Africa. I think that in God's sight the three are missionaries, not only the one on the foreign field, but the two who, staying at home, love the work as much as the missionary loves it, and make as much self-denial in giving as she makes in going. Is not that what God wants of each one of us,—that we should all be missionaries, whether we go or stay, that we should all love this work, and that those who are obliged to remain at home should make as much sacrifice in giving as the missionary makes in going? Who is under more obligation to give the gospel to the heathen than is every one of us? To whom does the commandment, "Go ye into all the world and preach the gospel to every creature," apply more strongly than to us? As an illustration of what may be done if one is really in earnest, let me tell you of the giving of a poor woman, living in Lowell, Mass., and named Sarah Hosmer. She heard that a young man might be educated in the Nestorian Mission Seminary in Persia for fifty dollars. Working in a factory, she saved this amount and sent it to Persia; and a Christian young man was educated, and went out as a preacher of Christ to his own people. She thought she would like to do it again. She did it five times. Five times she earned and saved fifty dollars, and five young men were educated and went out to preach the Lord Jesus Christ in Nestoria. When more than sixty years of age, she desired to send out one more preacher of Christ, and, living in an attic, she took in sewing until she had accomplished her cherished purpose; and she thus sent out the sixth preacher of Christ in Nestoria. I think she was a missionary. I believe the Lord Jesus Christ will say to her one day, "Inasmuch as you did it unto one of the least of these in Nestoria, you did it unto me." We are told of the poor native Christians on the Euphrates, that they conscientiously set apart one-tenth of their entire income to the service of God in obedience to his commands; and that wherever there are ten Christian families, they are enabled, by means of these tithes, to provide for the support of a native evangelist who shall devote his whole time to Christian work.

In view of such examples as this, I ask you the question, Would it not be possible for each Y. P. S. C. E. of sixty members to support one missionary in the foreign field? I would not like to ask you to give to the foreign missionary cause something that would be easy for you to give, something that would cost you no sacrifice. I would not like to ask you to give as I once heard a lady ask at a drawing-room meeting, who said, "I am coming around soon with my subscription paper for the missionary cause, and I want you each to give fifty cents or a dollar. You will never feel it." I thought, Is that the way to give to the foreign missionary cause,—a thousand millions of heathen and Mohammedans needing the gospel, and these people are being asked to give something that they will "never feel"? Is that what God asks from us? Is that the way in which God gave to us, giving something that He did not feel? No; He opened heaven and poured out His treasures; He gave His only begotten Son; He gave the best He had to give. Our hearts are glad this afternoon because God loved us so. Shall we not give back to Him in a way to make His heart glad? Shall not fathers and mothers give their sons and daughters for the foreign missionary work? Shall not young men and young women give themselves to Christ for this great work, if He shall call them? and shall not every one of us pour out our treasures and show the Lord Jesus that we love Him with our whole heart, soul, strength, and mind? Is not that what Christ asks of each one of us? Does He not say to us, "Ye are not your own; ye are bought with a price"? If we do not even own ourselves, how can we own anything else besides? If we have given to God the greater gift of our hearts, how can we keep back from Him the lesser gift of our possessions? Between His heart and ours there should be no "mine" and "thine:" it should all be "thine." Is not this what Christ means when He says, "Whosoever he be of you that forsaketh not all that he hath, he cannot be my disciple"? Does he mean it? I used to think that He did not mean it, that he only said those words to the people of eighteen hundred years ago. But I think, in the presence of the opium traffic in China, in the presence of the slave trade in Africa, in the presence of the awful liquor traffic at home and abroad, in the presence of all the woes and sins and miseries that afflict humanity,—I think it is time that every Christian should be wholly consecrated to Jesus Christ. I think it is time that we should give up all that we have to Him, to be at His disposal, to be used as He shall direct. [*Applause.*] I think Livingstone understood this truth when, in the early history of his missionary career, he made this resolve: "I will place no value on anything I have or may possess, except in relation to the kingdom of Christ. If anything I have will advance the interests of that kingdom, it shall be given or kept, as by keeping or giving it I shall most promote the glory of Him to whom I owe all my hopes, both for time and for eternity. May grace be given me to adhere to this." And on the last birthday but one of his eventful life, he wrote in his diary these words: "My Jesus, my Lord, my life, my all, I again dedicate my whole self to Thee." Shall we say less than that, we, redeemed by the blood of Christ, we, called to be His disciples, shall we say less than that? "My Jesus, my Lord, my life, my all, I again dedicate my whole life to Thee," and let us make our motto the words of that beautiful hymn which we so often sing: —

"Take my life and let it be
Consecrated, Lord, to Thee;
Take my moments and my days,
Let them flow in ceaseless praise.

Take my love; my Lord, I pour
At thy feet its treasure-store;
Take myself, and I will be
Ever, only, all for Thee."

[*Prolonged applause.*]

At this point in the exercises, before the address on "The Child at Work," the seats in the two middle sections on the floor of the hall were vacated by request from the platform, and several hundred children filed into the hall, under the lead of Miss Nettie Harrington, of Minneapolis, all singing "Onward, Christian soldiers."

Dr. Farrar: The next speaker, Mrs. Alice May Scudder, is well known to Christian Endeavorers through that column or two which she edits in *The Golden Rule* on juvenile work. She will speak to us at this time on "The Child at Work." [*Loud applause.*]

ADDRESS OF MRS. ALICE MAY SCUDDER.

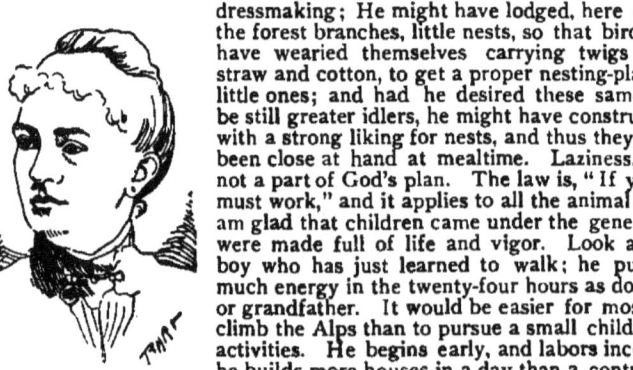

God designed everything that has life for work. He might have put perennial leaves on the trees and thus have saved them much of their spring dressmaking; He might have lodged, here and there in the forest branches, little nests, so that birds need not have wearied themselves carrying twigs and twine, straw and cotton, to get a proper nesting-place for their little ones; and had he desired these same birdies to be still greater idlers, he might have constructed worms with a strong liking for nests, and thus they would have been close at hand at mealtime. Laziness, however, is not a part of God's plan. The law is, "If you live you must work," and it applies to all the animal creation. I am glad that children came under the general rule and were made full of life and vigor. Look at that baby boy who has just learned to walk; he puts forth as much energy in the twenty-four hours as does his father or grandfather. It would be easier for most people to climb the Alps than to pursue a small child in his daily activities. He begins early, and labors incessantly, for he builds more houses in a day than a contractor could complete in a year. Earthquakes are frequent in babyland. That active boy must also see everything; like the hero in "Helen's Babies," he "wants to see the wheels go round," and it is lift him up and lift him down all day long, that he may peep at this or that. Try to rest your nerves a little by urging him to take a seat, and you soon feel the little feet kicking against you, or — worse yet — your best furniture. His hands are never quiet, and his head is so constantly in motion that it is often a question on which part of his body it was placed: neither is his tongue quiet, but it runs on like an eight-day clock, only, oftentimes, not to so good a purpose. This is the picture of a strong, healthy child: and the two words "perpetual motion" might have sufficed for his description.

Now, is this incessant activity discouraging? No; on the contrary, it is exactly the condition of things that we most desire. The danger to the young arises not from activity, but from a misdirection of their energies. Children need good educators who, like Edison, shall catch the lightning and control it for useful purposes; otherwise they will surely work iniquity. We hear a good deal about the innocence of childhood, but such talk is largely poetic fancy. Facts show that there are very few children who grow up entirely ignorant of the giant evils of the day. Most parents know only too well how early their little ones will be indoctrinated in sin. Every neighborhood has children who are Satan's emissaries, seeking to draw those who are pure and good into his diabolical labor union; and parents ought not to feel safe until their Tommy or their Susie is a positive Christian worker. Many people, however, are so blind that they think it unnecessary for children to become Christians, but their eyes would be opened if they could have a glance into the true conditions of family life all over our land; they would be appalled to see hundreds, yes thousands, of young men and women in our so-called best families, who, if justice had done its perfect work, would lay aside their silks and broadcloths to appear in a convict's garb. Only a few weeks ago a friend of mine had a call from a newly made acquaintance, a young lady of wealth. She came with a beautiful bouquet, and begged the privilege of going to her friend's room to place it on her bureau, "to give her a surprise," as she said, "on her return." She accomplished her purpose; for there was great surprise when it was discovered that when she put down the flowers she took up a pair of costly diamond ear-rings, and they were never seen or heard of more.

I know four mothers who have seen their sons under eighteen years of age behind prison bars, and so gentlemanly in appearance were these sons, that you never could have dreamed that they were to be counted among the criminals of the land. Criminals, however, they all were, and if you search for the reasons, you will find that back in childhood they commenced to do little crooked things. Be not deceived, friends, multitudes are going astray in childhood, and it is because they are not given active Christian work to do early in life. The old adage is not yet obsolete that "Satan finds work for idle hands to do," and if the children of our land are to be saved from misdoing, we must emphasize mightily the fact that children will work, and if their energy is not expended "for Christ and the church," then it will be for Satan and his kingdom. The young men and women who are firm in times of temptation are such as love the Lord their God and serve him; it is not those weak specimens of humanity who feel no responsibility towards God or man, but delight to do their own sweet pleasure.

Thus we have seen that many of the children of America are doing that which is positively evil, and we shall find many more who are working at that which, if not positively evil, is almost valueless.

Yonder sits a little girl, sewing industriously; see her needle fly as she hums a pretty song. What is she so intent upon? A dress for her doll. Good work, do you say? Yes, better than evil work, better than idleness, but, after all, work that is misdirected. Suppose that child should have in her hands a dress for some little one who is motherless or destitute, would not her work be of far more value, while it would require no greater expenditure of energy? There was a great cry raised all over the land because Frances Willard talked of annihilating dolls, but I think she only desired to say that which I wish to emphasize this afternoon. Let the children utilize their labor and affection for flesh and blood, instead of for sawdust and bisque. Suppose all the stitches taken for dolls' apparel should be transferred to clothes for unfortunate little ones, and all the love expended by young hearts on inanimate puppet creation could be given to neglected little souls, would there be, think you, so much want and suffering in the world? I know that it has not been customary to expect much from children, but if their possible energies could be summed up and put to some valuable work, there would be the power of a Niagara. The missionary boards have caught this idea and utilized it, with a manifest increase in their treasuries.

But just at this point I seem to hear some one say, "What a cruel proposition! By such a plan the children would be robbed of all their pleasures and become prematurely old. Better let them be free from care in childhood, for they will find plenty to do later." Yes, friends, there will always be plenty to do, but in eighty cases out of a hundred the child who lives for self-enjoyment until it is eighteen or twenty, will continue with no higher aspirations ever afterwards. You are not placing burdens upon children when you give them useful work to do. I know some little girls who are supporting a child in the Home of the Homeless; and when the motherless darling comes to spend the day with them, and they give her a little hat they have trimmed for her, or they see her delight at eating once more at a home table, they do not feel that their life has been robbed of its sunshine, nor that they are growing prematurely old; on the contrary, they have had the pleasure of doing for others, and this, I believe, is generally conceded to give the greatest happiness known to man.

Children play church, and play preach. Why not let them go to a Junior Endeavor meeting where the worship may be real? I saw two little girls once arrange their blocks in the form of a church; and when it was completed, they placed some paper dolls in what was intended for the pews. They then arranged a row of other paper dolls, both feminine and masculine, against the walls. On inquiry, I ascertained that this latter company were "to unite with the church." Thinking this too solemn a ceremony to be used in play, I objected; but my censure was met with a flood of tears, and these words, "Oh mamma, please don't make us stop; for we have had great work to convert these people; and if you don't let them join the church, it will spoil everything." The ceremony was allowed to go on; but I thought, What a pity it is that children who are so anxious to carry on the Lord's work cannot have better material than paper dolls to work upon! That incident occurred more than eight years ago, when children engaged very little in religious work, but now they can have work in abundance to do for their Master. The negative piety of olden times, which called for children who could sit still all day Sunday and look sanctimonious, is past; we ask today for children who can lead meetings and pray, who can talk of religion in the same tone and with the same will with which they speak of tennis or croquet, who can comfort the sick and convert the well; in fact, children who can do deeds of righteousness as naturally as they breathe the air. The little ones of today must be taught to have the same spirit that Jesus had when a boy, and to cry when any seek to arrest them in their labors, "Wist ye not that I must be about my Father's business?"

We hear a great deal today about skilled workmen; and this is exactly the object of Junior Endeavor societies,—to coax and encourage, and by setting high ideals to make men that shall be approved of God. We do not want the next generation to be what Richard Baxter called "wheelbarrow Christians, who only go where they are shoved," but we want rather a multitude of men and women like Helen Chalmers, who devoted her life to work among the drunken men and their families in the city of Edinburgh, who lived in the midst of their poverty and suffering in one of their alleys, going about on dark nights with her little lantern, hunting up the fallen and wretched, and bringing them to her meetings, to hear of Jesus. We shall have, and we have now, boys with higher ambitions than to be circus clowns or policemen. We have embryo clergymen and missionaries today in our Junior societies, and we need them, for ministers are a commodity that is growing scarcer every day. But with all this promise we must still cry, like Oliver Twist, for more. I therefore lay the task of educating at least one child "for Christ and the church" upon every

Christian Endeavorer in our land. It is a tiny duty to perform, and yet if the million Endeavorers in our land should do this simple little thing, we should have at our next annual Convention an army of workers of more than two millions. The Bible enjoins us to bring the children to the Master, and chiefly, I believe, that they may work for Him. I think He set a high value on small acts, just to encourage those who are young and timid. He made a great thing of giving a cup of cold water, and possibly He had a child in mind when He did so. Our Saviour always set an example by working Himself. He did not say to his disciples, "I 'll rest, while you do this or that," as the lazy little girl did, who lost her dollie and told her mother to go and hunt, while she prayed. Our Master gave His whole time to work for others, and if children are to be true disciples, they must love the Lord with all their heart, and all their soul, and all their mind, and all their strength, which text can never be interpreted as asking children to sit down and look pious. No, they must be up and at work, for we are not trying to prepare substitutes for the great Christian Endeavor army, but we are aiming to double our ranks, hoping thereby to close in old Satan and vanquish him. We need soldiers in every part of our field, and we must employ only the best Christian methods in their training. Discipline them, then, by the Christian Endeavor methods, for without a shade of hesitation I can say that they are the best. I know no other that will so perfectly develop the children in every direction; with a system for work broad enough to evangelize the world, with interdenominational advantages, with high aspirations, what can we ask for more? If the children can drink in the true spirit of Christian Endeavor and live up to our grand motto, "For Christ and the church," the boys and girls of today will not, when older, ask so frequently, "Where can I make the most money?" "Where can I find a rich husband?" but they will ask, "Where can I do the most effective work for my Master?" and if it shall be that God's Holy Spirit shall point them to the heart of a poor district, as in the case of the heroine of the "Children of Gibeon," there they will be found well prepared to carry on the great work.

But some may ask, "Are not other methods of instruction for work equally good? Will not a pastor's class do as well as a Junior Endeavor society?" The reply is that a pastor's class is insufficient in many ways, for being a member of it is very much like being a Christian outside of the church. The children miss the stimulus that comes from being in a great movement, and they lose the inspiration that comes from numbers. Most pastor's classes, too, are only for instruction, while in a Junior Endeavor society the children do more than acquire knowledge, for in it they are taught to develop every part of their being. The meetings are theirs to lead and participate in, the committee work is theirs to expand; and it is just this element of responsibility that charms children, and makes them doubly useful. Have you noticed what a difference it makes in a child's working capacity whether the weeds are to be taken from mother's flower garden or from a little garden of their own? Their zeal seems not to flag when they labor under their own responsibility, while, on the contrary, it often takes much encouraging, with sometimes an admixture of punishment, to complete the task that others direct. There is nothing that brings out the mettle in children so much as giving them some important work to do. Religion used to look unattractive to children, simply because there was nothing for them to do. They used to sing such songs as, "There 'll be something in heaven for children to do;" but if that hymn were to be sung by Junior Endeavorers it would have to be revised to read, "There is something on earth for children to do." Why wait until we reach heaven when there are such possibilities of accomplishment wrapped up in each child? Every boy and girl reminds me of a nest of boxes. Open them out and every box may be put to effective use; keep them closed and undeveloped, and not one will be of any service. Our business, then, for the coming year, is threefold. We are to quicken to still greater effort those who are already active; we are to turn misdirected labor into more fruitful channels, to stir up the indifferent, who can easily be led to do evil, and to teach them to labor for Christ and His kingdom.

Let us keep in mind this illustration which comes to us from fairy lore: There was once a little girl who called on a fairy godmother to send some one to dress her each day, and the old witch, being obliging, complied. This made the child very happy until one day she chanced to think it would be very hard for her when her helpful friends left her; so she called again for the godmother, asking her to make their visits permanent. The old witch consented, saying, "I have placed the ten fairies who helped you on your ten pretty little fingers, and there they shall remain forever." Now this is exactly what Christian Endeavorers desire to do to the children who are idling away precious moments; they wish to place ten kinds of committee work on their ten pretty little fingers to remain there forever. If missionary, prayer-meeting, pastor's aid, social, literary, entertainment, Sunday-school, flower, introduction, and executive committee work can be placed on the finger tips of the children of America, we need have no fears for the future; but let our little ones grow up inactive and godless, and who can foretell the result? No grander work has ever been designed for this fair land than that which may be accomplished under the Christian Endeavor system, which is able, when rightly carried out, to throttle infidelity and all its adherent evils, and to make the desert places rejoice and blossom as the rose. The responsibility of becoming leaders in so grand a movement must not be lightly brushed aside as a cobweb, for Christ's orders are too emphatic. "Feed my lambs," is only a synonym for "Form Junior Christian Endeavor societies," and all present are urged to obey the Saviour's command and from this moment do all in their power to bring the children under the care of "Christ and the church." The outlook is very hopeful, for we are much in the condition in which our country was during the late war, when Gen. Sheridan wrote to Gen. Grant, "Things are in shape to push." Back went a telegram from Grant saying, "Push things." And these are the two words I wish to brand on every one here present. If you forget all else, remember your orders are to "push things."

And you who are leaders are to remember that you are in Christ's stead to these little ones. His words are, "Whoso shall receive one such little child in my name, receiveth me." You must not, therefore, rest satisfied until every boy and girl under your care becomes a devoted follower of our Master, being able to lead a meeting and offer a prayer.

Enter into your work with an entire spirit of devotion, having always uppermost in your heart the spiritual training of the little ones. Observe prayerfully the consecration meetings, emphasize the temperance lessons, and strive to enforce through your committees this important teaching of our Saviour's, that they must be "doers of the word and not hearers only." If God has called you to this work, centre your energies on it, for it requires much time and study to conduct a Junior Endeavor society well. There can be no slipshod planning, for we are laying the foundations of a temple that is to be occupied by the Holy Ghost. Make the children conversant with God's holy word and inspiring Christian songs, and open their eyes wide that they may see those who are lost in the darkness of sin both here and in foreign lands. Do all this, and whatsoever else your judgment may direct, and great shall be your reward. Happy the persons who can at the judgment encircle the great white throne with children whom they have brought to the Master. No nobler purpose can one have in life than to direct the energies of children to earnest Christian service.

"Live for something, have a purpose,
And that purpose keep in view;
Drifting like a helmless vessel
Thou canst ne'er to life be true.
Half the wrecks that strew life's ocean,
If some star had been their guide,
Might have now been riding safely;
But they drifted with the tide."

Mrs. Scudder's address was followed by the hymn, "Precious Jewels," in the singing of which the small army of children in the midst of the congregation took a prominent part.

Dr. Farrar: Our next speaker needs no introduction to a Minneapolis audience. This last winter, in Boston, he conducted one of the most stirring series of meetings, I suppose, that was ever held in that city in the interests of men. Some 2,200 men gathered daily in Tremont Temple, and a large number were converted. Mr. John G. Woolley, the eloquent temperance evangelist, will speak to us on the great question of "Gospel Temperance." [*Loud applause.*]

ADDRESS OF MR. JOHN G. WOOLLEY.

I want to commence by thanking the chairman of this meeting for speaking kindly of the cause that I represent. I am very often made to feel that to introduce the temperance cause amongst happy Christian people jars upon their good taste and their sense of fitness; and I almost felt as I sat here today that perhaps it would do some violence to your sense of harmony for me to introduce into the splendid jubilation of this meeting this most discouraging kind of Christian endeavor that I am permitted under God to represent here today. I am glad, my friends, that the committee have seen fit to have this matter presented to you a little while; and I thank God that I have been permitted to be the person to present it, although I am perfectly conscious of my utter inability to do it as it ought to be done.

I am not a man given to looking on the dark side of things. If I were, I should despise myself, and I certainly should have been dead long ago; but as I listened to your secretary reading, the other evening, the splendid record of your work for the last year, as I heard him boast and you exult over the fact that New York State has some two thousand and more societies of Christian Endeavor, I could not help thinking that in New York City alone there are ten thousand societies of devilish success, and that they get their right to succeed and their power to succeed by the laws of the country that you and I—God forgive us!—make. But I do not complain, I count it a great joy to be permitted to speak to this gathering today upon this subject; for I believe—and it has been dawning upon me as I have sat here day after day and looked into your faces—that this is the greatest temperance meeting that was ever assembled. [*Applause.*] You are certainly the greatest in numbers; but numbers do not count very much in the sight of God. The church is a great society in numbers, but the church lacks a good deal yet of being square on the question of temperance. [*Applause.*] I noticed that you applauded, a while ago, a remark of one of my predecessors upon the platform here, when she spoke about the great need for a sweeping revival of religion in this country, and when she promised you that you would have it if you should get to be liberal and generous in giving money and sending missionaries to convert the world. I want to tell you something that comes nearer, it seems to me, to the point than that, although I quite agree with her in her proposition. If the Christian men of America would get square with God upon the question of the lawful dramshop in America, there would be such a revival of religion in this country as was never dreamed of before. [*Loud applause.*] Can the Christian men of America abolish the dramshop? I don't know whether they can or not; but the Christian men of America can get square with God about the dramshop, and that is power. If your son comes to my town, and goes to hell through the painted door of the dramshop that we permit to be there, I can look you in the face, when you come after him, and say, "I had no hand in his death;" and every Christian man ought to stand on that ground, whether the dramshops go on or whether they go down. [*Applause.*] It is an awful thought for you Christian men to have, that, if you could have today the power to look into the faces that are here in front of you,—you who sit on the rostrum,—and to tell by a look what was to happen in the lives of these people whom you see here, you would not dare to confront these faces, because I am talking today to women who are to be the wives of drunkards; I am talking to those who are to be the mothers of drunken sons; I am talking to boys who are going to fill drunkards' graves. We cannot help that, maybe; but you and I can get our hands clean of the blood of the innocent; and that is a good way for a Christian man to do. [*Applause.*]

I am to speak about gospel temperance. I intend to consider the subject in the most elementary view of it. That is easy enough intrinsically, but practically difficult. The trouble is, there is such variety of definitions. The phrase is a lexicographical ghost, visible, vocal, voluble, volatile, vanishing. Three years ago I became a gospel temperance missionary. My first appointment was for a month of nightly meetings. At the fourth meeting a man arose and said, in substance, he was a Christian, and a good one, but that I was too gentle to suit him; and later the committee, evidently of the same mind, told me they wanted the old political parties skinned. Being neither a butcher nor a taxidermist, I withdrew with such grace as I could, and left them, poorer but wiser, for I had learned that gospel temperance was but another name for vivisection.

My next appointment was in another State. The leading citizen of the place, a deacon of the church, said if I spoke on gospel temperance he would stand by me, but warned me to leave his party alone. I made the speech so coldly rejected for its excess of gospel in the other State. Before I finished, a howling mob was stoning me. A blind old man sitting on the platform was struck by a rock, and my wife stood at the door, and kept the crowd from killing me till I had done. We were escorted to our hotel between two lines of Caucasian savages, insulting us at every step, meanwhile yelping the name of their candidate, a Christian man. Then I knew that gospel temperance was a hideous discord with a treble of righteousness and a diapason of expediency, and loud and soft pedals of politics; and I said, God helping me, I'll never sound it; and I never did. [*Applause.*] Then I came to this sweet city of my heart and home, preaching the same thing from the same Bible as I was moved by the Holy Ghost. I prepared my sermons on my knees in those days; and a good Christian woman, a member of my committee, and my friend, said: "You are violating your pledge; you are not preaching gospel temperance. You must not speak against high license." I learned then that gospel temperance was a bombastic and flimsy paradox, composed of a gospel that had to be free, and temperance that had to be sold, a gospel that had to be proclaimed, and temperance that had to be smothered, and I said, So help me God, I'll never teach it; and I never did.

But I kept on. Part of my friends and helpers withdrew, deeply offended, because I said a Christless temperance pledge was untrustworthy; and then I learned that gospel temperance was a wretched sham, with God put in a parenthesis, or spoken in a low breath, or left out; and I said, God helping me, I'll know nothing but Jesus Christ crucified and risen, and walking the earth in all the ways of men; and I never did. [*Loud applause.*]

Now there is danger that the confusion of tongues among the workers will end as Babel ended. The blunder of Babel was at the bottom of it, not at the top; and I propose that in this temperance reform we stop building a top on it, and dig for the foundation that was laid in Jesus Christ. [*Applause.*] What we want is to focus on the centre of the subject, and then we shall be able to work on broad lines, and get the knack of putting our hand to everything that is Christlike in temperance endeavor. We cannot all play the same instruments, but we can all be in the right key.

A woman here in Minneapolis stopped at the gutter's side, and spread her handkerchief over a drunken man's face. He was a stranger, and repulsive enough, but she did it for Jesus' sake. I call that gospel temperance. A woman in this city, an invalid, totally strange to me, who had never seen me, and whom I had never seen, prayed every day at twelve o'clock for three years for me before I was saved. I call that gospel temperance. [*Applause.*] When, four years ago, I said that religion was a lie, and fled from the wreck of a fair name and a good estate, Edwin Sidney Williams put money in my pocket, and a letter for Christians and officers and morgue-keepers, signed with his name like this: "In the name of Jesus Christ, the Saviour of men, help this man." I call that gospel temperance. [*Applause.*]

I walked the streets of New York City one August day, starving, but I was sober. It is sometimes an awful thing to be sober. The play of my life was over; the light was burned out. I was a ruined man, godless and hopeless; and that is hell, whether it happen to a man in this world or another. I saw the three witches, Starvation, Beggary, and Crime, stirring a black broth for me on the bleakest moor of life that ever the fanged hounds of appetite and remorse hunted a man over. But I was sober!

> "And as a man with difficult, short breath,
> Forespent with toiling, 'scaped from sea to shore,
> Turns to the perilous wide waste and stands
> At gaze,"

so I looked back upon the wreck of my life that day. All was lost. Father had died, calling me to come from the saloon and see him die. Mother had died, calling upon me to stay out of the saloon and see her die. Wife was worse than widowed, children worse than orphaned,—shelterless but for the grace of creditors and God's sky that shelters all; and the future was an infinity of pitch. But I was sober. If I had said I had left off drink forever, no man who knew me would have believed me. If I had been able to telegraph my wife I was going home, she would have answered, though it broke her heart, "You must not come home." If I asked for employment, no man would trust me. The asylums would not receive me, for I was sane; nor the hospitals, for I was not sick; nor the morgue, for I was not dead. I had not been to bed, for I had no bed. I remembered nothing of the night before, or of the morning, but I was sober. I thought I was going mad. I washed my face at the fountain in Union Square and crossed over to Eighth Avenue. At the corner of Twenty-first Street I saw the sign of Stephen Merritt; you know him, some of you; all the angels know him well. I had never seen him, but had heard of him. It was not food I thought of, but an overwhelming desire filled me to touch the hand of a good man. I entered. A man with the joy of the Lord in his face came to meet me, with his hand extended; and as he grasped mine, I said, "I don't know why I came —." The sentence was never finished, for I burst into tears, and then I told him who and what I was. I said not a word about money or hunger. I had forgotten both. He said: "You need the woods. Did you ever go to camp meeting? I have a tent on the Hudson at the camp meeting. There 's a boat at one o'clock. You can catch it. Go out and rest, and perhaps you 'll enjoy the sermons, too. I 'll be out in three days." Then he snatched up a pen, and wrote a letter to a Christian woman, and read it to me before he closed it. "This is *my friend*, John G. Woolley, of Minneapolis; show him my tent, and do for him as you would do for me." Then he slipped a five-dollar bill into my hand, and said, "Good-by; see you Monday," and, pretending he was called, was gone before I said a word. [*Loud applause.*] I call that gospel temperance, and this incident will reveal to some of you the secret of my belief in the woods and five-dollar bills as a means of grace.

And when a young man simply declines a glass of wine, giving the name of Jesus for the reason, I call that gospel temperance. [*Loud applause.*] And when a young woman with Christian tact and grace demands, as Christian ladies can demand, for Jesus' sake, who never once reproached a woman, abstinence as a prerequisite to her respect, I call that gospel temperance. [*Loud applause.*] And when the honored wife of Minnesota's spotless Senator, who died with his glass reversed, Mrs. William Windom, refused to serve wine at her table according to the custom, saying she would rather offend a few than to tempt any, I call that gospel temperance. [*Loud applause.*]

And when a Christian man stands up and votes the will of God, touching drink, into the ballot box, and does it for His sake and in His name, though he stands alone among a million, and against overwhelming odds of policy or politics or worldly wis lom, I call that gospel temperance. [*Loud applause.*]

And when a Christian man, however good and true, stands with the crowd and for the policy of it, or the revenue of it, or the difficulty of it, or the-best-that-can-be-done-now-ness of it, for free trade's sake, or tariff's sake, or silver's sake, or fair election's sake, with or without a Sunday law, with or without a patrol limit, with or without public sentiment, with a low price or a high one, with long hours or short, in a dramshop, drug store, or hotel, in his own town, or in Alaska or Africa, votes for the sale of drink, or fails to vote against it,—I do not call that gospel temperance. [*Great applause, renewed and intensified when the Des Moines delegation unfurled a banner inscribed: "Des Moines,—the largest city in the West without saloons. A schoolhouse on every hilltop, and no saloon in the valley."*]

It needs the gentleness and charity of Jesus Christ to be a temperance evangelist, and no such man will ever have power until he lays down his theories at the feet of the Son of God. I think I have done that. Let me show you what I brought from there. If I seem dogmatic, it is because I must be brief. A position to be strong must be simple. The temperance question in most minds is complex; hence the strategies, diplomacies, truces, compromises, and defeats. Conscience is the main shaft of the mind, and the gospel is the gear that belts us to God's mind. There is no confusion in the mind in gear.

And now, please God, I am going to maintain this proposition. The Bible is anti-alcohol. I know the learning of it, the arguments of the spirituous scholars of the church, the *oinos, yayin, gleukos;* and I assert that the word of God is against alcohol, not intemperance in alcohol, and there's the kernel of this subject.

Do I deny that Jesus made alcohol at Cana? Of course I deny it; what He made there was *oinos*, and no respectable Greek scholar will say that means necessarily or ordinarily any more than grape juice. But were not the men "well drunk," and did not the master pronounce the wine of the miracle the best of all? I deny that the men were drunk. No Greek scholar will say that *methuo* must mean "intoxicate;" but suppose they were drunk. Am I then to admit against the plain bulk of the book, and against the known character of Jesus, that He made alcohol, on the testimony of a mushy compliment of a tipsy toastmaster, speaking fair the giver of the feast, when the language itself admits another meaning? Do you tell me that He who saved me from the hell of drunkenness, and gave me back to the wife from whom drink had driven me, went to a wedding where men were drunk, and made more alcohol for them to drink? Then I say, Away with the nonsense that marriage is a sacrament, a holy rite; it is nothing but a contract like a bond or policy of insurance. Widen the doors of your divorce courts, and let us hear no more of the ridiculous canons of the church. The Head of the church sanctioned and abetted drunkenness at the only wedding He ever saw! He never did it. He could not have done it. Jesus said, "The words that I speak, they are life." Alcohol is chemical death. Jesus said, "I am the bread of life." Alcohol is post-mortem bread. Jesus said, "I am the resurrection and the life." To be alcohol is the hell of fruit and grain. "This is life eternal that they might know Jesus Christ." Do you tell me that water knew the voice of Jesus Christ, and died, and rotted, and putrefied to alcohol in an instant, and that "this beginning of miracles did Jesus in Cana of Galilee, and manifested forth his glory" in the shame of men?

But what about the Lord's Supper? The hush of the Oriental evening had fallen on Palestine. Scarcely any sound was audible, save now and then the flutter of a late-returning sparrow, or the stridor of some sullen locust, rasping off the last bright edge of the sinking day. Darkness lay in puddles in the valley, which ran together like drops of ink on a glass, as night rose like a black tide up the hillside where a lonely man was standing; it crept to his feet, but he took no notice of it; to his waist, his head, then it covered him; his face was almost transparent in its paleness; he was motionless; his eyes were open, but seemed fixed upon some object in the farthest sky; and as he looked he seemed to listen with his whole soul; he looked down presently, drew his cloak about him, and moved towards the city gate. The stars came out timidly. The city lights glared haughtily. The night flowers by the wayside opened an instant as he passed, then closed again. His sandals were dusty, and he seemed weary. He passed up the Jericho road, round by the south of Olivet towards the east gate. It was the time of the Passover and he had sent his disciples to the city to prepare his last supper, for this lonely man with dusty sandals was Jesus of Nazareth on his way to Gethsemane and Calvary. He was the last to arrive at the upper room where the table was set. It was harvest time. As they had come on, Peter had plucked a small sheaf of yellow grain for the table; and John, the beloved, had got a basket of the ripest, sweetest grapes, and pressed from some with his own hands a cup of wine for the Master, and some were on the table in bunches; and when He came, all sat down to eat. He asked a blessing, the sweetest they had ever heard. Then He took the loaf; He looked surprised, and said, "Why, John, this is fermented bread. What does this mean? Have you forgotten the Scripture? Seven days shall ye eat unleavened bread. Even the first day ye shall put leaven out of your homes, for whosoever eateth leavened bread from the first day until the seventh, that soul shall be cut off from Israel. Take it away quickly, and bring unleavened bread." When that was done, He broke it among them, and said, "Have you never noticed that 'ferment' or 'yeast' is never used in the Scripture except to signify evil? and this is to remind you of my body broken for you." Then He took the cup; and as He saw the color of it, and thought of His bloody death now so near, He prayed again, then just touched the wine before passing it to the disciples, stopped suddenly, and said: "Why, this is unfermented wine;" and John said, "Yes, it is fruit of the vine. I pressed it out for you from ripe grapes. I thought you'd like it and I loved to do it so." And then Jesus said, "Judas will have to go and bring some alcoholic wine."

Son of God, forgive this if it is sacrilege! My friends, there was no alcohol at the last supper. What! alcohol, the death-sweat of grapes, an emblem of the blood of everlasting life? That cannot be. But listen; let Jesus testify: "I say unto you, I will not drink henceforth of this fruit of the vine, until that day when I drink it *new* with you in my Father's kingdom." When we sit down at the marriage supper of the Lamb, we are to drink the same kind of wine they drank that night in Jerusalem. It is to be *new*, made on the spot, the fruit of the vintage of the year one of the new heaven and earth. Alcohol cannot be new. It is expressed decomposition. It is fluid old age, the *rigor mortis* of vintages past and gone.

There will be no alcohol in heaven. Listen; let Jesus testify: "And God shall wipe all tears from their eyes; and there shall be no more death; neither sorrow nor crying, neither shall there be any more pain. . . . And there shall in no wise enter into it anything that defileth, neither whatsoever worketh abomination, or maketh a lie." No tears in heaven? Then there will be no alcohol. No death? no sorrow? no crying? no pain? no defilement? no abomination? no lying? Then there can be no alcohol, for alcohol contains them all. And listen to what John saw: "And death and hell were cast into the lake of fire." That includes alcohol. Abolish death, and alcohol will be impossible. Let hotter flames lick hell out of being, and alcohol, being sourceless and purposeless, would cease forever. Make haste, O God, fulfilling that Apocalypse!

The Bible is against alcohol. It curses it from Genesis to Malachi. There will be none at the marriage supper of the Lamb. There was none at the last supper of our Lord. There was none at the Cana wedding. There ought to be none anywhere. [*Applause.*] There is, but I'll not touch it. Other men will, but I'll dissuade them; and as they fall, I'll lift upon them in the name of Jesus Christ. And still they'll drink, and men will sell it to them, and government permit it, but not with my consent. [*Applause.*] I call that gospel temperance.

One word, and I am through. I think you are destined to be the greatest temperance society in the world. [*Applause.*] I have preached from the beginning to this minute of my little ministry that the whole gospel must be preached to save men. I do not believe in a little, one-sided gospel, just to save men from drunkenness, from tobacco, from blasphemy and licentiousness. If a man wants to be saved by Jesus Christ, he must go for cleanness; and by that token I expect the Y. P. S. C. E. in this country, in this world, to be God's greatest temperance society. May God keep the curse of drink from every life that is here today. May God bless every enterprise that is undertaken by the Y. P. S. C. E. [*Loud applause.*]

The afternoon session closed with singing the doxology, and the benediction by Rev. J. T. Beckley, D.D., of Philadelphia.

SUNDAY EVENING.

In spite of the greatly increased heat of the day, the vast auditorium was packed with delegates and their friends before the time of the evening session began. Several thousand, in fact, were turned away; and for these an outdoor meeting had been arranged, held in the amphitheatre designed for witnessing the display of fireworks in connection with the Exposition. Some three or four thousand attended this meeting in the open air. Rev. R. N. McKaig, D.D., presided, Col. Johnson, of Minneapolis, led the singing, and addresses were made by Rev. Messrs. W. F. McCauley, of Ohio; G. L. Morrill, of Minneapolis; F. O. Holman, of St. Paul; and T. L. Johnson, the colored missionary from Africa. Mr. R. E. Burleigh, the cornetist of the Convention, assisted in the singing, and the meeting proved very successful.

The praise service that began the exercises within the building was even more enthusiastic than usual, the delegates doubtless realizing that it was the last time that they should gather for this delightful exercise. One notable feature of the song service was the rendering of the "Farewell Song" by the choir, in which occurred the reference to meeting next year at New York and the following year at Montreal. The music of the song was peculiarly attractive, and the words, simple as they were, appealed so directly to the audience that the song was applauded to the echo, and the choir had to sing it over and over again.

MUSICAL DIRECTOR LINDSAY.

At 7.40 o'clock Dr. Clark called the assembly to order, and gave out in succession two of the most popular hymns of the Convention, "Showers of Blessing," and "Throw out the Life-Line." It is needless to say that they were sung as they had not been sung before. A selection from the Scriptures was read by Rev. W. P. Landon, of St. Paul; and Rev. J. T. Beckley, D.D., of

Philadelphia, led in prayer. "Bringing in the Sheaves" was the next hymn, and the last string of notices, telegrams, etc., was read.

The Committee on Resolutions, through Rev. H. B. Grose, presented a supplementary report, containing resolutions on the liquor traffic, the systematic study of the Bible, and the closing of the World's Fair on Sunday. The reading of the resolutions was received with great applause, and they were unanimously adopted.

Rev. B. F. Boller, for the Committee on Nominations, presented the following list of honorary vice-presidents for the ensuing year, the announcement of each name being followed by applause:

Rev. O. H. Tiffany, D.D., LL.D., Minneapolis; Rev. H. T. McEwen, New York City; Rev. R. E. Colwell, Louisville, Ky.; Rev. Elbert R. Dille, D.D., Oakland, Cal.; Rev. James A. Worden, D.D., Philadelphia; Rev. William Patterson, Toronto, Can.; Rev. R. M. Tennon, D.D., Ft. Worth, Texas; Rev. Chas. F. Deems, D.D., New York City; Rev. Daniel E. Bushnell, D.D., Chattanooga, Tenn.; Rev. J. F. Cowan, Pittsburg, Penn.; Rev. J. L. Parsons, St. Louis, Mo.; Rev. A. DeW. Mason, Brooklyn, N. Y.; Rev. L. A. Crandall, D.D., Cleveland, Ohio; Rev. Smith Baker, D.D., Minneapolis, Minn.; Rev. R. R. Meredith, D.D., Brooklyn, N. Y.; Rev. Thomas E. Vassar, D.D., Kansas City, Mo.; Rev. J. J. Hall, D.D., Raleigh, N. C.; Rev. J. A. Rondthaler, D.D., Indianapolis, Ind.; Rev. A. A. Fulton, Canton, China; Rev. A. J. Turkle, Omaha, Neb.; Rev. J. B. Jordan, Pawtucket, R. I.; Rev. E. S. Ray, Topeka, Kan.; Rev. Alfred C. Hathaway, Richmond, Ind.; Rev. Frank R. Millspaugh, Minneapolis, Minn.; Rev. Hugh Walker, Birmingham, Ala.; Mr. Breedlove Smith, New Orleans, La.; Rev. A. B. Cristy, Albuquerque, New Mexico; Rev. W. E. Judkins, D.D., Richmond, Va.

The report of the committee was adopted and the officers declared elected.

Secretary Baer, who had recovered from his illness and was able to be present this evening, next arose to address the audience. He was received with applause and the Chautauqua salute.

SECRETARY BAER: Having been out of the sessions of the Convention for two days, let me say that the first thing that greeted my eyes as I came in here tonight was that banner on the gallery opposite, "Montreal, 1893." [*Applause.*] When I left the hall Friday night, I feared that our Canadian friends felt so badly over their disappointment that they would not get over it; and I am glad that there are the same Christian Endeavorers there that there have been in every State that has been disappointed in the years gone by.

The Committee of '91 wish me to announce the number of delegates to this Convention. The registration shows 11,000 delegates, with an estimated representation more than that of almost 3,000, for the committee have given out so many programmes. But 11,000 have registered, and that makes a decided advance over the registration at St. Louis last year, which was 8,100. [*Applause.*]

The audience then united in singing the familiar hymn, "Jesus, lover of my soul."

President Clark: I have learned since returning from St. Paul, where I went this afternoon, that during my absence from Minneapolis and the Convention, an attempt was made to send me out of the country. [*Laughter.*] I want to say that I thank my friends very heartily for the kindness of their intention; I appreciate most sincerely the motive that underlay that action; but I want to say that I entirely approve of and believe in the final action that was taken, as thoroughly in accordance with our Christian Endeavor principles. For we do not believe in levying even the semblance of a tax upon any one for any such purpose as this or any purpose whatsoever. Yet, let me say that I also appreciate most heartily the intention of the Committee of '91, as I understand, to make this more and more a world-wide movement; and I think I can assure them, in behalf of the Trustees of the United Society, that we will do everything that we can, consistently with Christian Endeavor principles, to make this during the coming year more than ever a world-wide movement, that we will mark this beginning of the second decade of Christian Endeavor by making more strenuous efforts to send the glad message around all the world. This same request, which was embodied in the request from the Committee of '91, which came before you, has also come to me from missionaries in all parts of the world; and I think we can say to our brethren in foreign lands, as well as to you who are here, that everything will be done to enable Christian Endeavor to girdle the earth. [*Applause.*]

Let me also say, at this last opportunity that I shall have of saying anything on such a subject, that I desire to thank this great audience, and all who are represented by them, who are not here now, and who have been here in the past, for their exceeding courtesy and kindness and patience. It is no easy task to preside over such a great throng,—I am sure, however, that it must have taxed your patience far more than mine,—but it has been made as easy as it possibly could be by your most considerate and affectionate kindness during all these sessions. Let me say that a great many requests have come to us on the platform which could not be regarded. We have been asked to boom everything, from a penny pamphlet to a railroad; and it has been impossible to boom anything outside of the Christian Endeavor movement. [*Applause.*] There have been many personal requests that could not receive attention, as we could not take the time of ten thousand people always for the sake of one person, unless it was a matter of great importance. There have been hundreds and hundreds of people in this audience whom it would have given the management of this Convention great pleasure and delight to have recognized if it had been possible. There have been many distinguished ministers here whose faces have not been seen on the platform, and whose voices have not been heard from the platform. They have come here to listen, because they love the Christian Endeavor Society; and one of the most delightful things of all this Convention is that no one has come here to see or be seen, that no one has had an axe to grind, that no one has come here for any personal purpose, or for the sake of officialism of any kind. But we have come here for one purpose,—to honor our Lord and to gain the inspiration of this Convention. Because of that, this Convention has been so delightful and so fraternal in all its aspects; because of that, my task here as presiding officer has been so exceedingly delightful.

Let me say, also, that we have not been able, perhaps, in every case to recognize every State as we would desire. I am sure that no one will misunderstand this. There are forty-four States in the Union; there are a number of Territories as well; there are quite a number of Provinces of which we think just as much as of the States; there are foreign countries as well. You can see the task before any one who attempts to do anything of this sort and does not remember that this is an *international* Convention. Heretofore this movement has been, and I believe it always will be in the future, free from all sectional jealousies and from all personal desires for aggrandizement or anything of that sort. We come together on the broad platform of fellowship and love, to serve and honor the Lord Jesus Christ. [*Applause.*] A great many telegrams of greeting have been received; I suppose hundreds of them. Every one of them will be replied to in behalf of this Convention by the committee that has this matter in charge.

Now may I make one request of you? This is the holy Sabbath day. This is the closing meeting of our Convention. This is the climax of all, when we hope to come nearer to the heart of Jesus Christ our Lord than we have at any moment of the Convention, for this is the evening of our consecration service. May I ask of you that, during the rest of this session, even to the very close, there may be no applause, no hand-clapping, no cheers or demonstrations of any kind? Is it not more appropriate, in accordance with the day and the service of this hour, that this closing meeting should be held in silence so far as the audience is concerned, and that we show our appreciation and devout reverence by refraining from this applause, which at other times has been so delightful and cheering to us?

And now, dear friends, take this Convention home with you. You have a weighty responsibility, every one of you who has been here, in the sight of God, for these days of privilege. Take this Convention home, not only to your own society but to all the societies you can reach. Make an effort to tell the good news of this Convention to every one. Appoint local union meetings, district meetings, and carry wherever you can the glad tidings from Minneapolis and this tenth international Christian Endeavor Convention. Multiply it, O friends, multiply it fourteen thousand times in all this land.

Now we shall have the pleasure of listening to an address from Bishop Mahlon Norris Gilbert, of the Protestant Episcopal Church of Minnesota.

ADDRESS OF BISHOP M. N. GILBERT, D.D.

I bow in reverence most profound before this wonderful gathering of consecrated people, for I see here, I am sure, the evidences of God's Holy Spirit acting in individual hearts; and when in the presence of that Spirit of God, we should stand with heads uncovered and hearts touched, and with reverential feelings should acknowledge that sacred presence. And so, too, may I say to you, dear friends, who are gathered here in such vast numbers, that I stand here tonight not simply representing any one division of Christendom, not simply as the spokesman of the Protestant Episcopal Church, but rather as representing Christ, as you are representing Him, and being in the same grand fellowship, belonging to the same magnificent brotherhood, and inspired by the same purpose. As your chairman has said, this is no sectional convention. It represents no States; it represents no divisions; but it represents the international idea that sweeps around the vast circle of the globe. So it seems to me that every speaker who stands here represents, not any one church, not any one division, but the majesty and the power of the Lord Jesus Christ, with the determination in his heart that his words shall be spoken for Him and for Him alone.

This meeting has been a revelation to me. As I have sat during these sessions, listening to the speeches and feeling the inspiration of this gathering, it has seemed to me as though my mind, in a certain way, had been uncovered. I can understand now how this movement has passed into the history of the years, and how it is like all the mighty movements in the past that have resulted in the upspringing and the outspreading of God's kingdom over the whole world. So I recognize this as being part and parcel, nay, as being a kind of culmination of historic data, as being a kind of gathering-point of all that has been working in the hearts and minds of men for the years that are gone. For have we not been waiting for this? Is it not true that every soul that has prayed to God through these eighteen Christian centuries, that every heart that has been bowed before the power of the divine Master, that every witness that has gone up to his God from amid the flames, or from Flavian amphitheatre, or from the mouths of savage beasts and savage men — do we not recognize, I say, that this is the veritable culmination of all those wonderful prophecies and those wonderful revelations of the outpourings of the Spirit that have gone before? It seems to me so; and it seems to me that I am not exaggerating the importance of this movement when I say that it seems to have reached down to the very springs of human life, that it has taken the young heart in its freshness and its enthusiasm,— the grain in all its potential fruitfulness,— taken it and spread it out before the Lord, and offered it as a sacrifice of a sweet-smelling savor. It seems to me that in getting down to the very heart of the younger generation, and in enkindling their love and their ardor, we are doing that which shall propel the vast forces of Christianity on until the knowledge of Christ shall cover the world.

And why not see another fulfilment, as it were, of prophecy in this? for I believe that we are approaching the last time; I believe that the last times will come when the gospel shall be preached to every man underneath the whole heaven. When I heard tonight that out of this gathering many had volunteered to go across the seas, and when I study the history of the religious movements of the last few years and see that never before has there been such a volunteering of individuals to preach the gospel everywhere, do I not read therein the fact that the fulness of the times is at hand, and that soon shall be fulfilled all prophecy, and that the knowledge of Christ shall cover the earth as the waters cover the sea?

And then one other thought, for I must not tarry long tonight, full as you are of enthusiasm. I wish simply to say this: that this grand meeting is the focus of enthusiasm, the enthusiasm that speaks for the individual, in communities, in States, in the nation. Like the rivulets that come down from the virgin snows of mountain summits, sparkling and rushing, and singing their glad notes, and forming the mighty river, so now the individual and the national and the denominational streams of enthusiasm have united here to form a mighty river, which shall flow on and out into all lands. I see it pictured to me as my mind's eye ranges over the outreachings of this vast hall; I hear it speaking down to me in the enthusiasm that comes from over the border, for we are all one nation in Christ; I hear it speaking to me from my dear native State, the Empire State, as she comes here with her voices all attuned to the one note for Christ and His love; I seem to hear it coming to me out of Southland, which is no longer divided, but which is one with us in the determination to bring Christ to the knowledge of all; yea, I see these streams of enthusiasm coming, perhaps slowly, but nevertheless really, from across the seas, from China and the islands of the sea, and gathering here. What does it mean? It means that all these streams of enthusiasm have gathered here with an increased volume and a mightier flood than they could attain by simply flowing in their individual channels.

And then, what is enthusiasm? for is not that the thought before you tonight? It is in my mind, for I see here tonight the very focus of that enthusiasm that has been burning and bubbling and speaking itself out through all these days that have gone. What is enthusiam? Did you ever think of the meaning of the word? Did you ever look up its derivation? It is from the Greek *en* and *theos*,— the inner god, as the old heathen called it, the divine inspiration. So the Christian interprets it as being the Holy Spirit of God within us. So enthusiasm, when it is given to Christ, is divine It speaks itself in works, in actions, in love, in prayer. My friends, this enthusiasm, this God within us, cannot be limited by any narrow human condition; it cannot be confined by any mere individual interpretation or twisting thereof; for if it be the Spirit of God, then it will sweep over your heads, nay, through your hearts, out into all lands and into all hearts.

And then, dear friends, suppose you take this enthusiasm,— for is there man, woman, or child before me tonight that has not the feeling of consecrated enthusiasm within his heart? — suppose you bring it down practically and take this enthusiasm and carry it home with you; for enthusiasm is not noise, it is not mere gathering, it is not mere music and song, though it may uplift the soul, though it may be manifest in a mighty gathering from all corners of the earth. Enthusiasm is, as I have said, the divine Spirit of God within us; and therefore it will show itself in action wherever we go. Suppose that enthusiasm went with you to your homes and your churches, nay, suppose that enthusiasm filled up your churches on Sunday evening; suppose that enthusiasm made your prayer meetings not formal, but full of the grace of God; suppose that enthusiasm should make the liturgy of which our church is so proud full of all its divine meaning, until it should touch every heart that listened thereto; suppose that enthusiasm, speaking itself out in words, and following you to your homes, should touch some weak soul that trembled, and that needed inspiration, would it not be worth everything? Ah, dear friends, what a mighty possibility lies before this Convention! Here you are one; tomorrow you will be separated into your separate integers; and unless there has risen within your hearts that power which shall carry you into action, then indeed will your gathering be a kind of mockery and a kind of disdain to your souls.

I simply want to say one word in conclusion, and that is this. Some of you have noticed, perhaps, that in this age of the world enthusiasm in certain quarters is at a discount. It is a part of what may be called the cultus of mere society to hold itself back in a kind of disdainful position from what is called the ebullition of enthusiasm. It tries to hold itself so that it shall kill out all inspiration of the inner feelings of the heart. It would have love, but it would not have itself surprised; it would have a kind of fashionable devotion, which would be satisfied with pew rentals, but not with the souls in those pews, which would be satisfied with a flourishing church, but not with a church that was bubbling over with the enthusiasm of God's Holy Spirit. Nay, nay, my friends; what we need, all of us, is the enthusiasm that St. Paul had when standing before Festus in the days of old, when Festus cried out, "Much learning doth make thee mad;" or such enthusiasm as St. Peter and the other apostles had on that day of Pentecost, when men looking at them and not understanding it, said that they were drunk with new wine; such enthusiasm as St. Chrysostom had when he bent the whole populace of Constantinople underneath the power of his Christ-inspired voice; such enthusiasm as the noble Savonarola had, in controlling the very destinies of the prenatal Reformation and guiding it into the magnificent channels of the sixteenth century; such enthusiasm as John Wesley had, who served not only to send missionaries out into this new land, but also to break the bands of Erastianism, which were killing out the spirit of God in our church, and to send out into it new thrills of life, which the Church of England and the Episcopal Church in this country are feeling to their finger tips today. I say that is the kind of enthusiasm which the world despises; but that is the enthusiasm which we are proud of and which we will stand for — will we not, dear brethren? — through Jesus Christ our Lord.

Go forth, go forth, dear friends, with this "inner God" in your hearts. Go forth from this consecrated hour with that spirit alive and burning. Make new lamps of your life with the oil of Christian gladness and Christian endeavor. And as some of you will go to the westward, and will stand, as I have done, on the very Point of Inspiration, which looks out over the mighty cañon of the Yellowstone, and will see the wonders and beauties and magnificence of God's creation there, in all their sublimity and awe, as you receive a new inspiration, let it be coupled with the inspiration of this time. So, as you go back to your homes, there shall flow out into your churches, into your lives, into your children, into your friends, such a power of the Spirit of God that this Pentecostal time here in Minneapolis shall be felt throughout this whole land, and shall spread like a mighty torrent over the whole round world. May God speed the day.

At the close of Bishop Gilbert's address the audience sung the appropriate hymn, "Holy Spirit, Light divine."

President Clark: After the Mizpah benediction has been united in by all of us at the close of the consecration service, the Tenth International Christian Endeavor Convention will stand adjourned. The closing address, on "The Secret of Power," will be given by Rev. J. W. Chapman. D.D., pastor of the Bethany Presbyterian Church, Philadelphia, who will also have charge of the consecration service.

ADDRESS OF REV. J. WILBUR CHAPMAN, D.D.

Some one has recently said that the church is behind the age, and this is true; the same person has ventured the assertion that the religion of Christ is behind the young people of the age, and this is likewise true; and for both of these things we thank God. The church and religion are behind the age and the young people of the age, as the wind is behind the sails of the ship, pushing her into the harbor, where she is free from the power of the storm. By this same religion the young people are being lifted up to better living, purer manhood and womanhood, and better still, to the measure of the stature of the fulness of Christ, to the only perfect manhood the world knows. This is power. Passing along the streets, I have many times read a sign like this. "Power wanted," meaning that it was a desirable thing to turn the wheels of the business by the power of steam or its equivalent. It is a sign that should be set upon the

Christian church, and upon this great Society; for, with all that we already posess, we ought still to be longing for more, yet more. I have also many times read a sign that to us is significant; it is, "Power to let," and that should be written across the pages of this blessed book, the Bible, for there is here the secret of power, and we may all possess the thing itself if we are willing to pay the price. There is nothing of which we stand in so great need today, and there is nothing that we may have so easily if we will meet the conditions. Sometimes a very little thing may prevent our possession of it, however. In the city of Philadelphia, at one time, one of the most magnificent engines ever sent out from the Corliss shops at Providence suddenly stopped. The assistant engineer looked it all over, and could not understand why it should refuse to go on; it seemed perfect. The chief engineer examined it with no better success; after the most careful search he said that apparently nothing was the matter with the engine. As a last resort, a message was sent to the maker in Providence; and he, too, was on the eve of giving up in despair, when, in walking over the hard cement floor, his foot touched a little, thin steel wedge. He heard the sound of it, stooped and picked it up, and then exclaimed, "Here is the difficulty." It was almost the smallest thing about the engine, and yet it stood in the way of power. When it was put in its proper place, the great wheels began to revolve, and everything was right again. But I have known smaller things than that to stand between a Christian and power. But there is really a secret in connection with the possession of power.

I read the other day that a company in the State of New York had just taken out papers for the purpose of obtaining the permission of the State to lay hold upon the power of the great Falls of Niagara. They intend to transmit that power to the cities and towns round about, to set the factories running, and in some cases to light the streets with electricity. How strange it is that the power has been there ever since God set the waters running, but men are just now laying hold upon it. Did you never think that there was latent power, in even greater abundance, in the church of Christ? O that we were filled with the Spirit of God, baptized with the Holy Ghost. For this is the real "secret of power." I am speaking of that kind of power which I am sure the Master had in His mind, when, in reply to the disciples' question as to why they could not cast out the unclean spirit from the demoniac boy, He said, "This kind goeth not out but by prayer and fasting." There is such a thing as being a Christian and being without power; that is, having the Holy Ghost "in you" for life. But there is no such thing as being a happy Christian or a useful Christian without having the Holy Ghost "on you;" that is, for power in service.

Yet there are many who do not know what they are losing in not possessing this blessing. John Ericsson and Ole Bull were boys together in their native land. Ericsson grew up to be the man of hard mechanical skill, and Ole Bull became the musician, swaying the world by his power of music. They met at one time in the city of New York, and Ole Bull asked his old friend to come and hear him play. He did not come, and so Ole Bull asked him the second time, and the third; and then he said to him, "If you don't come around and hear me play tonight, I will come and play for you;" and Ericsson said to him, "Don't you bring your violin into my shop, for I don't care for music." But the next day Ole Bull entered the shop and said, "John, there is something the matter with my violin," and they talked about tones and semi-tones, and fibres of wood, when Ole Bull said, "I will show you how it is;" and he drew the bow across the strings, as he alone could do it. In an instant, men in the shop began to leave their work, and to press around him, drawn by an irresistible spell. Ericsson was of the number. The great musician played on, until the great factory was filled with harmony, and suddenly he stopped. When the spell had been broken, John Ericsson, with the tears streaming down his cheeks, came towards his old friend saying, "Play on, play on! I never knew what was lacking in my life before." O, young people of the Christian Endeavor societies, the wide world round, the only thing that is lacking in our lives today, that which would give us happiness, purity, peace, power, is the indwelling of the Holy Spirit of God.

"Come Holy Spirit, heavenly Dove,
With all Thy quickening powers;
Kindle a flame of sacred love
In these cold hearts of ours."

I would that I might give you the secret; I will try to do it. Partly from my own experience, but more largely from the experience of others, I would hold up before you the following suggestions.

Secret the first: A consistent life. There can be no abiding power in your life or mine until the day comes when we shall keep our conduct abreast of our profession; there must be something back of our professions, and that is a consistent life. It is beautiful to hear in the prayer meeting one who is gifted in speech and in prayer, but I am persuaded that there is something far more beautiful, and that is for one to be able from Monday morning until Saturday night to live Christ. Here is a power that infidelity cannot assail or unbelief deny. If you are travelling through an orange country, you are all the time sensible of the fact that the orange blossoms are about you; the fragrance is wafted to you the last thing at night, the first thing in the morning, and it even makes your sleep the sweeter. There is a sweetness like that about the life that "is hid with Christ in God."

It is said that not many years ago a man made his way into the old Water Street Mission, where Jerry McAuley did so wonderful a work for his Master. This man was a perfect wreck; sin had left its mark on his face, in his speech, and on every part of his body. Naturally be would be a man at least six feet tall, but sin had so bound him down that he was not more than four feet high; he looked like a dwarf; his speech had been so affected that no one could understand what he tried to say. Under the power of God he was converted. By an almost miraculous display of that power the bands were loosed that bound him down, and he stood again as God had made him; but his power of speech never returned. It has long been the custom in the Mission for those who have been saved to tell often the story of what Christ has done for them. This poor fellow was always denied that privilege, for they could not understand his message. I have been told that he would sit with the tears streaming down his cheeks as he listened to the others speaking. At last it occurred to him that there was a way in which he could have his part in the meeting. It is said that when all the others had finished, he would rise before them, and would stand first a dwarf, as sin had made him, a prisoner; and then, with every eye upon him, he would rise to the full dignity of his Christian manhood, and stand for a moment as Christ had made him, free; and this was a more eloquent testimony than any words he could have uttered. O young people, this is power. Live Christ in the world, and show to the world the change that the indwelling of Christ hath wrought in you. Sitting at the breakfast table this morning at the West Hotel, I overheard two men talking together about this great Convention. They were not of our number; they did not wear our badge, either in their faces or on their coats. One said to the other, "What is this gathering?" the answer was, "It is the Christian Endeavor Convention." "Christian Endeavor, what is that?" "Well, I suppose it is endeavoring to be Christians," was the reply. But, do you know, young people? this is not the best idea of our great Society. Being a Christian is accepting Christ as your substitute, sacrifice, taking Him at His word, and then never giving the matter an anxious thought. But being a Christian Endeavorer is doing all the good you can, to all the people you can, doing it quickly, for the night is coming when we cannot work. In other words, to be a Christian Endeavorer means this, almost more than anything else, Be Consistent. The badge that we wear in this little pin, C. E., as we read it in one way, stands for Christian Endeavor; but did you ever think that if you reverse the same letters, they have another message for us? for "E. C." means Ever Consistent, and that is always power.

One of the artists in the olden days was cast into prison for a crime of which he was innocent. He was given his paints and brushes, but not a thing on which he might paint, and his only light was from a little window high up in the side of the wall. One day a man stood looking in through the grating of his cell door, and said to him, "I wish you would paint me a picture." "I would," said the artist, "if I had anything on which to paint it." The man looked around him, and found on the floor of the prison corridor an old soiled napkin. "Paint it on that," he said, and the artist began working on and on, until the picture was complete. Afterwards it was placed in one of the old cathedrals, a most marvellous picture of Christ. What a wonder that such a change could be wrought, — an old soiled napkin changed into the picture of Him who was the rose of Sharon for beauty, and the lily of the valley for fragrance. But I know something more remarkable than that, namely, that we can be so changed that we shall not only act Him, but actually look like Him. This is power.

Secret the second: Our dependence is entirely upon God. Seeking to know just what this has meant to the people who have already attained, my mind takes in such characters as Elijah and Jacob, Peter and Paul, and in these modern days, Andrews and Welsh, Brainerd and Evans, and a host of others. Do not be discouraged when you hear such names as these. They were men of like passions with ourselves, weak where we are weak, failing where we have failed, yet working wonders, having power with men, but, better still, having power with God, not because of anything in themselves, but because they entirely submitted to God, and He could use them. It is useless to cry out in despairing tones, "Where is the God of Elijah?" He is here, He is our God, He is the "same yesterday, and today, and forever." We have only to emulate their faith, and to stand as they did in the very presence-chamber of God, to be filled to overflowing with the same power that possessed them. Referring again to Niagara, I have been told that in the transmitting of the power of the great cataract, it might be sent along almost any kind of wire, and that the question was not at all as to that, but altogether as to the power itself. And the question for us is not as to whether we are weak in ourselves, but whether we are entirely submissive to God. In the manufactories round about us I am sure it would be possible to unhitch the bands that connect the machinery with the great engine, and to substitute hand power; twelve or fifteen men might send the wheels round after a fashion, but it would be a poor way in which to do the work. Then, with the same machinery attached to the ponderous engine, you could do in an hour ten times as much work as before, and at about one-tenth the cost. It is the same machinery, but the difference lies in the power that drives it. It is never a question as to our abilities or qualifications, but of the power behind us. If it is the power of man, it is not surprising that the results are so poor. But if we link ourselves with the eternal power of God, nothing will be impossible to us. "All things are possible to him that believeth." Jesus Christ is the reservoir in which the power of God is stored; keep in touch with Him and you have learned the secret of power. Every soul that has ever had great power with men, with God, has been much in prayer. Are you willing to pay the price? Elijah locked up the heavens and held the keys, so that there was no rain for years, but he prayed once more, and the skies were covered with clouds, which broke in blessing on the burning earth. Jacob wrestled with the Son of God Himself, until from being Jacob, the supplanter, he was Israel, the prince, having power with God and men. Bishop Andrews spent days at a time in prayer. John Walsh, night after night, never closed his eyes, but kept them open toward Jerusalem above, that he might receive a blessing from on high, and he did. Fletcher of Madeley often would say in the midst of his classes, "Young men, I must retire to my room, that I may pour out my soul before God;" and at times they would go with him, and pray until the very windows of heaven seemed to be opened above them. It is said that John Livingston, the night before he preached his wonderful sermon in the Kirk, in Shotts, in 1630, spent the whole of the night in the fields in prayer, crying out unto God for power. What wonder was it that hundreds came the next day pressing into the Kingdom? O beloved, God is the same; today He is just as easily moved; if we would but take Him at His word, and put Him to the test, we could shake this city to its very depths, and through the city we could shake the world.

Secret the third: Make a definite consecration of yourselves to God. We have had consecration services before. But do you remember any particular time when you gave yourself to God in consecration for service? I believe that it is a possible thing for one to be a Christian, and never to be able to tell the moment when one was converted, just as I should be sure that I were living, even if I did not know my birthday. But I do not think that it is a possible thing for one to have much power in the service of God until one has made the matter of consecration to God a definite thing. If, in looking over the past, you feel that you cannot recall such a time, then, I beseech you, let this be the time: Sunday evening, July 12, I gave myself to God, once and forever. It may be that some of you feel that you cannot give up everything to God, you are not yet willing. Then let me give you a sentence that Rev. F. B. Meyer, of London, has given to me, and for which I shall never cease to thank him: "Tell God that you are willing to be made willing about everything." I plead for entire consecration. In the days of old Rome, when the *sacramentum*, or oath, was given to the soldiers, the leader of the detachment that was to be sworn to live and die for the senate and the people of Rome read over at large the *sacramentum*, and then the right-hand man held up his right hand, and repeated the words, "The same for me," and down it went along the line until the last left-hand man held up his right hand in what he thought the most holy attitude, and swore the same oath. Are we thus ready? Who will say it? My time for God, my thought for God, my strength for God, my all, my all, my body, soul, and spirit for Him. Who will say it? "The same for me," "The same for me."

Secret the fourth: To be so possessed of the mind and spirit of Christ that we shall have a perfect passion for souls. It is the spirit of Moses when pleading for the children of Israel. "Let them come back," he cried unto God; "but if not, blot me, I pray thee, out of thy book which thou hast written." It is the spirit of Paul, when he said, "I say the truth in Christ, I lie not, my conscience also bearing me witness in the Holy Ghost, that I have great heaviness and continual sorrow in my heart. For I could wish that myself were accursed from Christ, for my brethren, my kinsmen according to the flesh." It is the spirit of John Knox, when he cried out, "O God, give me Scotland, or I die;" then God gave him Scotland. It is the spirit of a Greater than them all, when on the mountain top He cried out, with the tears streaming down His cheeks, "O Jerusalem, Jerusalem." Do you know that if the young people of the Society of Christian Endeavor had this same spirit, before another convention like this could be assembled, we should be able to say that thousands, yea, hundreds of thousands of the young people of America, had been saved; and we should almost think that the millennium had come? Not a great while ago, in the city of London, Mr. Spurgeon, in an address before the ministers of the city, told of the journeys of the census-taker through the metropolis. He came to one house in particular. Without, all was neat and clean; within, it was even better; the floor was spotless, the two old people who lived there looked the perfect picture of peace and happiness. "You must be very happy here," said the census-taker, "you have nothing to worry you, and you are away from the cares of the world; I should think that you would be very happy." The old woman looked at him for a moment, and then said, "No, we're not happy; we once had happiness here, our house was filled with little children; but they have been gone these many days, and now there is neither chick nor child about us; and from morning till night he sits there and looks at me, and I sit here and look at him, and it goes on in that way until we almost hate the sight of each other." There is no happiness, said that great preacher, in the church, until we see round about us the children in Christ Jesus. You are a stranger to it, if you have never led a soul to Christ; your society does not know real joy until you are distinguished for leading the lost into the Kingdom; neither the church nor the minister can know the beginning of joy in service until the cry is heard, "What must I do to be saved?" and then is followed by that gladder cry, "I have found Him, I have found Him." At the State Christian Endeavor convention in Connecticut, I heard Col. Hadley, of St. Bartholomew Mission, in New York, give the secret of their being able to lead so many drunkards into the Kingdom and into the liberty of the sons of God. He said that they met at the beginning of each year with their workers, and that then on their knees they pledged themselves before God that they would, during the year, do their very best to lead at least one drunkard to God. If they failed for six months, they were not discouraged; for they had six months longer in which to work. And the marvellous part of it all to me was that he made the statement that almost nine out of ten were saved, when a real, honest, determined effort was made to lead them to Christ. I believe this is the solution of the question as to how we are to lead our young people to Christ. If we should, here tonight, before God and this multitude of people, say, With His help, I will this year try to lead at least one soul to Christ; I will write the name down in my memory; I will pray for him, I will work for him, I will make any sacrifice for him, I believe that before six months had passed away we should see our friends coming. I can almost hear them now, coming like doves to their windows. Do you remember the conflict waging between the forces on the other side of the sea, when the Scotch troops were discouraged, and were on the eve of falling back? To do this was to be defeated. If only the reinforcements would come! They had been expecting them for hours. Already the line is breaking, when suddenly a young Scotch girl, who had been bending with her ear to the ground, listening, sprung to her feet, her face radiant, her hair thrown back from her forehead, until she looked like one from another world, and she shouted until the farthest soldier heard her voice, "I hear them coming, I hear them coming, I hear them coming." And Scotland won the day, for every soldier fought with renewed courage until the troops arrived. I stand this moment with my eyes closed, looking into the next year, listening for the results of this great gathering of the children of God. Hark, hark! I hear them coming, I hear them coming, I hear them coming, five hundred thousand strong, I hear them coming, the souls we have led to Christ. And there is joy that fills the earth, and reaches to the sky, and comes again upon us like the showers of His mercy. Yea, it is a joy that fills the heart of God. For if "there is joy in the presence of the angels of God over one sinner that repenteth," what do you think of the joy of five hundred thousand and more brought to Him?

Dr. Chapman closed his address with brief invocation of the Holy Spirit, and after a moment of silent prayer he started the hymn, "Come, Holy Spirit, heavenly Dove." Then he called upon the several State delegations to voice their consecration briefly.

Indiana was the first to respond, with the Scripture text: "Search me, O God, and know my heart," etc., followed by one verse of the hymn, "My faith looks up to Thee."

Ohio united in the hymn, "Once again our pledge we renew."

Minnesota sung, "Consecrate me now to Thy service."

Connecticut repeated the text, "Come out from among them, and be ye separate," etc., followed by a pledge for a more consistent life.

In this manner responses were heard from all the various delegations present, and frequently the hymn selected would be taken up and sung by the whole congregation. Many individuals also gave their personal testimonies. After the list had been gone through with, Dr. Chapman appealed to those present who were not Christians, and who desired the prayers of the audience, to rise. Several rose on the floor and in the gallery, and Dr. Chapman offered a brief prayer in their behalf. Dr. Chapman then asked all in the audience who would promise that with God's help they would try and lead at least one soul to Christ during the year to rise and hold up their hands. Nearly the entire audience rose, and with uplifted hands united in singing, "But drops of grief can ne'er repay." While they were still standing, and with hands still uplifted, Dr. Wayland Hoyt led in the following prayer of consecration :—

"O Lord Jesus, Thou didst utterly give Thyself for us. We do now utterly yield ourselves to Thee for this service. We will attempt to win souls for Thee. Accept our consecration; give us souls; put upon us the power of the Holy Spirit. Be Thou in us and upon us, O Thou empowering Spirit, and as never before, because we consecrate ourselves to Thee with earnest and full hearts. May Thy kingdom come, O Lord, through us, to thy glory. For Jesus' sake. Amen."

Mr. Sankey then sung "Man of sorrows," the audience uniting in the refrain, "Hallelujah, what a Saviour!"

Dr. Clark then gave out the first and last verses of the hymn, "God be with you till we meet again," which was sung with wonderful expressiveness; and the Convention closed with the Mizpah benediction: "The Lord watch between thee and me, when we are absent one from another."

But though the exercises were over, the spirit and enthusiasm of the meeting were not. At Dr. Clark's request, the delegates as they left the hall sung together the favorite hymn, "At the cross." As they went down the stairs, they caught up the hymn, "Shall we gather at the river?" Reaching the open air, "Blest be the tie that binds," was sung yet once again. When taking the electric cars to go to their various places of entertainment, "Nearer, my God, to Thee," was the favorite; and as each car carried away its heavy load of passengers, some Christian song would be wafted back on the air. It was an impressive sight as these cars pursued their different directions, each one carrying its company of young people who woke the night echoes with their songs of faith and hope and mutual love. Passers-by everywhere stopped to observe and listen, for it was a decidedly unusual sight in this city of many conventions.

So far as the young people themselves were concerned, there were heard many expressions of regret that the delightful feast of fellowship that they had enjoyed for four days was over; but along with the feeling of sadness there was the universal purpose to live stronger and better lives because of the mighty inspiration received at the Convention of 1891.

Rev. H. W. GLEASON, Scribe.

THE STATISTICS.

The following statistics as to the number of societies are taken from the General Secretary's records, June 20, 1891.

Alabama, 44; Alaska, 1; Arkansas, 83; Arizona, 5; California, 387; Colorado, 150; Connecticut, 534; Deleware, 26; District of Columbia, 52; Florida, 104; Georgia, 77; Idaho, 10; Illinois, 1,043; Indiana, 512; Indian Territory, 28; Iowa, 786; Kansas, 652; Kentucky, 108; Louisiana, 21; Maine, 334; Maryland, 131; Massachusetts, 918; Michigan, 536; Minnesota, 413; Mississippi, 26; Missouri, 530; Montana, 36; Nebraska, 335; Nevada, 1; New Mexico, 7; New Hampshire, 210; New Jersey, 546; New York, 2,354; North Carolina, 24; North Dakota, 33; Ohio, 1,061; Oregon, 133; Oklahoma, 13; Pennsylvania, 1,463; Rhode Island, 92; South Carolina, 35; South Dakota, 114; Tennessee, 114; Texas, 116; Utah, 35; Vermont, 237; Virginia, 48; Washington, 119; West Virginia, 49; Wisconsin, 466; Wyoming, 9; Floating Societies, 4.

In the Canadian Provinces: Ontario, 458; Nova Scotia, 186; Quebec, 63; Prince Edward Island, 17; British Columbia, 25; New Brunswick, 36; Newfoundland, 15; Manitoba, 11; Cape Breton, 8; Northwest Territories, 10.

In foreign lands: England, 120; Mexico, 5; Bermuda, 1; China, 7; Japan, 3; Ireland, 2; India, 30; Micronesian Islands, 2; Spain, 1; Scotland, 1; West Indies, 4; Samoa, 8; Turkey, 12; Africa, 5; Australia, 82

SUPERINTENDENTS.

STATES AND TERRITORIES.

Alabama — Rev. Horace Porter, New Decatur.*
Alaska — Rev. A. E. Austin, Sitka.†
Arizona — Mr. O. S. Cameron, Phœnix City.†
Arkansas — Mr. R. W. Porter, Little Rock.*
California — Mr. Edwin B. Hays, Los Angeles.*
Colorado — Mr. J. W. Barrows, Box 1544, Denver.*
Connecticut — Rev. C. S. Nash, Hartford.*
Delaware — Rev. Geo. E. Thompson, Wilmington.*
District of Columbia — Mr. W. H. H. Smith, 2122 H St., Washington.*
Florida — Mr. F. A. Curtis, Orlando.*
Georgia — Mr. A. B. Carrier, Atlanta.*
Idaho — Rev. J. H. Barton, Boise City.†
Illinois — Mr. Chas. B. Holdrege, Bloomington.*
Indiana — Mr. W. J. Lewis, Evansville.*
Indian Territory — Rev. M. J. Williams, Muskogee.†
Iowa — Rev. J. K. Fowler, D. D., Cedar Rapids.*
Kansas — Rev. Geo. S. Swezey, Peabody.*
Kentucky — Rev. Geo. B. Overton, D. D., Louisville.*
Louisiana — Rev. Fitzgerald S. Parker, New Iberia.†
Maine — Mr. V. Richard Foss, Portland.*
Maryland — Rev. O. F. Gregory, D. D., 504 N. Broadway, Baltimore.*
Massachusetts — Rev. Lawrence Phelps, Chelsea.*
Michigan — Rev. C. H. Irving, West Bay City.*
Minnesota — Mr. W. P. Landon, House of Hope, St. Paul.*
Missouri — Mr. George B. Graff, St. Louis, Mo.*
Mississippi — Mr. E. F. George, Meridian.†
Montana — Mr. G. C. Tilly, Helena.†
Nebraska — Rev. S. R. Boyd, Omaha, Neb.*
Nevada — Rev. George R. Bird, Carson City.†
New Hampshire — Mr. W. P. Fiske, Concord.*
New Jersey — Rev. G. S. Sykes, Beverly.*
New Mexico — Rev. A. B. Cristy, Albuquerque.*
New York — Rev. H. C. Farrar, D. D., Albany.*
North Carolina — Rev. J. J. Hall, D. D., Raleigh.*
North Dakota — Mr. R. M. Carothers, Grand Forks.*
Ohio — Rev. W. F. McCauley, Dayton.*

Oklahoma — Mr. Wm. Blincoe, Guthrie.†
Oregon — Dr. C. R. Templeton, Portland.*
Pennsylvania — Rev. Geo. B. Stewart, Harrisburg.*
Rhode Island — Mr. Frederic H. Fuller, 261 Brook St., Providence.*
South Carolina — Mr. J. L. Wilson, Society Hill.†
South Dakota — Miss Esther A. Clark, Yankton.*
Tennessee — Mr. E. P. Loose, Nashville.*
Texas — Mr. E. F. Groene, Ft. Worth.*
Utah — Rev. J. Brainerd Thrall, Salt Lake City.*
Vermont — Rev. P. McMillan, Woodstock.*
Virginia — Mr. J. R. Durrett, Richmond.†
Washington — Mr. F. W. Hill, Tacoma.*
West Virginia — Rev. R. B. Whitehead, Fairmount.*
Wisconsin — Rev. W. O. Carrier, Wausau.*
Wyoming — Mr. M. M. Mason, Cheyenne.†

PROVINCES.

British Columbia — Rev. Thomas Rogers, Vancouver.†
Cape Breton — Rev. John Murray, Sydney.†
Manitoba — Mr. J. W. C. Swan, Winnipeg.†
New Brunswick — Rev. T. F. Fotheringham, St. John.†
Northwest Territories — Dr. W. D. Cowan, Regina.†
Nova Scotia — Mr. John S. Smith, Halifax.†
Ontario — Mr. R. J. Colville, Peterboro.*
Prince Edward Island — Miss Laird, Charlottetown.†
Quebec — Rev. George H. Wells, D. D., Montreal.*

FOREIGN AND MISSIONARY LANDS.

Africa — Rev. Chas. Newton Ransom, Adams, Natal, South Africa.†
Australia — Mr. J. B. Jackson, Hon. Sec'y, Victorian Section, Melbourne.*
Brazil — Miss Clara E. Hough, Caixa 14, Citadel-de-San-Paul.†
Ceylon — Miss M. W. Leitch, Jaffna College.†
China — Rev. A. A. Fulton, Canton, and Rev. Geo. H. Hubbard, Foo Chow.†
Great Britain — Mr. Chas. Waters, Hon. Sec'y, British Section, London.*
India — Rev. John S. Chandler, Periakulam, Madura.†
Japan — Mr. Arthur T. Hill, Kobe.†
Mexico — Rev. James D. Eaton, Chihuahua.†
Norway — Mr. Edvart Ellefsen, Skien.†
Sandwich Islands — Dr. W. O. Smith, Honolulu.†
Samoa; South Seas — Rev. J. E. Newell, Malua Institute.†
Switzerland — Mr. Angnot Seeli, Bern.†
Spain — Miss Catherine H. Barbour, San Sebastian.†
Turkey, Eastern — Miss Emily C. Wheeler, Harpoot.†
Turkey — Rev. G. H. Gregorian, Yozghad.†
West Indies — Rev. C. S. Bullock, Port Antonio, Jamaica.†

* President of State, territorial or provincial union, and a representative, *ex officio*, of the United Society.
† Representative appointed by the United Society.

CONTENTS.

COVER.

OFFICERS OF THE

UNITED SOCIETY OF CHRISTIAN ENDEAVOR.

PRESIDENT.

Rev. FRANCIS E. CLARK, D.D., Boston, Mass

GENERAL SECRETARY.

Mr. J. W. BAER, Boston. Mass

TREASURER.

Mr. WILLIAM SHAW. Boston. Mass

TRUSTEES.

Rev. C. A. Dickinson.
Rev. R. W. Brokaw.
Rev. N. Boynton.
Mr. Choate Burnham.
Rev. John H. Barrows, D.D.
Rev. S. V. Leech, D.D.
Rev. Teunis S. Hamlin, D.D.
Rev. P. S. Henson, D.D.
Rev. J. T. Beckley, D.D.
Bishop Samuel Fallows, D.D.
Rev. R. L. Swain. Ph.D.
Rev. W. W. Andrews.
Pres. Merrill E. Gates, LL.D.
Rev. J. Z. Tyler.
Rev. James L. Hill. D.D.
Rev. H. B. Grose.
Mr. W. H. Pennell.
Mr. W. J. Van Patten.
Rev. Wayland Hoyt, D.D.
Hon. John Wanamaker.
Rev. George H. Wells, D.D.
Rev. H. C. Farrar, D.D.
Rev. W. H. McMillen, D.D.
Rev. W. J. Darby.
Rev. M. Rhodes, D.D.
Rev. Gilby C. Kelly, D.D.
Pres. Wm. R. Harper, Ph.D.
Rev. D. J. Burrell, D.D.

AUDITOR.

Mr. F. H. KIDDER, Boston, Mass

OFFICE.

50 BROMFIELD STREET, BOSTON, MASS.

www.ingramcontent.com/pod-product-compliance
Lightning Source LLC
Chambersburg PA
CBHW031354040426
42444CB00005B/289
9781621712787